An Introduction to Theatre Design

This introduction to theatre design explains the theories, strategies, and tools of practical design work for the undergraduate student.

Through its numerous illustrated case studies and analysis of key terms, students will build an understanding of the design process and be able to:

- Identify the fundamentals of theatre design and scenography
- Recognize the role of individual design areas such as scenery, costume, lighting, and sound
- Develop both conceptual and analytical thinking
- Communicate their own understanding of complex design work
- Trace the traditions of stage design, from Sebastiano Serlio to Julie Taymor.

Demonstrating the dynamics of good design through the work of influential designers, Stephen Di Benedetto also looks in depth at script analysis, stylistic considerations, and the importance of collaboration to the designer's craft.

This is an essential guide for students and teachers of theatre design. Readers will form not only a strong ability to explain and understand the process of design, but also the basic skills required to conceive and realize designs of their own.

Stephen Di Benedetto is Associate Professor of Theatre History and Theory at the University of Miami, USA, specializing in scenographic design and the senses in performance. He is author of *The Provocation of the Senses in Contemporary Theatre* (2010).

An Introduction
to Theatre Design

Stephen Di Benedetto

Routledge
Taylor & Francis Group

LONDON AND NEW YORK

First published 2012
by Routledge
2 Park Square, Milton Park, Abingdon, Oxon OX14 4RN

Simultaneously published in the USA and Canada
by Routledge
711 Third Avenue, New York, NY 10017

Routledge is an imprint of the Taylor & Francis Group, an informa business

British Library Cataloguing in Publication Data
A catalogue record for this book is available from the British Library

Library of Congress Cataloging-in-Publication Data
Di Benedetto, Stephen.
    An introduction to theatre design / Stephen Di Benedetto.
       p. cm.
    Includes bibliographical references and index.
    1. Theaters—Stage-setting and scenery. I. Title.
    PN2091.S8.D45 2012
    792.02'5–dc23   2011031826

ISBN: 978-0-415-54753-6 (hbk)
ISBN: 978-0-415-54754-3 (pbk)
ISBN: 978-0-203-13386-6 (ebk)

Typeset in FS Albert and Gill Sans
by Keystroke, Station Road, Codsall, Wolverhampton

Contents

V

Preface

This book is designed as a supplement to introductory design classes. While specific practices differ around the world, the basic aesthetic concepts used to create designs are common. With all the advances in technology that began in the last century the design elements of production have become increasingly important and increasingly complicated to execute. By no means are the examples in the book representative of definitive design practices, however, they are common enough that they will be familiar to a general university audience. Generally, the practitioners included here have won multiple Olivier or Tony awards for their designs. Descriptions of working practices as well as quotes from the designers have been extracted from trade publications, monographs on specific designers, and from production reviews. The designers' own websites and the educational material provided by the producing theatres that these designers work at have been invaluable. Increasingly, recorded interviews with designers are available in both the United Kingdom and the United States. Students should be encouraged to search for podcasts that will give them access to these designers' views and descriptions of practice. The case studies are included as supplements to the activities that instructors will assign to teach how to make settings, costumes, lighting, or aural effects.

I am fascinated by the continually evolving practices of designers as they find new ways to evoke new interpretations of classic plays and musicals. The worlds that these designers create for the actors provide a background for action and create visual variety and interest for the audience. In my experience, the images that are made possible through the work of the designers and the feelings they evoke are the means by which I remember the performances I attend. Designers are often the unsung heroes of a production because their work is less often recognized publically. How many plays that you have gone to do you know who designed the sets, lighting, costumes, or sounds? Yet their work is the underpinning of our experience and understanding of a performance. I hope that by spending a few hours appreciating the complexity of the decisions that designers make to bring what looks obvious to life, perhaps we can more publically celebrate the creativity of the theatrical designers who create the spectacles that we love.

Miami, Florida

Acknowledgments

This project could not have been completed without the help of so many over the last couple of years. First I must thank Talia Rogers and Ben Piggott for their generous patience, encouragement, and advice that guided me through this and other simultaneous projects. Special thanks go out to my colleagues Robert Perry, Michiko Kitayama-Skinner, and April Soroko at the University of Miami for taking time out of their production schedules to critique chapters, and to Anthony Di Benedetto and Maria Gali Stampino for their advice organizing and honing ideas. As well, the comments that anonymous readers have offered have been indispensible in shaping the book. My summer honors research student, Bethley Cameron, went to great lengths early on to find material and offer a student's perspective on the book. Thanks as well to my students from Script Analysis for Designers and Theatre History who participated in the project. Finally, Juliet and Francesca you will always have my undying gratitude for your everlasting support.

Routledge would like to thank all of those who have allowed their words and imagery to be reproduced. If any words or images have been inadvertently reproduced without the correct permission or been miscredited in any way, the errors will be rectified in future editions of the book.

The theatre designer's job

Key Topics:

℮ What do theatrical designers do?

- Set design, costume design, lighting design, and sound design

℮ An overview of the designer's job from conception to realization

- Ground plan, rendering, models, load-in, and tech rehearsals

℮ Types of theatre spaces

- Proscenium, thrust stage, arena, black box, non-theatre spaces

℮ Designers looking at the world

- Peformance designers and scenographers

Examples:

- *August: Osage County* (2008) / Todd Rosenthal
- *Hamlet* (1909) / Edward Gordon Craig
- *Death of a Salesman* (1949) / Jo Mielziner
- The proscenium configuration
- Berkeley Rep's thrust stage
- An adapted proscenium configuration
- A three-quarter thrust configuration
- *H.G.* (1995) / Robert Wilson

Theatre is a collaborative art and it is hard to define where particular visual ideas come from and why they take on the final form that they do in production. A theatre designer is a person who creates and organizes one of the visual or aural aspects of a stage production. Theatrical designers sometimes seem mysterious to actors and audiences because their work takes place out of sight. Where do their ideas come from? Why do they make the choices they do? How can one evaluate the creativity of their work? There is no simple answer to these questions since theatre production is an ephemeral art that disappears as soon as it is created. One must first learn to read those images like we do play texts in order to understand what the role and skills of the designer were as the designs were created.

There are four main types of designers that create the visual and aural world of a play. They are the set designer, costume designer, light designer, and sound designer. While they all make use of the same principles and elements of composition their tasks differ slightly. Even these divisions are artificial, for a set designer often works as a costumer, in the United Kingdom, or even as a director at times. This chapter outlines the basic job descriptions of each type of designer and begins to show you their approach to the design process.

What do theatrical designers do?

A theatre designer is a person who creates and organizes the visual or aural aspects of a stage production. Based on practical necessity, convention has developed in such a way that the set designer leads the design process. The **set design** is often the first thing audiences see when they walk into a theatre. This is their first look at the production and can set its tone, reveal the time or locale, set up the basic style, establish mood and atmosphere, and introduce the production's concept. It can suggest a lot about the kind of people who will inhabit this stage world before we meet them. The scenic designer collaborates with the director and the other designers to create a production concept that integrates actors, text, and environment. Once built, the adjustment of specific details of the set design is less flexible than those of costume, for example, because being a fixed set of staging it is expensive to change. Consequently the set designer will have initiated the colors and tones, and the general feelings of the picture that the audience sees onstage.

Scenery, costumes, lighting, and sound work together with the actors to create an ever-changing event. For example, if you look at Todd Rosenthal's set for *August: Osage County*, we can see the Weston home, but we cannot develop an understanding of the nuances of protagonist Beverley's life in the absence of the

© Todd Rosenthal

This full model of Todd Rosenthal's set for the original Broadway production of *August: Osage County* (2008) shows the basic configuration for the Weston family home. However, it does not tell us anything about the secrets that each of the family members have, or the traumatic arguments that will unfold here. It is only after we see the actors and listen to the text that we can see what elements in the set reinforce the dark undertones of the major themes. Rosenthal does not create separate rooms for each location, but rather divides the space into distinct zones. These rooms are understood to be real spaces. Rosenthal leaves the further definitions of these spaces to the lighting designer and the actors. For example, Ann Wrightson, the lighting designer, may only light one zone at a time to concentrate the audience's attention, or use light to reveal more than one zone to suggest activities in one zone affect the zone where the scene occurs. Rosenthal selected details to evoke the social context of real spaces.

other aspects of the theatrical design. We cannot know that the windows are blacked out because the characters refuse to acknowledge certain facts about the family. The setting on its own cannot provide us with the meaning of the play; it needs to be integrated with the embodiment of the text by the actor as well. By the end of the play we will understand that the house helps illustrate the history of the conflicts between the different family members.

The scene designer is responsible for the creation of the stage set. It can be anything from a bare stage to a huge spectacle complete with exploding volcanoes or waterfalls. No matter whether it is simple or complex, every set has a design. Even the act of arranging chairs as part of Eugene Ionesco's *The Chairs* can be considered as design practice. Related to stage design, is the job of production designer in the film industry. Whether a film is set on location or in a studio, the designers create a real object down to the last detail. Different from theatre design, the film medium's detail, texture, and surface detail are more important than the overall look since the camera sees close up detail more than long shots. On the other hand, scene design for the stage differs from interior decorating in that it creates an environment and an atmosphere that are not finished until occupied by performers.

There is a great deal more to good set design than just making pretty pictures for performers to stand in. Effective set design involves supporting the idea of the play and the director's interpretation, creating a dynamic space, which feeds the action of the play, the blocking, and the performances. Of equal importance, the set must give the audience, as well as the actors, a powerful and accurate sense of time and place.

Deborah Dennison

A designer does not create a space that speaks on its own, but creates a space that is defined by the actions of the actors inhabiting that space. Besides creating an environment, the scene designer also has to develop a design concept with a central design metaphor in order to distinguish realism from non-realism, to establish time and place, to set tone and style, to coordinate with other elements, and to deal with practical considerations of how the stage space will be used. The scenic designer does not work in isolation; the costume designer is responsible for the selection or creation of the outfits and accessories worn by performers, lighting reveals hidden aspects of the setting establishing such things as time of day, and sound designers handle the sounds and the amplification necessary to hear or to create mood or effect. Thus, we have to characterize the environmental conditions that the actors inhabit. Are the characters sitting around in a factory, and if so, when? Is it a safe place, decrepit, or abandoned? At a glance the audience will be encouraged to make judgments about that space.

Scenery, similarly to playwriting, directing, and acting is firmly rooted in everyday life. The choices that we make from the type of house that we buy to the neighborhood we live in show something about us. Does your living room have a television in it or bookshelves? These objects communicate different things about us and reveal our traditions, family background and perhaps even what we would like to become. When we first encounter a new room we are influenced by where we are, the temperature, the furniture, the seating configuration, whether it is a loud or quiet space, whether we are sitting on a new soft, black leather sofa or a blue polyester chair from the 1970s. Color, light quality, and temperature will affect our mood and how we see the world. We process this information quickly in our day-to-day interactions. We pick up whether we have walked into a dive bar or an exclusive nightclub. Is the space open and airy, or enclosed and dark? Immediately we understand whose place it is and what the owner is trying to convey about this place, and the types of activities that take place in the space. In theatre we take this knowledge for granted and make use of it to create fictional settings for audiences. Stage designers do not merely reproduce settings as if they were real, but rather deliberately choose elements to shape an audience's impression of the worlds depicted within the play.

We are so acculturated to the presence of physical environments in each play that so closely suit its mood and meaning that we forget that theatre has not always been like this. Throughout most of theatre history the position of scenic designer did not exist – theatre makers used stock scenery or merely the space itself to serve as a setting. In Ancient Greece the *skene* was a fixed configuration used for all plays, while in the Renaissance there were only three stock sets (the civic, the domestic, and the pastoral) to serve for each genre of play. Therefore scenery did not differ considerably from production to production. Even today show-specific scenery is rare in traditional Asian theatres. For example, the Japanese *Noh* theatre has a stage that uses the same basic configuration of the stage and the ramp for all of their settings. They stand in for the location of all the plays. There is no literal representation of a real space, but rather it is a symbolic space that stands in for the location and context established by the music and the movements of the performers. Where couches, tables, and other scenic elements suggested a plausibly real space in *August: Osage County*, this space is fluid and is defined by use and convention. It is not meant to depict the world naturalistically. This type of platform scenery is used to indicate location because the action of the play is more important than the spectacle. Specificity in design became important in the early nineteenth century and not common until the twentieth century with the introduction of the ever-changing spectacle of melodrama and the desire to depict specific realistic locations. This was not possible until Adolphe Appia and Gordon Craig were able to liberate the representational stage from a static configuration into a practical playing space that is designed through the constantly changing dynamics of lighting, backdrops, and flats. Once the convention of creating localized setting became common, designers began to tailor their settings to the specific requirements of each play. Thus, for centuries the theatre used little more than the theatre space itself, with little embellishment, to stand in for environments. Likewise, prior to the late nineteenth century costume was not tailored specifically for each production. Actors chose their own costume from their private wardrobe, choosing garments that best showed off their features rather than with an eye to denoting status or character. Today costumes are chosen to support the definition of a particular character, not to show off the actor's best features. Now we shape space to evoke moods and contribute to the audiences' overall understanding of what the costumed characters unfold in front of their eyes.

Next in the hierarchy of designers comes the costume designer whose task is the visual embellishment of the actors on stage. The costume designer's job is to transform the words of the film or play script into clothing and create the look of the characters. **Costume design** helps the actor to create believable characters by creating a visual narrative through the language of clothing. Within the framework of the director's vision, costume designers will typically seek to dress actors to enhance a character's persona, and/or to create an evolving palette of color, changing social status or period through the visual design of garments and other means of dressing, distorting, and enhancing the body.

Everybody has the ability to understand costume. We do it every day when we meet someone new. Our first impression of people we meet is likely to be influenced by their appearance. Are they neatly dressed in a suit or covered in tattered rags? Often the clothes we choose to wear reflect the way we feel and the way we want others to feel about us, while other times they reflect our circumstances or ability to care for ourselves. Our everyday interactions have taught us to assess how clothes reflect the people who wear them. Costumers harness that knowledge to show us who these characters are that we will be watching. At a glance the audience gains a huge amount of information about the status of, and relationship between, the characters. Before Miss Julie opens her mouth, her elegant, beautifully fitted white silk dress shows us something different about her than Jean's black livery coat. A simple adjustment to the costume, a bloodstain on her bodice and a torn shoulder seam, or a straight razor sticking out of her clutch purse, enriches the audience's perception of the character they see on stage. Even the type and quality of the materials used tells a story. The flow and weight of cloth may give information about the weight of the atmosphere – heaviness and thickness, diaphanous and airy all evoke related feelings in actors and audiences.

A fashion designer has a very different job than that of a costumer. High fashion reflects innovation and concept rather than a practical garment – it is defined to reflect the social and cultural world of the moment. The clothes that we see models wear are examples of a notion of style that will be obsolete in a season, rather than the reflection of the people who wear outfits in everyday life. In other words, fashion is about the display or defining of the fashion of a time and costume design is about representing or defining character. On the other hand, a theatrical designer has to imagine the people living in the clothes, behaving as they would in the time of the play to create a convincing picture of the characters. Costume designing is a balanced mixture of invention and practicality. Everything a designer tries to do with a design is chosen to strengthen the performance of the actors and the concept of the director. Most often, the work of the designers is scarcely noticed by the audience.

Lighting design shapes the way that audiences see the setting and costumes. The **lighting designer**'s task is to illuminate the actors so that the audience may see them while at the same time evoking mood or atmosphere. The scenic and costume designer know that their products look different under the lighting designer's colored lights. Therefore it takes careful planning to ensure that the team will not have to make costly changes late in the game once lighting is added into the composition. A lighting designer handles all forms of illumination on the stage: the color of the lights, the mixture of the colors, the number of the lights, the intensity and brightness of the lights, the angle at which the lights strike the performers, and the length of time required for lights to come up or fade out. The light designer uses light to depict time of day and to evoke mood. We are all familiar with the ways in which light can affect our mood – on a bright and sunny day it is easier to get out of bed cheerfully, while on a cloudy, grey day it feels better to snuggle under the covers. It is the lighting designer's task to set up these moods to color the audience's perception of the actor's actions. Lighting also helps to delineate different spaces on the stage, and to provide what looks like natural light to illuminate the setting and the actors.

Lighting was slow to develop as an art form through history. At first lighting was not necessary since most theatre took place outdoors during the day. As time passed and theatre moved indoors, candles and oil lamps were used to illuminate the stage. Since the house remained lit and the candlepower was weak little could be seen beyond the proscenium arch. It was not until the development of high-powered gaslights and electricity that the space behind the proscenium could be illuminated and therefore inhabited by the actors. Technological advancement necessitated the function of the lighting. When Appia and Craig both argued for the use of light as a creator of mood, light became an important component of building a visual world for a play. They used light to provide visibility, but they also used light and shadow to create mood, establish time and place, provide focus for the stage compositions, and establish a rhythm of visual movement. If you look at Craig's conceptual drawing, you can see how he depicts a setting for *Hamlet*. His use of light and shadow create an ominous mood and highlight the protagonist's relationship to the court. Thus the lighting designer uses brightness, color, and direc-

© Victoria and Albert Museum, London

tion to guide the audience's eye to the points of focus that the director wants to highlight. What would George Bernard Shaw's *Salome* be without the light of the full moon falling on John the Baptist's severed head?

> When I read a play for the first time I dream a bit but always try to stay aware of the part that others will play in development of the landscape of the production. Early on I learned that to be too specific about lighting ideas at this stage would lead to frustration and disappointment if a set was designed that would make it impossible to implement my ideas. For me the ideal way to begin is with a meeting of everyone involved early enough to throw ideas back and forth freely before any design has been developed.
>
> **Jennifer Tipton**

Edward Gordon Craig, sketch for "To be or not to be," *Hamlet* (1909) uses light and shadow to define the atmosphere of the scenic location. Notice the way in which shadow is used to create a melancholy mood. As well, the repetition of the sculptural figures and columns fading into infinity give the speech a metaphysical tone. In the collaborative process the sketch is used to give the director and other members of the design team an idea of the light qualities that the lighting designer will be composing during the technical rehearsal. There is no really effective way to show precisely what the final lighting effects will look like.

If lighting is designed well, it will be in harmony with the other elements of the performance, because it acts as the glue that unifies all the other elements. Light reflects off the setting and costume to give color to the composition and the level of illumination will evoke a sense of mood. In that way it enhances the communication between the performers and their collaborators (writers, designers, composers, and choreographers) and the audience. The colors, shapes, and lines of lighting mix with the other elements to give shape to the three-dimensional world of the stage. A related field, though not visual, is that of sound which infuses itself with the other strands of media to contribute to the overall feeling of the composition.

In contrast to the visual forms of design, the **sound design** is a relatively new addition to the production design. It has become as complex and nuanced as the other disciplines in recent years as a result of increasingly sophisticated amplification and sound manipulation technology. Usually, the incorporation of the aural components with the visual components comes later in the process. The sound designer attempts to set the mood and tempo of the production in a similar way to the lighting designer. A sound designer may create sounds that never existed in life or may modify real sounds to create a fantasy world. No less important than the rest of the production team, a sound designer creates an overall soundscape that suits the performance space and contributes to the unified artistic vision of production. Sound designers understand and work with the acoustic of the performance space, select and facilitate the use of microphones, and acquire, edit, and facilitate the appropriate use of sound effects and music. There are two basic types of sound design, technical sound design and conceptual sound design. The technical side of sound design is common on Broadway and in the West End and the conceptual style of sound design is more peculiar to regional theatres or experimental venues. Both styles are equally important and sometimes they are both made use of in production. Technical sound designers are hired to design the sound system and to tune all necessary equipment to attain the best sound quality for performance. On the other hand, a conceptual sound designer collaborates with a director to determine what musical themes and ideas should be crafted to establish a mood or setting. Also, in collaboration with the music director a conceptual sound designer might choose or compose some specific music or noise for the play.

No matter the task assigned, theatre designers work as collaborators adjusting their interpretations and their choices to best serve the director's central concept. It is a job where compromise and flexibility are critical in order to create a unified composition. How designers collaborate in light of their individual tasks comes next.

An overview of the designer's job from conception to realization

Like any other difficult task, stage designs do not emerge fully formed out of the designers' heads. They require a period of gestation and development, informed by thought, research, and experimentation. The steps of the designer's work process include analysis, research, drawing, rendering, model building, drafting, and load-in. At each step they are in contact with their other collaborators considering the aesthetics of the stage images. Therefore, as a team they are responsible for the visual appearance of everything, including props, costume, make-up, and the set. We will explore in detail each type of designer's job in later chapters; however, a basic overview is necessary to set the stage. In general, the design process may begin months before the actors are hired when the designers collaborate with the director to conceive of the visual elements for performance. The first thing that the designers will want to know is what the play is about. After each designer reads the play, they chat together with the director about their ideas of where they might place their **playing areas** on the stage to establish the **ground plan**, and they discuss the themes in the play. Early discussion with the director will establish the story, style, colors, and period. The initial reading of the script to many designers is a key to the whole process of the project. The ideas, emotions, and visual pictures that arise from this first reading of the script may be the most valuable of the whole design process. The world that the characters live in will be apparent in the script, although it takes work to discover it. It is more than the literal representation of location, character, or the time of day; it is a world of atmosphere as much as it is a political, historical, and social environment. Identifying an atmosphere may be an elusive process. Our first impressions of a play are often unimpeded by research and analytical thinking. The most important task is to dig out the secrets of the background of the story and the characters before the design process begins.

> Our first job was to decide which configuration of audience and playing space would work best for all the plays. Each has quite specific needs in terms of entrances and exits, and the studio has its own character to consider as well. After looking at options like playing in the round and in traverse, we saw that a "proscenium" style gave us the best options. We then made a set of grey walls, and a grey floor to make a shell inside the studio, hiding distracting details in the architecture, and giving us a neutral clean base on which to build. Next came our proscenium which arches over the space, dividing it into two areas; one very directly in touch with the audience in front, and one more recessive, dream-like space behind. It also provided us with extra entrances and a surface to project onto. We chose grey because it is very kind to skin tones, and shows off other colours (in props and clothes for example) beautifully.
>
> **Jessica Curtis**

Talking about the ideas with the other members of the production team is essential during the early stages of the design process. This means that each of the designers has to be good at communicating ideas and thoughts with the group. The most difficult ideas to talk about are often the ones that seem either too vague to discuss or too impractical to achieve. However, as these ideas are introduced in discussion they can become clearer and more possible, while others can be discarded after thought. The perspectives and experiences of the production team can help refine ideas so new solutions emerge to problems that once seemed insurmountable. The best and most creative results can grow out of the discussion.

> I still do not fully comprehend what happens when, having read and researched and discussed and avoided for as long as I apparently need to, I finally sit down to draw. Like I said, ideas are magic. Because what goes down on the paper is rarely exactly what I thought I was going to draw. Sort of like automatic writing. As if my hand has a more direct line to the creative process than my brain, which has been up till then preoccupied with the craft process but is finally willing to step out of the way for a while. And yet, without drawing it, I can't fully *imagine* it. Those ideas from nowhere are often sketchy or wild-eyed. They need the discipline of the craft to bring them into line, that is, help them into a form that can be realized in the real world, the world of parameters, theatre measurements, budgets and collaborators.
>
> **Marjorie Kellogg**

Once a project has been accepted, the designer begins to think about the play and look to the world to begin to search for a conceptual idea to explore with the director and other designers. To do this, designers will often begin by playing with images on paper. Sketching is a form of thinking, like putting words on the page to try and figure out what you think. Some artists like to use pencil, others charcoal, while others use collage. When the design team meets the director to brainstorm, these visual representations may be used to help the director and other designers formulate a more refined production concept. During these discussions many designers will continue to make rough sketches of ideas on the spot. The preliminary small sketches of the characters inhabiting the set in costume or in a group scene show the progression of the action through the play so that there is something tangible to discuss in secondary meetings. Designers use the early meetings to gain understanding of the genre of the production so that it can be reflected in the feeling and style of the refined designs. In later meeting, the set designer and the costume designer will have exchanged ideas about the colors and lighting. By the time the final series of production meetings start to happen the designs will have been completed.

When the designers are on their own they develop sketches to give the director in secondary meetings, in which they can discuss those ideas. The next stage of the process comes when a more formal production concept has been agreed upon. It is at this point that **renderings** are produced. Jo Mielziner's renderings for Willy Loman's house were more detailed than the sketches and give a sense of the mood the team was trying to create through light, shadow, and position of the characters. Renderings are two-dimensional representations of setting, lighting, and costume used to make design more concrete than they were in the initial consultations. These are not finished products, but are used to communicate more fully formed ideas to

A SALESMAN   DES. by Jo MIELZINER   1 8 9 2 R IG

Courtesy of Jules Fisher

the director and other designers. They are working drawings that will be adjusted as a result of input and collaboration from the other members of the design team. At each stage of the process the designers continually refine and adjust their expression in concert with the other collaborators in the process.

Based on those initial stages, the scenic designer carefully makes a **white card model**, or a simple, unadorned sketch model made at an early stage in the design process that is flexible enough to experiment with space, structure, and form; a quick and uninhibited method of three-dimensional sketching. For example, the technical staff will discuss the white card model with the ground plan laid out for reference. The team spends hours looking at the various models, sketches, renderings, and story boards depicting different moments in the production. They examine the material to try and determine how the actors will use the space, move through the space, and how the space will transform from one state to the next over the duration of the production. Careful planning ensures that last-minute surprises are manageable. Collaboration is at the heart of the designer's job. Once this model has been approved, a more precise, realistically textured and painted model follows. It is a three-dimensional representation of what the design will look like at a particular moment. The **full model** is built to scale and represents the setting on the stage in which the performance will take place. The figures made to scale can be moved in the environment. Set pieces can be lifted in and out, lighting effects can be tested, and color, patterns, and textures are evident. These full models give a good sense of what the product will look like in production. Depending on the type of space that is

Jo Mielziner's sketches for Arthur Miller's *Death of a Salesman* (1949) show the process of how the designer tests ideas to see how they will look during production. The ideas for any set evolve in the focus of the designer over a period of months. These sketches show some the development of Mielziner's beginning ideas for the Loman home. The characters are depicted in several different scenes. The composition of the images changed over time. As well, the different arrangements to change the focus of the action to center stage for some scenes give a different feeling than the scenes that take place on stage-right and stage-left. One is enclosed, cocooned from the outside world, while the other is open and amidst the rest of the world.

Courtesy of Jules Fisher

In this sketch the background is barely indicated. Instead the arrangement of actors within the context of the structure of the family environment is seen against the context of society itself. The background and the mid-ground impinge upon the action between the characters that the audience focuses upon. Playing with arrangements helps the production team understand how aesthetic balance affects the audience's perception of the action. As well, different visual arrangements can tease out different themes. This experimental drawing reveals what might be possible in production.

depicted it may contain hanging back drops, furniture, architecture, and even miniature figures representing the actors on stage. Lighting designers, who may use flashlights and other effects to simulate lighting effects, can use this model. This realization of the design in miniature will allow the design team to envision the design in action.

Models are especially useful for the director, since many directors have a hard time conceptualizing how things will look in three dimensions. Think for a moment about designing a room in your house. When you move in you have furniture, curtains, paintings, and other props. You will not necessarily know how they will look in a new space, or whether they will even fit until you try them. In the theatre it is expensive to build scenery and to acquire props and furniture. By building a model the designer can try out what possibilities exist for how the actors use the space and what things will look like before the objects are built or purchased. The more small adjustments are made throughout the design process the fewer large adjustments there will be during the technical rehearsals. It is best to look for problems before they happen and plan for contingencies to avoid problems and large expenses. It is a constant wrestling match between what the designer would like and what is practical to have. As well, one must have the flexibility to accommodate for changes that occur with the inclusion of the other design elements and the director's and actors' use of the stage and setting. If a character needs to do deep-knee lunges and they are dressed in armor on a raked stage, some problems are sure to emerge.

Once the designs have been agreed upon it is time to begin the fabrication of the design. To do that the scene shop or costume shop needs instruction on building the scenery. **True views** of the scenery and costume are needed to aid the shop to build the designs. These renderings are formal documents that resemble an architect's blueprints of a building, showing various views of the scenery to scale with precise instructions on how the objects are to be put together. These are given to the technical director so that he or she may fabricate the necessary objects and be certain that they fit on the stage and match the drawings and renderings that the design team has agreed upon.

The design team returns to the theatre during **load-in** and for the **technical rehearsals**. At this point the built scenery and costumes are placed on stage and lit by the lighting designer. Now the designers have a chance to give notes and make adjustments according to how it looks in three dimensions. Changes will be necessary as a result of the colored light hitting the scenery and the costumes. The team will consider what needs to be adjusted to create an aesthetic **balance** between the different design elements. They will see if some surface or object might not be reflecting the light or achieving the desired effect. These changes will contribute to the overall look and mood of the play. Hopefully, the design team has spotted many of these problems during the modeling period, because radical changes at this point are expensive.

Every designer goes about his or her task differently in creating the stage world, but they all share a common goal – to create an environment within which the actors evoke a convincing character. This means that designers must work as a team and that they must work in concert with the director so that each element on the stage is compatible. A design team is hired to work with the director to create an environment that will communicate the meaning of a specific production and in which the actors can perform. A theatrical environment is never neutral, rather it is the physical and visual balance to the words of the play and the actors' performance. A good design is created in concert with the integration of actor, text, and environment. Bad designs are those that detract from a performance. For example, if a costume looks inappropriate on a character, the actor's work may be more difficult; or if in a setting an element draws pointless attention through spectacle when spectacle is not called for, or in lighting by not providing enough spectacle when spectacle is clearly called for, by confusing combinations of color that pull audience focus to the wrong place on stage.

> I try to attend as many design meetings as I can, even if the lighting is not discussed specifically. The best way to understand how to light a show is to completely immerse oneself in it. During the lengthy set design process for *The Lion King*, I attended most of the meetings between Julie Taymor and Richard Hudson (scenic designer) over a period of several months. When Richard was preparing a formal design presentation, I participated by lighting each of several models he and his assistants had created. This was an incredibly useful exercise, as I gained insights into lighting the production that would have been difficult to discover working only at the drafting table. Although my

13

attendance and participation in all the design meetings didn't necessarily result in a specific list of lighting notes, it did give me a deeper understanding of the world of *The Lion King*, Julie's approach to staging the piece, and the overall style of production.

Donald Holder

Designers make use of the same skills that we do in everyday life to signify characteristics such as age, class, wealth, and health. We encounter the forms of scenic design in everyday life – the carefully planned décor of a restaurant or hotel lobby. In the same sense we often shape the spaces around us to reflect what we would like the world to see us as by hanging posters of jazz legends on our walls to seem cool and hip, or by painting our walls with graffiti to show how unconventional we are. Designers choose clothes that in a particular environment will lead audiences to make judgments about who the characters are. If you think about going to a job interview, we will choose clothes that will reflect our success and seriousness for the job. Our clothes say something about us. Each of these visual displays will show the world about which groups, ideas, and concepts we wish to be associated with.

Theatre designers work with the environments of human life and the materials of the world: Light and shadow, fabric and color, wood and canvas, plastic and metal and paint. While we may put silk bedding on our beds in pale neutral tones to suggest sensuality and make our bed inviting, the designer will choose similar materials to achieve the same effect. However, the materials and objects placed onstage are not always utilitarian and real. They look real. Fabrics, colors, and textures may not read under the harsh light of the stage as they do with the soft lights of our bedrooms. Therefore the fabrics must be manipulated to seem real. Real life is limited through the skills of theatrical make-believe to appear convincing so that our bodies and eyes are tricked in to perceiving the world as real. It does not matter if we are talking about a bedroom in the president's house or what we think a martian bed may look like. The job of the designer is to make it look plausible and reasonable in the given frame that we are displaying. To accomplish all of this, the designers must deal with the practical limits of the stage space and the offstage areas.

Types of theatre spaces

Designers do not create sets, costumes, lighting, and sound effects for an imaginary space. They must work within the constraints of the preexisting spaces of the theatres where the production will be performed. In dealing with created or found space, the designer must plan the entire environment, the audience area as well as the stage area. There are five basic stage configurations: the proscenium (sometimes called the picture frame); Arena, circle, or theatre in the round; the thrust or three-quarter round, the black box; and found space.

What I've always been fascinated with in the pictorial aspect of the theatre is the mystery of stage depths. One of the shocks when you work in America is that theatres are generally shallower; always with massive wing space, but a shallow stage. It's the opposite here; we have more depth, but narrow wings.

Bill Dudley

The atmosphere and environment of theatrical space plays a large part in setting the time of the event. Each style of configuration has advantages and disadvantages. Designers need to understand how these spaces work to best use them as a part of their designs. For example, if we tried to place Willy Loman's house as designed by Mielziner on an arena stage rather than on a picture frame stage, the audience behind the house could not see the actors performing in front of the house. In the same sense, if the lighting designer angled his or her lighting instrument the same way for an arena stage as they do for a proscenium stage, those lights directed toward the walls of the setting would blind the audience. Settings and lighting must take the style of stage into consideration so that they can be sure the audience can see the actors performing. Scenery provides convincing settings for the performers. The scenic designer is responsible for creating the physical and visual environments in which the actors and actresses perform.

The **proscenium** space is the most familiar type of theatre, because it was the most common form of theatre building in the eighteenth, nineteenth, and twentieth

© Massimo Listri/Corbis

Here is a standard proscenium configuration. The columns accentuate the frame that surrounds the abyss of the stage. The audience's eye is directed towards the center of the space. The form has not changed much in several hundred years because it frames and accentuates what happens behind the proscenium in an organized fashion.

The interior of the Thrust Stage at the Tony Award-winning Berkeley Repertory Theatre. Photo by Kevin Berne

This is the interior of Berkeley Rep's thrust stage. The audience is positioned along three sides of the stage and actors can exit and enter at the rear. The voms are used as audience entrances, but can also be used by actors for their entrances. It gives the audience a sense that the characters come out of the audience. It is an intimate arrangement. Often the comings and goings of the audience can be as much a part of the show as the action on the stage.

centuries. The proscenium configuration looks like a framed opening in a wall that the audience look into. That hole is the proscenium arch and it creates a picture frame that controls the point of view of the audience as they watch the action of the play unfold. The whole audience is directly facing the stage and looks through the opening of the picture frame. The proscenium was originated as a way to accentuate the illusion of perspective that designers were trying to create with the painted scenery behind the actors. It has transformed into a picture frame stage that contains the movement of actors in the three-dimensional volume of the setting. It has the potential for elaborate scene shifts and visual displays transforming a drawing room into a city street. The obvious advantage of this type of space is the ability to control focus. The mechanics of the stage can remain out of sight, hidden from the audience. Scenery, lighting, costumes, and sound are designed to move toward the audience. It creates a distancing effect and the proscenium creates a barrier between actors and audience. Proscenium houses tend to be bigger, serving more patrons and the audience can all see most of the stage at all times. Good examples of proscenium stages are the McGuire Proscenium Stage at the Guthrie in Minneapolis and the Royal Haymarket Theatre in London.

A **thrust stage**, or **three-quarter round** stage, extends into the audience on three sides and is connected to the backstage area at its upstage end. Similar to an arena stage, the audience in a thrust stage theatre may view the stage from three or more sides. It is a platform stage where entrances and exits usually are made at the rear. The thrust stage is a combination of scenic features of the proscenium and the intimacy of the arena stage. Because the audience sits on three sides of the stage, focus becomes an issue, since nothing can be hidden away. In contrast to the proscenium stage, only one wall and the stage floor are available for scenic design. As a result they become essential elements, whether left completely blank or filled with ornate detailing, because they are the only visual elements beyond the costumes that the audience is able to focus upon. Not only are we able to see the actors but we can see the other spectators as they watch as well. Since the role of the setting is minimized, this can be an advantage for costume designers since the audience can pay attention to costume detail. Audience members are closer and can see more detail and are more intimate with the setting and actors. For lighting and sound the designers are afforded a large palette. Light can be projected upon the stage floor and become a focal point, creating space, time, mood, and patterns. Lighting designers can use a gobo to create sunlight through the trees or abstract designs. Their biggest challenge is to light the stage without spilling over into the audience, blinding the audience, or calling unnecessary attention to the

This proscenium configuration has been adapted into a theatre in the round. As you can see on the round stage, anything that has height or volume would block the sightlines of a quarter of the audience. We also can see how we are aware of our fellow audience members. Everyone is in the glare of the lights.

Photo copyright Matt Humphrey, Set Design: Rob Howell

spectators. In other words it can distract focus. The audience can be wrapped in sound from multiple directions. The balance of sound in the space is important so that everyone hears equally well. When the sound balance is off it can destroy the effects. Good examples of thrust stages are The Swan Theatre in Stratford or the Wurtele Thrust at the Guthrie in Minneapolis.

An **arena** theatre places the playing space in the center with the audience surrounding the perimeter of the stage in a circle or square. Boxing rings and circus tents are the most familiar versions of this style of stage. A theatre in the round has no place for curtains or large units of scenery because the audience surrounds the action. Like the thrust stage, the stage floor becomes an essential surface on which to work. As well, scenic elements hung over the stage can be an important means of conveying setting or mood. The audience is closer than in a thrust stage. A successful design must be simple, for anything of any mass or height will block the sight lines. Like the thrust stage, costume detail and balance and focus for lighting and sound are essential. Since the audience is aware of the others watching and they are close to the actors, the physical and psychological proximity is high. This closeness heightens the sense of a shared experience. A good example of an arena stage is The Fichandler Theatre at Arena Stage, Washington, D.C.

A **black box** theatre is a generic term for a smaller sized theatre often with fewer than one hundred seats, the walls being painted black to deemphasize them, and with flexible seating capabilities. Depending on how much equipment is installed in this space, it can be adapted for whatever the production team wants. It can be configured differently each time it is used – a season in a black box theatre can be staged as a proscenium for one show, the next in the round, and a third as a thrust. It all depends upon what type of theatrical invitation the production team wants to exploit as a means of expression. These spaces are extremely flexible, almost like a black palette. These are intimate spaces where actors and audience are at close quarters, and audiences can see the detail in the setting, costumes, and facial expressions of the actors. The Cottesloe Theatre in London, which can hold up to three hundred patrons, is a good example of a space that can be adapted differently for each production.

Found, environmental, or **created spaces** take on several forms, the use of non-theatre buildings, the adaptation of a space to suit the need of an individual production, the use of nature, geography, and the use of architecture to affect the environment. Performances that do not take place in a formal theatre building can be said to be environmental or as site-specific theatres. Control over the design ranges from none, to intricate creation within the space. These are similar to performances of Christian Cycle plays done inside a cathedral or on the church square. Basically this involves the adaptation of existing spaces for production. Take for example Robert

This black box theatre has been configured in a three-quarter thrust configuration. Notice that we can see the black painted walls along the perimeter and that the lighting instruments and second level are visible. Since the seats are light and positioned on risers they can be moved easily. This adaptable space is popular today since it creates an intimate relationship with the audience and can accommodate different staging configurations. This style also gives flexibility to the designer to create expensive elaborate stage settings or cheaper minimal settings. Experimental companies love black box configurations.

Image courtesy of Milo Smith Tower Theater, Central Washington University

© Artangel

Wilson's installation *H.G.* (1995) that took place in the underground vaults of the old Clink in South London. He took advantage of the rhythmic quality of the colonnade to create a hospital ward. The decrepit nature of the building added to the destructive atmosphere that the influenza epidemic had upon society at the end of the nineteenth century. He made use of the space's qualities to help him evoke mood. Site-specific productions have multiple focuses such as street theatre or a music festival where multiple bands are playing on structures built in a large open space, or the circus tent pitched in each town as it travels across the country. How different is it to watch *Hamlet* in the ruins of the theatre of Verona than it is in the Covent Garden Opera House? What does the space add to the production? An environmental stage may be as intimate as a living room or as big as the wide open prairies. Street corners, alleyways, churches, toilets, town halls, palaces, warehouses, and the forest have all been used as theatrical settings.

Experimental theatre groups often make spectators aware of the performance environment. Shape and location (indoor or outdoor) and the shape and character of the theatre building affect the environment. Take for instance Peter Brook's theatre, the Bouffes du Nord. It is an old crumbling proscenium theatre that has been transformed into a found space. The interior of the space sets a particular mood to the performance. This is in contrast to the open concrete configuration of the Oliver Theatre in London. The nature of the material played in the theatre is affected by these material conditions. It changes the experiences of the audiences as they watch the play unfold. Audiences cannot but be affected by the material of their surroundings. How hot and cold and how confined or enlarged affects how audiences understand the images that unfold in front of them on stage.

> The core of the theatre is the actor and the audience, and the word, and what designers do with all our bits and pieces is to try and prepare an enchanted space, where the audience is asked to play make believe. Anything that breaks down the laws of physics can lend itself to the time frame of how a play reads – the time it's supposed to cover, and the real time of performance.
>
> **Bill Dudley**

Designers looking at the world

There are a whole host of skills that a designer cultivates over a lifetime of practice. Designers are inquisitive and are interested in everything that the world has to offer as a potential inspiration for elements within their work. They are attuned to the visual world and draw from it constantly. Woody Allen has said that genius knows from where to steal; as such, designers are avid museum-goers, visiting the great art, design, fashion, and furniture museums in the cities that they work in. Designers are called upon to contemplate the ways that others have drawn upon the principles and elements of design to create compositions. They look to the world around us at paintings, sculptures, photographs, architecture, and nature, and they pour through images that they find in magazines and on the Internet. Some photograph, paint, sculpt, or even write novels in their spare time. They scavenge the streets for ideas, materials, and inspirations. Have you ever noticed that not one of the doors on the houses on your street matches? Designers seek out those observations by spending time in nature, looking for textures, patterns, colors, and shapes that may help them in some future project. How is the color or texture of clay different than mud? For example the Spanish designer Romón B. Ivars found that the orange netting used at construction sites could be used as a dress form, and that garbage bags are great as reflective surfaces.

Have you ever noticed how objects and machines we use every day can evoke other objects or machines? Take for example a car – its sleek lines and low profile can evoke the sleek form of a jaguar, or its forbidding shape and immense size conjure up one of the warships that made up the flotilla of ships called the Armada. These ideas help inspire the shapes that make up the look of the vehicle. The practical nature of what makes a car go combined with the safety features and other practical concerns are coupled with qualities of other objects to create a desirable commodity. Theatrical designers use the same principles and elements to conceive of the images that we see on stage. For example, for Peter Brook's famous staging of *A Midsummer Night's Dream*, the costume designer used the lines of a bird's feathers in a fairy costume. The actress's features were elongated into a beak and her make-up was conceived of in a way to accentuate that shape. As well, her dress is made to look like feathers. Theatrical designers look to the world to use shapes and compositions that we are familiar with to lead us to read the actor's actions in a particular way. It is through these subtle cues that we begin to understand the action of the play.

Television design shows such as *Color Splash Miami* have made interior design a popular pastime, but while the concepts are similar to what theatre designers do, theatre designers do more than create aesthetically pleasing living environments. They make use of the same basic principles of composition that other visual artists use, as well as designers of video games, cars, and airplanes; however their practice is utilized for different ends. While all forms of design make use of the elements and principles of design in the creation of objects, there is a difference between objects made for theatre and objects made for everyday usage. Theatre or other visual designers are attentive to their function as well as their aesthetic appeal. The theatre tries to evoke details for another aim; while clothing may try to flatter the individual, a costumer may make unflattering clothes to transform the actor or actress into an unappealing character, or to mask gender or beauty to aid the actor in their per-formance. The design helps the actor influence the audience perception of their character. They may design unbalanced and ugly compositions to make a point or to communicate something unsettling to the audience. Designers make use of their tools and philosophies to create mimetic expression, so they create an environment that is unbalanced in structure to communicate dysfunction or instability. Whereas a car designer may try and visually create appealing shapes that are wind resistant and form and function work hand in hand, the function of the theatre form may be to communicate something dysfunctional.

It is important to note that no matter how realistic the production, it is not a real space. These worlds are sometimes imitations of the real world, sometimes not. In either case they are make-believe worlds made up of familiar materials used often in novel ways. Theatre designers are not making a literal representation of reality. Even for the most naturalistic or domestic drama such as *Death of a Salesman* or *August: Osage County*, the performance space is not the four-walled room it pretends to be, any more than the actors are the people that they present to the audience using the words of the script. And it would not be any different than using everyday furniture present in a room as the setting. Thus designers use line, color, movement, texture, and shape to create a semblance of the real world. It is a constructed world that is made up of symbols and other recognizable elements drawn from past cultural production.

The goal of design is to contribute to the overall harmony of the product of collaboration between the different elements of design. All performance prac-titioners need to be aware of how much visual information is potentially available to the audience, and need to hone their skills in both reading the intentional cues, and spotting the potentially distracting stimuli to eliminate them. While we tend to overlook distracting visual elements in our day-to-day lives such as glare on a projection screen at a meeting, in a play extraneous information leads audiences

21

away from the harmonic elements of expression made use of during performance. Those particularly concerned with the visual elements of performance steal ideas from wherever they can to create dynamic environments. Creating stimulating images on stage requires us to observe with a critical eye and not just look.

Designers are problem solvers. They often have a limited palette to work with and must find solutions to compositional problems that arise during collaboration. For example, a light source may reflect on the surface of a floor and distract from the audience's focus. How can the lighting designer make a change to achieve a desired effect? Designers look to the art world for ideas. While looking at images from other art forms as inspiration the theatre designer will search for interesting compositions, techniques, or manners of rendering a particular mood or feeling. A set designer may look at the ways in which the artist arranges the figure in the volume of the environment. Is there a transition between the architecture on the horizontal to the walls of the vertical? What is the relationship of the figure to the other objects in the frame? The costume designer may look at the way in which the texture contributes to the definition of the personality of the figure, or how the draping of cloth hangs on the frame of the figure's body and what it conveys about his or her stature. A lighting designer will ask where the light sources are within the image. How could that look be reproduced in the performance? What is evident from this image beyond surface meaning? How is that information being communicated? What role is light playing in creating meaning and directing interpretation? All these observations may become useful in a later project when a solution to a design problem arises.

Designers are students of culture and society as much as they are theatre artists. They must be familiar with the styles and traditions of the world's cultures so that they can draw upon their themes and motifs to evoke different times and places. For example, John Conklin's opera sets owe a debt to eighteenth-century civic design. He makes use of the rhythmic pattern of the architectural details to give his setting a sense of authority and grandeur. He may draw from the features of a Palladio-inspired building to speak to an audience's associations with eighteenth-century life. He counts on our cultural preconceptions to color our response to his setting in the context of the production. While the features of the eighteenth-century building were conceived to fit into the context of the street in which it was built, Conklin's rendering is meant to be the setting of the play. It stands in for a place. Rather than reproduce a real cityscape, his opera sets often evoke paintings from the great masters. In this way he is able to provide a setting that adheres to the audience's conception of what the world of an opera ought to look like.

In the same sense, Eiko Ishioka's designs for *M-Butterfly* drew both from Peking Opera and Chinese communist propaganda poster design. For *M-Butterfly* she juxtaposed the blown-up propaganda poster with the characters performing on the platform in the foreground. The visual concept is a direct copy of the style of communist propaganda art. Political ideology and biased cultural stereotypes are central themes within the play. Massive, idealized figures dominate the background dwarfing the central character's actions. The private exchanges of the central characters are seen to have larger implications. The setting provides a context for the action as well as an aesthetically interesting image. Designers take from life to help the audience understand the play that they are watching. We understand the world we live in, so we can use those skills to understand the choices the production team makes to color our understanding of the action. The poster stood in as a controlling metaphor reminding the audience of the Butterfly's relationship to the government as she/he strolled in sleek feminine attire across the stage. To evoke the West's conception of femininity she contrasted governmental propaganda to the ways in which we depict gender, thus complementing the action of the plot. Designers draw from all sorts of sources to help find visual form for their interpretations of the play scripts. As such, designers work in other disciplines as well.

It is important to understand that designers use their skills in a variety of professions. For example, theatre designers often work in other fields outside of the theatre as a complement to their stage design work. Lighting designers are often hired to work in industrial design, lighting conferences, or other corporate events. For example a company may want the event to create an atmosphere of cheer for the employees. They may want to project a company logo or colors to echo the message they are trying to impart. Other designers may light rock concerts or fashion shows. Film production is another common related field, where set designers create a fixed setting that transforms over time; production designers may be called upon to transform existing locations, build sets for scenes or create new environments for the action to take place. Though these practices share similar aesthetic and conceptual features, the practical challenges are different. A set designer may need to accommodate entrances and exits, and limit sightlines, and a production designer may have to account for the space necessary for the camera apparatus and crew. Costume designers in the theatre need to create durable costumes that will withstand a long run and accentuate movement while film costumes need to be more detailed and elaborate because of the detail of the camera. Lighting designers need to cope with how the eye sees and the camera records, because light is perceived differently in a camera than the eyes, so different colors and intensities are used to create similar effects in the different media.

As well, within theatrical practice there are two emerging disciplines that give designers a more central role in the collaborative process. Both performance designers and scenographers take a more proactive role in conceiving of an event, controlling and collaborating with others to author works. **Performance designers** work in a variety of disciplines collaborating with designers, musicians, live artists, and other visual artists creating and coordinating the visual elements of a project. This is rather a new conception of theatre design that regards other aesthetic practices and theory as integral to the creation of theatrical representation. The term **scenography** also is used for a broader conception of the role of design in performance, where the control over the visible and conceptual elements is conceived as a *gesamtkunstwerk* – or total work of art. Rather than serving a representational function, the scenographer conceives of the design as the engine of the dramaturgy. Notable scenographers include Robert Wilson who is a director as well as set, costume, and lighting designer, and Julie Taymor who controls all aspects of performance design, which may also include dramaturgy and choreography. To understand the styles that designers work with we must move on to look at the traditions of stage design and the inherited conventions within which all theatre designers practice. The next chapter will take us on a tour of influential practices from theatre design history.

Traditions of stage design

2

Key Topics:

@ A brief survey of theatre design

- Ancient Greece, Rome, Medieval, Renaissance, 19th Century
- Lighting
- Spectacle and panorama
- Realistic setting
- New Stagecraft
- Edward Gordon Craig and the Über-marionette
- Bringing the avant garde to the mainstream
- Epic Theatre and the Bauhaus
- Practice in America and Great Britain
- Multimedia theatre design
- Appropriated spaces
- Innovation

Examples:

- Il Teatro Farnese, Parma
- Tragic Theatre stage set (1545) / Sebastiano Serlio
- The court masque
- *Parsifal* (1882) / Adolphe Appia
- *The Magnanimous Cuckold* (1922) / Lyubov Popova
- *The Triadic Ballet* (1922) / Oskar Schlemmer

Current design practice comes from a rich tradition of inherited assumptions about the role of the designer in production. A brief summary of the history of major design practices, including a history of sets, costumes, lights, and sound will provide the framework for understanding the origin of contemporary design practice. The chapter will then concentrate on how theories of the late nineteenth- and early twentieth-century theatre, as well as the advancement of technology, have influenced the current practices of contemporary designers. This section will highlight several influential styles and the technical developments in illumination that made three-dimensional representation in theatre possible, and suggest how technology has shaped the aesthetics of current practice.

Design practice is firmly rooted in the assumptions of the past. While each generation puts their own mark on the theatre of the day, the practices of the past have led us to what we do today. Some practices date back to the classical period, while others are invented as new technology changes what is possible to accomplish on the stage. During the Greek, Roman, and Elizabethan periods the rear wall of the theatre was the scenery, and generally the scene's location either was obvious, unimportant, or stated in a character's lines. Renaissance traditions in continental Europe made use of Italianate staging, which made popular the use of three stock locations. The tragic scene depicted civic space such as palaces, the comic scene depicted domestic spaces, and the pastoral scene depicted rural settings. However, it is not until the late nineteenth century that it became typical for a theatre company to design a setting specific to a production. Once technology made it easier to control the elements of design, then new practices were developed into the standard practices that we are familiar with today.

A brief survey of theatre design

Ancient Greek theatres were outdoor structures that took advantage of sloping hillsides for seating. Greek and Hellenistic theatre used the stage space itself to define the setting. Generally, the theatre space was made up of the skene, orchestra, and theatron. An *orchestra* is the place where the chorus danced and sung, while the protagonist, antagonist, and other lead characters performed on the *logeion*, or raised stage, in front of the *skene*, or scene building. Actors could make entrances and exits from doors in the skene onto the logeion. The *theatron* is where the audience watched from semi-circular benches built into the hillside. Between the theatron and skene were parodoi, or long ramps that led into the orchestra. The *parodoi* were used for the entrances and exits of the chorus. The façade of the skene served as the backdrop for action. Generally, the costumes used in tragedy were emblematic, where different masks and different robes indicated age and gender and could be read from the back of the theatron. Comic costumes were perhaps padded and the men wore phalli; other characters might have dressed as birds, frogs, and so on depending on the subject of the comedy. Performances were held during the day, so natural sunlight provided the lighting. Sound effects may have been used. Some historians speculate that pebbles may have been shaken inside of metal containers as a means of reproducing rain or thunder from behind the skene. Its spectacular scenic effects were carried out by the mechane, ekkyklema, and periaktoi. The most impressive device was the *mechane*, which is a crane that was used to lift actors above the acting area, allowing them to appear as gods flying in and out. Since violence was never depicted on stage, they used an *ekkyklema*, or rolling platform, to reveal corpses from behind the central door in the skene. As well, they may have used trap doors to enter and exit, and *periaktoi*, or painted triangular columns that revolved to show a change in location. While stage design was relatively generic, it allowed the audience to track characters and follow the action of the tragedy or comedy.

Roman theatre structures evolved from the basic configuration of Greek theatre buildings, though Roman theatres were a single architectural unit that was located inside the city. Most extant Roman theatres have a roofed house called the *scaena* at the back of the stage. Its façade, the *scaenae frons*, which served as the backdrop to the action, could be as high as three stories. At stage level, the scaenae had three doors used for entrances and exits. While there was a vestigial orchestra, it was not used as performance space. The only performance space was on the raised stage called the *pulpitum*. Spectators sat in the semi-circular *cavea*. As theatre competed with gladiatorial combat and other popular entertainments, the Roman theatres used more elaborate stage machinery. They had stage curtains, sliding panels, elaborate props, and even elevators to lift actors or animals to the pulpitum. The stage space could be flooded to stage mock navel battles. Similar to the Greeks, the Romans used emblematic clothing and masks to denote age, gender, and stock character type. These could be understood all the way from the top of the cavea. Roman architectural design comes down to us by way of Vitruvius's books of architecture. Renaissance scholars were so fascinated with classical culture, they used his designs to build what would become the first Italianate stages.

These children, twelve in all, being arranged, as I have said, on pedestals and clad like angels with gilt wings and caps of gold lace, took one another's hands when the time came, and extending their arms they appeared to be dancing, especially as the basin was always turning and moving. Inside this and above the heads of the angels were three circle or garlands of lights arranged with some tiny lanterns which could not turn over. These lights looked like stars from the ground, while the beams being covered with cotton resembled clouds.

Giorgio Vasari on the medieval machinery used to create effects.

Medieval theatre was different from classical theatre because it did not take place in a formal theatre building. Theatrical activities were performed in found spaces such as churches, town squares, courtyards, and banquet halls. Theatre was far more intimate, more like what we term site-specific theatre today. Audiences stand or sit in close proximity to the performers. Medieval theatre was religious in nature and developed out of Latin religious rituals within the church building. The stories of the bible were performed on **mansions** placed around the perimeter of the nave and baptistery within the church. Each mansion served as a sacred location for a single bible-story. As theatrical performances began to get more colloquial and performed in the vernacular they were forced outside of the church into the town square. The individual scenic locations of the mansion staging were retained. Generally, there were two types of stages in the medieval era: fixed and movable. **Fixed** or **stationary staging** refers to a series of mansions set up in available spaces such as courtyards or the town square arranged around the perimeter of the space. The structure of a mansion with a **platea** was retained from the performances inside of the church. **Movable** or **processional staging** is when **pageant wagons**, a mansion built onto a cart, would travel a set route, and the play would be performed at various locations. It can be thought of as something similar to a parade. Whether performances were held on the fixed mansion or the pageant wagon, all of these scenic locations were temporary. The guilds, or business unions, built these stages and took pride in decorating them and performing their assigned play. **Simultaneous staging**, the display of several locations at a time, was a distinctive characteristic of this style of performance. The guilds would organize the spaces so that Hell, earth and Heaven were separated. Location was apparent. For example, the **Hell Mouth** was a spectacular effect with smoke and fire issuing forth and the cries of the damned coming from inside. Costumed devils would run into the crowd and drag participants in. Even though they used ecclesiastical garments, and everyday clothing and props for effect, these were not realistic settings in any sense. Heavenly characters were designed to inspire awe and demons were designed to inspire terror. To accomplish this the guilds took pride in creating elaborate special effects, called **secrets**. Theatrical design was a chance for the amateur theatre makers to have fun and capture the audience's attention.

> Houses for Tragedies, must be made for great personages, for that actions of love, strange adveture, and cruell murthers (as you reade in ancient and moderne Tragedies) happen always in the houses of great Lords, Dukes, Princes, and Kings. Therefore in such cases you must make none but stately houses. . . . I have made all my Scenes of laths, covered with linen, yet sometime it is necessary to make some things rising or bossing out; which are to bee made of wood, like the houses on the left side, whereof the Pillars, although they shorten, stand all upon one base, with some stayres, all covered with cloth, the Cornices bearing out, which you must observe to the middle part . . .
>
> **Sebastiano Serlio**

©Atlantide Phototravel/Corbis

This is Il Teatro Farnese, which combines the façade of a Roman Theatre and a proscenium arch. The vestigial orchestra is used for seating, as is the horseshoe ring of seats. Behind the proscenium would have been a raked stage outfitted with wings and flats to create a perspective vista. The basic structure of this theatre is still in use today. The picture frame around the stage space is useful for designers in creating their compositions.

Conventional stage scenery as it is known on the Broadway and West End stage is a descendant of the Italian Renaissance. Generally, Renaissance design is based on the discovery of the rules for perspective, their application to the world of architecture, and a large infusion of funding from patronage. Leon Battista Alberti wrote *On Painting* in 1435, the first treatise outlining Filippo Brunelleschi's discovery of **linear perspective**, the mathematical system for creating the illusion of space and distance on a two-dimensional surface. This revolutionized pictorial representations of three-dimensional space. As businessmen grew wealthy they sought ways to display their wealth to their friends and their competition, and invested in the arts. The early evolution of the theatrical scenery is the work of a number of designers over the period between 1508 and 1638. Stage design was affected by the rediscovery of classical texts such as Vitruvius's books of architecture. Designers mimicked his advice on creating three basic settings to depict the tragic setting with a palace location, a comic setting with a street location, and a pastoral scene with a woodland location. They began to experiment with how they could use these principles to try and create a sense of perspective combining three-dimensional forms with two-dimensional **angled wings** and **painted backdrops**. These practices became more commonplace when Sebastiano Serlio (1475–1554) published *Dell'architettura* in

Serlio's Tragic Set depicts halls of government. Predating the proscenium, this would have been built recessed behind an apron where the actors would deliver their lines. The stage would have been raked to accentuate the perspective. About two-thirds of the way back there would have been a backdrop that had a perspective vista painted on that continued the street off in the distance. When the proscenium was introduced the buildings would have been set behind it. These generalized locations would have served as the backdrop to all of the tragedies performed at the theatre. It is a generalized locale.

© Fotolia.com

1545 detailing the design and construction of a court theatre. He advocates Vitruvius's three main stage settings, but imagines them in terms of Renaissance perspective design. He places the setting on a **raked stage** that has a flat portion at the front for actors and then the rear is sloped up toward the back wall to assist in the illusion of distance at back. His scenery is not meant to move and is constructed using the sets of angled wing and flats on the raked portion of the stage and a backdrop.

Another example of how classical ideas were rearticulated during the Renaissance is the construction of *Il teatro Olimpico*. The Olympic Academy commissioned Andrea Palladio and then Vincenzo Scamozzi (1552–1616) to build a classical theatre inside of an existing building. It looks like a miniature Roman theatre brought indoors. It has a wooden scenae frons, semi-circular seating, and five entrances including one at each end and three in the center. Contemporary Renaissance ideas were incorporated with the street scenes built in perspective behind each of the stage openings to help create the impression that the stage is a city square into which a number of streets lead. With the popularity of perspective scenery came the fashion for elaborate scenic spectacle, and designers continued to innovate and find ways to make the perspective more believable, and to try and vary the location over the course of a production. In 1606 Giovanni Battista Aleotti (1546–1636) made an innovation upon this idea with the introduction of the **flat wing**, which was a flat piece of scenery painted to look like the façade of a building. He also designed *Il Teatro Farnese*, built from 1618–1628, with a permanent proscenium arch. At one end of a rectangular structure was a stage area designed for deep-perspective scenery and spectacular effects. It was divided in half by two half walls, and had provision for three sets of side wings and a back shutter in the front and four sets of wings or shutters. The use of flat wings became common after 1638 when Nicola Sabbattini (1574–1654) published *The Manual for Constructing Theatrical Scenes and Machines*. He experimented to find ways to have greater flexibility in shifting scenery. Later, **sliding flats** replace flat wings, and then evolve into the **wing and groove system**. Giacomo Torelli (1608–1678) revolutionized scene shifting with the **chariot-and-pole system**, which remained popular until the late nineteenth century. When flat wings replaced angle wings, flats could be stacked behind each other and moved out of the way when the next flat was required in the wing and groove system. The chariot-and-pole system coordinated all of the flat changes at once by connecting all of the scenery using ropes and pulleys to a rolling chariot under the stage that could remove and place a scene simultaneously in a single motion. These systems were perfected in the public opera houses in Venice such as *il teatro San Cassiano*, where they experimented with angled flats turning like pages in a book or sliding into place on grooves. It popularized the **pit, box, and gallery** structure of seating to accommodate all classes while segregating by class. Proscenium staging like this becomes increasingly important to accommodate the new emphasis on spectacle, illusion, and perspective scenery.

> There yet remains an article to be mentioned, and of equal importance with the foregoing, though not sufficiently considered, and that erroneously; to wit, the illumination of the scenes. What wonderful things might not be produced by the light, when not dispensed in that equal manner, and by degrees, as is not the custom. Were it to be played off with a masterly artifice, distributing it in a strong mass on some parts of the stage, and by depriving others, as it were, at the same time; it is hardly credible what effects might be produced thereby; for instance, a *chiaro obscuro*, for strength and vivacity, not inferior to that so much admired in the prints of Rembrandt.
>
> **Algarotti, in the eighteenth century**

The growing taste for machinery and spectacular effects was encouraged by the growth of court masques, intermezzi, and opera that made increasingly elaborate use of spectacle and illusion. These effects were illuminated with candles and oil lamps that provided a general diffuse wash of light over the stage space. They mounted these lights on the front edge of the stage and on ladders between each pair of side wings. In the 1780s oil lamps were introduced to replace the candle as the lighting source. Generally chandeliers hung over the house and stage, with candles behind the proscenium arch and the wings and as footlights. They even managed lighting effects

The court masque was a form of festive courtly entertainment which flourished in sixteenth- and early seventeenth-century Europe. It involved music, dancing, singing, and acting, within an elaborate and expensive stage design. The host would hire a preeminent designer, commission a flattering neoclassical allegory, and hire some performers to fill in the roles. Often, the courtier guests at the party were active participants performing alongside the professionals. The costume above would have been worn by the guest/actor. While seeming elegant these entertainments were raucous drunken affairs. The spectacular settings and designs fueled scenic innovation in the Opera house.

by raising and lowering lights and creating lenses with containers filled with tinted liquid. Variations on these practices were in use across Europe and in the New World between the eighteenth and late nineteenth century. The most famous of the designers of this period, Philip James de Loutherbourg (1740–1812), a French painter, revolutionized English stage design. In a major exhibit he showed off the new effects that he was playing with. He created a model theatre, in which lights behind a canvas represented the moon and stars; the illusory appearance of running water produced by clear blue sheets of metal and gauze, with loose threads of silver, and so on, were his devices. In 1771 he went to London working for David Garrick, who paid him handsomely to become Drury Lane's resident designer. He incorporated his inventions and superintended the scene painting. For example he delighted audiences and amazed fellow artists with green trees that gradually became russet, and a moon that rose and lit the edges of passing clouds in his designs for Garrick's *The Christmas Tale*, and the pantomime, *1781–1782*. He is most famous for an entertainment called the *Eidophusikon*, which, using mirrors and pulleys, lights, gauzes, colored glass, and smoke showed the rise, progress, and result of a storm at sea that destroyed a great ship, the Halsewell, and the Fallen Angels raising the Palace of Pandemonium from Milton. It was not until the massive changes that took place in the nineteenth century that a scenic revolution occurred again.

Generally, the scenes should have a tone favorable to every color of the dresses, like Beuther's scenery, which has more or less of a brownish tinge, and brings out the color of the dresses with perfect freshness. If, however, the scene-painter is obliged to depart from so favorable an undecided tone, and to represent a red or yellow chamber, a white tent or a green garden, the actors should be clever enough to avoid similar colors in their dresses. If an actor in a red uniform and green breeches enters a red room, the upper part of his body vanishes, and only his legs are seen; if with the same dress, he enters a green garden, his legs vanish, and the upper part of his body is conspicuous. Thus I saw an actor in a white uniform and dark breeches, the upper part of whose body completely vanished in a white tent, while the legs disappeared against a dark background.

Johann Wolfgang von Goethe

The three major scenic trends that developed during the nineteenth century, especially in Europe, were historically accurate scenery, the development of the realistic box set, and a move away from two-dimensional painted scenery to three-dimensional spaces. These changes were in part due to the new technologies of limelight, gas, and electricity that enabled practitioners to make the volume of the stage set visible to audiences in convincing ways. William Capon (1757–1827) was the best known designer in England in the late eighteenth and early nineteenth century. He was noted for use of contemporaneous architectural styles in his settings as well as depicting local settings as backdrops for plays. Capon's painted backdrops depicted local vistas that were used as settings to plays, thus combining contemporary painting trends with theatrical taste. While experiments began in the early nineteenth century with historically accurate settings and costumes it was not until the later half of the century that accuracy would become desirable. William Charles Macready's production of *King John* was a watershed event introducing historically accurate costumes and scenery. However, his designer William Telbin (1813–1873) in later collaborations with Charles Kean made the practices more visible. Kean was convinced that he could improve upon Shakespeare by imagining it for the proscenium stage filled with perspective scenery. He applied historical detailing to all his Shakespeare and melodramas, illustrating the action with detailed street scenes filled with houses and crowds of costume characters. His production of Dion Boucicault's *The Corsican Brothers* in 1852 made use of elaborate stage tricks to reveal ghosts. This complex machinery became known as the "Corsican trap," which mimicked the gliding of a ghost across stage. The most famous image of a scene from this play is a tableau of a duel whose dying central figure is revealed when a background scrim is lit from behind. He began to use such elaborate devices for his melodramas as panoramic backgrounds, ghost traps, and vampire traps. Moving spectacle became all the rage.

The practice of lighting the theatre with candles and oil lamps was not ideal for illuminating the volume of the stage because the emission was poor and inconsistent. When **gas lighting** was first introduced in 1816 its advantages were immediately apparent. It was easier to control and it was considerably brighter. However, it smelled bad and it was prone to overheating and setting the wood and canvas of the scenery on fire. Designers sought to shape the light and to have control over which parts of the stage were lit at any one time, so in 1826 **limelight** was invented. Limelight uses a block of quicklime heated by oxygen and hydrogen to produce a sharp, highly controlled shaft of light that was used as a spotlight. These spotlights positioned in the balcony of the house or on the sides could illuminate a small area of the stage, the actor, or create an illusion like moonlight. By the late nineteenth century the **carbon arc lamp** was introduced and used instead because it was safer, had more control, and produced less heat. A carbon arc lamp works by hooking two carbon rods to an electrical source; current flows through the spaced rods as an arc of vaporizing carbon, producing an intense white light. By the early 1920s newer, safer **incandescent lights** replaced carbon arcs for general theatrical use. Electric light was safer, did not smell, and did not heat the stage space excessively. This made practical the use of box sets to depict location. **Box sets** moved away from the sliding flats that were common since the Renaissance, used to create the illusion of perspective. Actors could walk between the flats to enter and exit the stage. Rather with the box set designers created an illusion of an interior room by constructing three walls on the stage, with the convention that the audience was looking through an invisible forth wall positioned beneath the proscenium arch. It included architectural features such as doors and windows to add realism to entrances and exits. Box sets were introduced as early as the Renaissance but they did not catch on until Madame Vestris (1797–1856) began to use them in around 1832. They later became a feature of realist theatre, which emphasized the illusion of real spaces particular to each play.

> I turn my carpenters over to my scenic artist, who furnishes to them the plans. They then construct the scenery in my own shops, for I never have such work done by contract. I will allow nothing to be built out of canvas stretched on frames. Everything must be real. I have seen plays in which thrones creaked on which monarchs sat, and palace walls flapped when persons touched them. Nothing so destructive to the illusion or so ludicrous can happen on my stage.
>
> **David Belasco**

Between 1815 and 1850 as a result of the rise in popularity of **melodrama**, spectacle gained importance even though stock settings were still in widespread use. Large theatre auditoriums and a desire for productions featuring exotic locations, special effects, and scenic illusion led theatre producers to invest in theatre design. These developments coincided with the invention of the **panorama**, first exhibited by Robert Barker (1739–1806). This popular form of realistic landscape painting that offered a 360-degree view was considered theatre, even without the presence of actors. Viewers stood on a raised platform in the center of a circular exhibition space and turned themselves around as if looking at a scenic vista, or walked along the perimeter. Eventually moving panoramas were offered that scrolled past the viewer. Louis Daguerre introduced the diorama offering lighting effects that mimicked fog lifting from a bucolic scene or a storm brewing in the sky. His innovations are still in use in the form of the translucent drop where, depending on the lighting angle, a different scene can be seen on a backcloth. These innovations attracted mass audiences keen to see more spectacular effects as offered in melodramatic enter-tainments. In the conventional theatre the panorama was mounted at the back of the stage and the painted scene was scrolled past the audience. Scene locations could be presented quickly. These trends paved the way for a greater illusionism on the stage, as well as an increased experimentation with lighting effects.

Louis Daguerre (1787–1851) and Pierre Luc Charles Ciceri (1782–1868) experi-mented with **moving panoramas** and atmospheric scenic effects. Coupled with advances in lighting technology, these techniques led to greater realism on the stage.

Daguerre's moving panoramas allowed spectators to sit and watch two paintings scroll past them on proscenium-like stages over the course of 15 minutes depicting such places as the pyramids at Giza or the beaches and palm trees of Hawaii. He also used lighting techniques and semi-transparent scenery to show calm weather turn stormy or day change to night. Audiences still see techniques like his **translucent drop** on stage today. Depending on how the drop is lit, the painted images on the front and back can become visible and/or invisible. Ciceri was considered the most influential designer of the period. He opened a scenic studio in Paris and specialized in scenery that created a sense of local color or historical settings. This move to paint specialized depictions of locale, time, and place fostered an expectation for audiences that settings ought to be distinct to each show.

> Observe that I am not at all, so to speak, carried away by them. Their discordant settings, oddly erected, are infinitely less well painted than ours. They overdo the use of practicables, putting them everywhere. The costumes, splendid and ridiculously rich when they are strictly historical, are almost always in bad taste when, there being no documentary evidence, imagination and originality must be employed. Their lighting effects are very successful, but too often they are regulated without art. For instance, instead of moving gradually, a very beautiful ray from the setting sun that shone on the noble head of an old man dying in his armchair, all of a sudden passed across the stained-glass window at the exact moment that the good man died, with the sole purpose of providing a tableau.

> **André Antoine on Meiningen**

These developments made possible the fabrication of individualized settings for each new production. Architecture, costumes, stage decoration all could be reproduced to create localized settings and tailor-made productions. When this interest combined with technological developments and a new interest in philosophy and science, directors began to emerge to create unified realistic settings. The most important practitioner to influence the development of realistic setting was Georg II (1826–1914), the Duke of Saxe-Meiningen. His company championed historically accurate sets and costumes, though not as an end in themselves. Although he used a realistic style of production, the plays he presented were primarily romantic. He demanded intensives rehearsals with sets and costumes in place from the outset, and would not let actors tamper with designed costumes as they did in conventional practice. He paid attention to stage composition, blocking actors on the diagonal, and used trees instead of sky borders. Above all he wanted to create a unified composition. His acting company toured the major cities of Europe between 1874 and 1890 influencing production techniques from Paris to Moscow. In America the producer, director, and playwright David Belasco (1853–1931) is renowned for his emphasis on naturalistic detail. For example in 1912 he built Child's Restaurant, which was a fully functioning restaurant, on stage, for the *Governor's Lady*. Nevertheless, not everyone thought that this literal depiction of location was ideal for theatre production.

> [U]nder the domination of painted set, the lighting is completely dominated by the décor. . . Lighting itself is an element of the effects of which are limitless; once it is free, it becomes for us what the palette is for the painter. . . the actor no longer walks *in front* of painted lights and shadows; he is immersed in an atmosphere that is *destined for him*.
>
> **Adolphe Appia**

All of this realistic detail was an exciting development; however, at the end of the nineteenth century and in the beginning of the twentieth century two designers radically changed the ways in which traditional theatre companies conceived of scenic practice. These practices began a revolution not seen since the Renaissance in the way in which design practice was conceived. Both Adolphe Appia (1862–1928) and Edward Gordon Craig (1872–1966) disapproved of the convention of a three-dimensional actor standing on a flat floor surrounded by a mass of realistically painted canvas. Their ideas and designs challenged conventional practice and their designs became the basis for the **New Stagecraft**. Rather than strictly reproduce realistic painted locale, New Stagecraft technique represents settings through simplification and suggestion. They wanted to evoke location and atmosphere using

This rendering by Adolphe Appia for Wagner's *Parsifal* act I, scene I, demonstrates the way in which he advocated the complete use of the three dimensions of the stage space and the absence of realistic or picturesque elements. He attached particular importance to the text and to the actor, which for him were inseparable from the sets and lighting. Appia felt that the setting should evoke the mood and atmosphere of the action, not depict location literally. He used the background landscape to provide a transition between the mid-ground and background breaking up the horizontal and vertical. The trees in the foreground provide scale and rhythm to the image. The light and shadow convey mood. These techniques paved the way for contemporary stage practice.

Photo courtesy of Collection Suisse du Theatre, Bern

selected details that give a sense of place and leave the audience room to imagine the rest. Appia assumed that artistic unity was the fundamental goal of theatrical production and that contemporary practice failed to achieve this with the contradictions of placing an actor's form against a two-dimensional backdrop. He broke down why this fails to create a unified composition. He describes three conflicting visual elements: a moving three-dimensional actor; the perpendicular scenery and the horizontal floor; and the two-dimensional setting. To unify these elements he advocated the use of three-dimensional forms such as steps, ramps, or platforms to enhance actors' movements. These forms also provide a transition between the horizontal floor and the upright scenery. Light was the key to fuse all the visual elements into a unified whole. Appia laid out these ideas in *The Staging of Wagner's Musical Dramas* (1895), *Music and Stage Setting* (1899), and *The Work of Living Art* (1921). He described three types of stage light: **diffused light**, which is a general wash of the stage space, **creative light**, which composes highlights and shadows on the stage, and **painted light**, which is the painted highlights and shadows on the two-dimensional scenery. He considered light to be the counterpart to music, changing moment to moment in response to shifting moods, emotions, and actions. Diffused light and creative light should be composed as music to allow for shifting light to create an inner drama that flows and changes with music, and that the intensity, color, and direction of the light should reflect the changing atmosphere or mood of the production. Accomplishing this was difficult given the technical limitations at the end of the nineteenth century. However, his theories about light distribution, brightness, and color are the foundation of contemporary stage lighting practice.

> By means of suggestion you may bring on the stage a sense of all things – the rain, the sun, the wind, the snow, the hail, the intense heat – but you will never bring them there by attempting to wrestle and close with Nature, in order so that you may seize some of her treasure and lay it before the eyes of the multitude. By means of suggestion in movement you may translate all the passions and the thoughts of the vast numbers of people, or by means of the same you can assist your actor to convey the thoughts and emotions of the particular character he impersonates. Actuality, accuracy of detail, is useless upon the stage . . .
>
> **Gordon Craig**

Edward Gordon Craig's ideas were so controversial that he was notorious across Europe. Though his practices were seldom seen in production, an exhibition of his designs in 1902, the publication of *The Art of Theatre* in 1905, *On The Art of Theatre* in 1911, *Towards a New Theatre* in 1932, *The Theatre Advancing* in 1919, and his periodical *The Mask* advocated a radical departure from the painterly practices of the nineteenth-century stage. Craig, like Appia, thought of the theatre as a distinct art form where a master artist fuses actions, words, line, color, and rhythm as a painter, sculptor, or composer would. Another idea that made Craig unpopular was that of the *Über-marionette*, that conceived of the actor as a super-puppet that served as a controlled visual element following the designer's demands. He shared Appia's concern that the three-dimensional volume of the stage space needed to be broken up using platforms, steps, and ramps. He also replaced the parallel rows of canvas flats with a series of tall screens that were meant to suggest the essence of the local. Both designers preferred abstraction to realistic reproduction because they felt that it better approximated the poetic nature of artistic representation. Both Appia and Craig influenced the trend in the early twentieth century toward a simplified décor, three-dimensional settings, flexibility in both scenery and lighting, and directional lighting.

The non-realist theatre practitioners substituted their own subjective visions for the so-called realist and naturalist depictions of the world. They used abstraction and distortion to depict that which they felt was beneath the surface of reality. Experiments by designers in the various movements helped develop a range of techniques that made use of the elements and principles of design in an abstract palette to create the visual world of the stage. Avant-garde designers worked on the symbolist stage, the dada stage, the surrealist performance events, and on the futurist stage. These designers sought to use color, movement, shape, form, lighting, and sound to create their stage worlds. Each manipulated the principle of practice as a means of staying true to their idealized styles. Their practices freed conventional theatre from the need to create unnecessarily realistic reproductions of the world.

> *Let's renovate the stage.* The absolutely new character that our innovation will give the theatre is *the abolition of the painted stage.* The stage will no longer be a coloured backdrop but a *colourless electromechanical architecture, powerfully vitalized by chromatic emanations from a luminous source,* produced by electric reflectors with multicoloured panes of glass, arranged, coordinated analogically with the psyche of each scenic action.
>
> **Enrico Prampolini**

One major leap forward toward incorporating the avant-garde theatre practices into mainstream theatre was with the work of the director Max Reinhardt (1873–1943). He made common the approach to production that it was necessary to look to the dramatic text to find out which tools would best serve the production. His production teams mixed and matched techniques derived from the whole range of design practices available at the time. This careful attention to design as a means to serve the text is the basis of many of the most conventional production approaches today. As well, he was not content to rely on a proscenium stage, but rather he experimented with a revolving stage playing with different arrangements between actors and audiences. He brought these ideas to Great Britain and the United States. Reinhardt did not use abstract settings, but he was willing to adopt any of the new stagecraft techniques to his spectacles if they suited the action. Unlike the popular theatre's exploitation of machinery and technical devices to dazzle audiences, his tempered vision made the incorporation of new technology and new concepts a sustainable practice.

A further influential company which affected conventional stage practice in Great Britain and later the United States was the Ballets Russes. Little was known of the Russian art practices of the time, and as a result when Sergei Diaghilev (1872–1929) brought his company on tour their unified compositions where movement, music, and décor were fused into an overall harmony created a stir. The work of the Ballets Russes was a rebellion against naturalistic spectacle that used wings and drops. Instead he hired contemporary painters to create the setting and costumes and they adopted new painterly art styles to convey mood and theme using the conventional stage devices. For example in 1921 he teamed up with Leon Bakst (1866–1924) to present *The Sleeping Princess*, which imitated the work of the Bibienas while employing new painting techniques and diagonal perspectives. They blended the old with the new. Their practice departed from illusionism, adopting instead a stylized representation of place designed to convey the mood and atmosphere of a time rather than distinct historical period representation.

Another Russian, Vsevolod Meyerhold (1874–1940) began to work as what we now term as scenographer – both director and designer appropriating text and finding visual forms for representing themes. He made use of a physical acting style called Biomechanics, where actors used their bodies as acrobats to create an outward expression of internal states, and made use of a design style called constructivism, which conceived of the stage as an acting machine. In Biomechanics enacting the appropriate kinetic pattern can induce a desired emotional response. The physical and emotional reflects replaced concentration on inner motivation. Using constructivist principles his design team stripped down the mechanisms of performance to their bare mechanical essence. For example his designer Lyubov Popova (1889–1924) created a setting for his infamous *Magnanimous Cuckold* (1922) that stripped the stage down and left it completely bare. She added in steps, platforms, slides, and uncovered flats. The back of the theatre was left bare. There was a huge disk resembling a hamster wheel with the letters painted across it, which turned at various speeds according to the emotional and rhythmic needs of the scene. The costumes were blue coveralls used by factory workers. The machine enabled the actions of the actors to come to the forefront while the lines, shapes, movements, rhythms, and textures accented the content of the play. These practices were in direct conflict with the realist practices of the Moscow Art Theatre and it took the introduction of several other techniques for designers in other parts of the world to adopt these tools for practice.

Though Erwin Piscator (1893–1966) developed its principles, Epic Theatre has become synonymous with Bertolt Brecht (1898–1956). This theatrical mode

Lyubov Popova's maquette for Meyerhold's production of the Flemish play *The Magnanimous Cuckold* shows the way in which the actors are provided multiple levels for use. The setting does not depict a literal space, but rather is a machine for acting. The platforms take up the volume of the stage space and dissect it at various depths and angles. The propellers and wheels rotated, providing a constantly changing visual image for the audience. Constructivist set design is an example of non-realistic theatre practices making use of abstract settings to evoke the themes of the production. The windmill blades in the upper right of the construction were meant to remind the audience of the play's Flemish origins.

Tretyakov Gallery, Moscow, Russia / The Bridgeman Art Library

combined features of expressionism and realism as a means of depicting documentary events geared to raise political awareness. Rather than providing natural environments in the form of a cityscape backdrop, the epic mode used a map as a backdrop to show the relationship of the town to the whole geopolitical context of the action. It made use of projection, film clips, and abstract acting machines. Multiple events may have occurred simultaneously on its stages. The painter Georg Grosz (1893–1959) designed Piscator's most famous production, *The Good Soldier Schweik*. He made cartoon-like sketches that were incorporated into the scenery. There were two treadmills that moved in opposite directions and maps, film clips, and projections used as a means of commenting on the action of the play as it unfolded. Brecht took these ideas further in his productions. He believed that locations ought to be suggested rather than constructed as a Naturalist would. The design should never seek to give an illusion of place in its entirety, but rather provide fragments of a location that would evoke the place, comment on the action, or provide a functional utility for the actors. He revealed the mechanics of constructing stage environments as a means of calling attention to the theatricality of the moment. He used the scenery as an extension of his alienation techniques that distanced the audience from the action so that they could think about and judge what they were watching.

Brecht's theories in staging were influenced by his collaboration with Caspar Neher (1897–1962). Neher chose to make selective use of real materials such as wood, leather, and metal rather than create a large-scale illusion like Andre Antoine or other practitioners of naturalism. Instead clothing and props were chosen as a means to create a connection between the stage action and life outside of the theatre. The common elements associated with Brechtian scenography are the half curtains suspended by rusty wires, visible lighting instruments, and working props chosen to remind audiences of the theatricality of the event. The scenic elements were another means for the audience to see a commentary on the action. Brecht worked closely with Neher as they rehearsed the actors and developed the scenery simultaneously in the rehearsal room. They did not seek to create an illusion, but rather use each element of production separately to evoke a poetic depiction of the context for the action.

> Work on the stage is a work of art. Work on the stage points to the unity of life through the multiplicity of the living. Unity is heralded by order in multiplicity. Order is the law of the work of art . . . Work on the stage encompasses the world of man. The stage produces life just as life produces life. The message of the inner man creates the inner man.
>
> **Lothar Schreye**

In line with the development of Epic Theatre practice is the influence of the Bauhaus upon stage design. Bauhaus was a school that combined crafts with all of the disciplines of the fine arts. The commonalities between all art practices were explored. Among their collaborative experiments were explorations of line, shape, color, movement, and sound meant for performance. The most commonly known is by Oskar Schlemmer (1888–1943). Schlemmer was not in a representational theatre, but a theatre of abstraction that used the elements of design as a pure art. He divided the stage into three elements. All theatre practice contains a man in space, light in motion, and architecture. His *Triadic Ballet* (1922) was made up of three dancers, three musical movements, and was a fusion of the three elements of dance, costume, and music. Concentrating on its form and movement, Schlemmer explored the body's spatial relationship to its architectural surroundings. His composition is based on the concept that mechanization demands that we hone our skills. His art practice reduced form and motion to the smallest number of shapes and movements, like the factory worker reduces his or her movements to the most economical gestures to do

© 2011, Estate Oskar Schlemmer, Munich

Oskar Schlemmer's costume design for the *Triadic Ballet* resembles a classical tutu in appearance, but is far from it in texture and form. Costumes are meant to disguise the body, so the wire changes the form of the human body. Its loops add movement and rhythm in its repetition. As well, its surface is shiny and will catch the light. He uses shape, form, texture, and color to provide visual interest. The elements and forms are as much the content of the dance as the movements of the dancer. Here costume is pared down to its most basic form.

the job. Therefore the function of costume was to emphasize the identity of the body or to change it so that an audience could read its abstracted expression. Costume and setting express the body's nature or it purposely misleads the audience regarding it. These practices allowed theatre artists to experiment with the visual elements of theatre as abstraction.

> The aesthetic methods of the stage-designer, like those of his director, are determined by factors not in themselves aesthetic. Design in the theatre today is nothing more than a kind of visual eloquence, integrally part of the act of interpreting a theme. Whether it illuminates the present or revives a fresh sense of the past, it will be vital only where it is a necessary factor in the struggle to impregnate spectators with a dramatist's idea. The style of modern stage setting, therefore, cannot be deduced from any formal concepts of pure beauty nor be evolved by avoiding any specific ugliness. Its beauty will be only the vividness with which it reflects dramatic ideas that a producer can bring to life, its finality, as form, no greater than the insight or the imagination of which audiences of today are capable.
>
> **Lee Simonson**

Although American designers were exposed to a number of styles from the continental avant-garde, Craig's concepts and his books became the most important influence over American design practice. Robert Edmund Jones (1887–1954) traveled to Europe and brought back the techniques he learned there. He shocked American audiences with a presentational setting for Anatole France's *The Man Who Married a Dumb Wife* in 1915. Jones's design departed from the realistic depiction of medieval architecture and instead presented a simple abstract setting. The stage is broken into a colorless geometric grid and suggested the period only through costume. Jones teamed up with Kenneth Macgowan (1888–1963) to publish *Continental Stagecraft* in 1922. They presented their impressions of the styles they saw in Europe and introduced the simplicity of design that is suggestive and symbolic, rather than a literal depiction of a setting complete with live grass and farm animals made popular by Belasco. They advocated a style that captured the essence of a real object with the minimum amount of detail. This was the key to making the extreme concepts of the avant-garde accessible to mainstream audiences. Norman Bel Geddes (1893–1958), like Appia and Craig made his mark on stagecraft primarily through projects that were never produced. His work is described as resembling Appia's designs on the scale of Craig's settings. He made use of modern lighting equipment offering him control over lighting the stage and flexibility in what he could achieve. These designers paved the way for Jo Mielziner and those he taught and inspired such as Ming Cho Lee. Emerging in the same generation were Tharron Musser and Jean Rosenthal, who are the doyens of lighting design, and Abe Feder, who established the contemporary practices of sound design and amplification which led to the recognition of the important function of sound. These pioneers paved the way for contemporary working relationships as well as basic operating procedures.

> A Stage Designer is, in a very real sense, a jack-of-all-trades. He can make blueprints and murals and patterns and light-plots. He can design fireplaces and bodices and bridges and wigs. He understands architecture, but is not an architect: can paint a portrait, but is not a painter: creates costumes, but is not a couturier. Although he is able to call upon any or all of these varied gifts at will, he is not concerned with any one of them to the exclusion of the others, nor is he interested in any one of them for its own sake. These talents are only the tools of his trade. His real calling is something quite different. He is an artist of occasions.

Robert Edmond Jones

In Great Britain non-realist practice sought to replace nineteenth-century attempts at illusionism, creating a sense of historical accuracy with theatricality. Craig's legacy is seen in the use of light to shape mood and atmosphere in production and Reinhardt's is a sense of eclecticism in theatre production. Notable designers in the mid-twentieth century who followed in their footsteps include the Motley Group (Margaret Harris, Sophia Harris, and Elizabeth Montgomery), who designed sets and costumes for Shakespearean and modern classics, opera, ballet, and motion pictures. They were known for their innovative set and costume designs that suggested the mood, architecture, and styles of the original setting of the play, but was not the rote duplication of stock scenery common at the time. On the other hand Oliver Messel (1904–1978) created painterly sets composed of borders, painted flats, cut cloths, and backcloths, accompanied by colorful and opulent costume designs, in a pastiche of historical styles. The transition point in theatre practice came after the Berliner Ensemble's visit to London which inspired Joan Littlewood's *Oh, What a Lovely War* (1963) that made use of Epic Theatre production techniques, freeing the stage from the proscenium illusionism that had been popular for so long. Her production flashed news bulletins on the back wall, presented projections and slides on screen, and exposed the materials of theatre practice such as lighting instruments and musicians. This freedom allowed designers such as John Bury (1925–2000) to make the floor an integral design element. He created a large mosaic circle in *The Physicists* and used a tilted circular disk for Wagner's *The Ring*. He used found materials such as metal and plastics to create texture paving the way for scenographers such as Pamela Howard. Ralph Koltai focused on creating an environment that serves as context for the actor picking up on kinetic theatre techniques from Eastern Europe. These designers paved the way for the use of avant-garde techniques in the construction of West End productions.

43

> [T]he relationship of scenic details, their capacity for association, creates from the abstract and undefined space of the stage a transformable, kinetic, dramatic space and movement. Dramatic space is psycho-plastic space, which means that it is elastic in its scope and alterable in its quality. It is space only when it needs to be space. It is a cheerful space if it needs to be cheerful. It certainly cannot be expressed by stiff flats that stand behind the action and have no contact with it.
>
> Josef Svoboda

Non-realistic design practices led to multimedia theatre design in the mid-twentieth century. One of the more influential practitioners of a design practice that used abstraction as a means of communication was Josef Svoboda (1920–2002). One of his best-known projects is the Laterna Magika, which is still in operation as a tourist attraction in Prague. The Laterna Magika techniques blend live actors with still and moving images. He mounted eight screens of various sizes on overhead tracks at varying distances, each could be moved independently. He created a collage of images using each screen to convey different aspects of the theme of the play through association. The stage incorporated treadmills and traps to keep in time with the images. His concept was that we as audience members would create our own associations with the images and the elements to combine them into our own composition. He discovered that he could use different levels of light to define the stage and call attention to images. He continued to experiment with simultaneous scenes. He experimented with reflective materials such as mirrors and other shiny surfaces. His legacy is a result of his experiments with low voltage light units to create a material light that served as an interactive setting and his continued use of projection. He experimented with a range of materials and technologies to work through Appia and Craig's ideas toward a kinetic theatre. To achieve a total immersive experience he included the audience within his conception of designed stage space. In *The Queen of Spades* (1976) he had playing cards as moving screens above the performers. Simultaneously images and films are projected upon the walls and ceiling. Light highlights the actors, but the whole space is used to evoke the mood, create the atmosphere, and comment upon the action. Here is a blend of styles used to bring out the themes of the opera and complement its music. These are early experiments in incorporating multiple media into a cohesive whole. His designs did not decorate the stage but rather created three-dimensional environments that could be synthesized with the actors' work to create a holistic meaning. Lighting was a critical element used to create movement, mood, and atmosphere as well as create energy for a dynamic representation. However, lighting worked in tandem with the scenery to create a composition whose elements were interrelated.

Returning to medieval theatre practice, contemporary theatre also makes use of found spaces or appropriated spaces as settings for their productions. Events like *Oh, What a Lovely War* exploited non-theatre spaces as a part of their counter-culture mandate. When removed from the conventions of the traditional theatre space a whole new host of design potentials open up. The whole space can be considered as a part of the design, or the space can contribute to the themes, mood, or atmosphere of the performance in a way that a proscenium theatre cannot. Robert Wilson's *Journey to Ka Mountain* was staged in the mountains of Iran; Le Théâtre du Soleil, an environmental theatre, performs in La Cartoucherie, a converted munitions factory. Their devised work often makes use of the entire theatre space. They have built barricades and dug trenches as a part of their production designs. As well, Peter Brook converted a dilapidated nineteenth-century Parisian melodrama house into a found space. There was no proscenium left and the company ripped out the house seats and converted it into a flexible theatre space. The ruined walls and leaks were kept. They often adapt the space adding elements such as dirt promontories or water features to space as part of their settings. In found spaces the environment becomes a part of the scenic design as well. Street theatre also allows for different design strategies. As often as new venues are found theatre practice absorbs the new practices into conventional theatre making. Today we make use of whichever eclectic tools best serve the goals of a production.

That is not to say that the age of innovation and experimentation is over. Today's practices will make way for new and exciting strategies that will change the way we construct, view, and interpret theatre designs. Advances in the sophistication of special effects in the film industry are training audiences to expect more from forms of visual entertainment. With the growing popularity of three-dimensional films and four-dimensional theme park entertainments, theatrical designers are searching for effective ways of incorporating mixed media technology into live performance. There are designers experimenting with virtual technology trying to integrate two-dimensional computer technology with three-dimensional performers, and designers experimenting with interactive scenery that responds to the performer's motions. Most recently there is Julie Taymor's collaboration with Glen Berger, Bono, and the Edge to create *Spider-Man: Turn off the Dark* at the Fox Woods Casino Theatre in New York, a comic book–rock opera–circus whose aim is to put the audience in the middle of a three-dimensional graphic novel that is meant to be just as thrilling as the movies. It uses projection and animation behind the proscenium, high velocity flying and special effects, pyrotechnics, and mechanized scenery. For example to create the comic book look the production team design graphics that have the look of a comic book and a pop-up book. Taymor sculpted masks of the villains and then took pictures that were then projected on the giant LED set. The acrobatic flying effects are computerized and fly actors over the audience. It is an immersive environment. Taymor worked as a scenographer involved in every aspect, until her resignation in March of 2011. As a result of the complexity of the conception the musical has accrued the largest production costs for a Broadway show ever, actors have been injured, and the technology to coordinate all the fast-paced scenography has not been perfected. Innovative theatre design is expensive. However, history

45

has proven that once this type of innovation occurs new possibilities of what theatre can be lead to new genres of entertainment and new conceptions of design practice.

The next chapter will define the basic visual concepts that designers use to create their sets, costumes, lights, and projections no matter the media or the time period. These elements and principles of design are the ways in which they conceive of the visual and spatial components used to build a production. While the designers and practices used as illustrations in this book are mainstream and only represent some of the most conventional commercial practices, their processes are recognized as representative of the building blocks for good design practice.

The vocabulary of visual thinking

3

> **Key Topics:**
>
> ℮ The elements of design
>
> - Line, shape and form, space, color, texture, movement
>
> ℮ The principles of design
>
> - Proportion, balance, rhythm, emphasis, contrast, unity, proximity, variety

Case Studies:

- Suggesting real spaces: *Serjeant Musgrave's Dance* and Jocelyn Herbert's design
- Robert Wilson designs *Alceste* with line, movement, and color
- *Shrek, The Musical*: Color, texture, shape, space, and a large green ogre

Example:

- *Lohengrin* (1998) / Robert Wilson

When audiences look at the spaces, props, costumes, and colors on the stage they read the arrangement of those visual components as if they are telling a story. This chapter introduces the basic principles and elements of the form and function of design components once they have been realized in production. The elements of line, shape and form, measure, position, color, value, texture, and space can be thought of as the things that make up the set, costume, lights, or sound design. The principles of balance, gradation, repetition, contrast, harmony, and unity can be thought of as the ways in which designers use the elements in the overall design of the theatrical production. How designers apply these principles determines how successful they are in creating a work of art. These concepts provide a vocabulary to describe the theatrical designer's aesthetic tools and how they are harnessed to create what audiences see on stage. This vocabulary provides a means for designers to talk to other theatre professionals to describe what they have seen or wish to see in production.

The elements of design

The six elements of design are like the parts of a machine. These parts do not amount to much on their own, but when they are combined in the right way they come together to make a successful production. They are line, shape and form, color, value, texture, and space. This section provides the basic definitions of each element of design as well as examples that demonstrate their characteristics and functions.

A **line** is the basic building block of visual design. It can be made up of an infinite number of points, or be seen as the moving path of a point. It can have different qualities, curved or straight, thick or thin, loose or precise, delicate or bold, expressive or controlled. Lines can show direction, draw your attention, outline an object, divide a space, or communicate a feeling. Designers often use **implied lines**, which are a trick of perception created by a series of points such as a series of people standing in a row. They also use a **perceived line** that is not present at all, but is a line that is imagined. For example in the group shot from *Shrek* where Donkey's eyes are looking toward Shrek's face a line can be imagined from one face to the next. The qualities of a line can evoke different feelings, for example a curved line may feel natural or organic, while a straight line may feel artificial or mechanical. A delicate line may feel soft and feminine, while a bold line may feel strong and masculine. Lines create contours and form, and are often used to convey a specific kind of feeling or point to an important feature in a design. They are also used to create perspective, and dominant directional lines are often adopted to create a sense of continuance in a composition. In addition, lines that are grouped together often create a sense of value, density, or texture.

> The lines in every piece relate to those four points and every time we moved something, even a couple of inches on stage, all the relationships changed and we had to redraft the entire piece. . . The perspective points gave the set an added sense of whimsy because it's clearly not realism. It's a very rigid whimsy because it is all parallel lines that's a lot of fun for the show and it made sense since spelling is rigid − it has right and wrong answers. Nobody realizes the technical mechanics that create the perspective but it gives it a firmer framework rather than just creating a wacky set.
>
> **Beowulf Borrit**

An important component of line is that is has **direction**. For example, they can be horizontal, diagonal, vertical, or oblique. Robert Wilson's thumbnail sketches below show the ways in which **horizontal** line can suggest a feeling of calmness, stability, and tranquility. Objects parallel to the earth are at rest in relation to gravity, and audiences understand compositions where horizontal lines dominate as quiet and restful in feeling. Wilson's drawings also show how **vertical** lines can communicate a feeling of loftiness and spirituality, or how erect lines seem to extend upwards beyond human reach, toward the sky. Extended perpendicular lines may suggest an overpowering grandeur, beyond ordinary human measure. The perpendicular lines in Lohengrin subtly evoke Lohengrin's supernatural origin. A set designer might create a façade with extended perpendicular lines as a backdrop for the beginning action of the *Bacchai*, where Pentheus imposes the order of law on his people. **Diagonal** lines suggest a feeling of movement or direction. Since objects in a diagonal position are unstable in relation to gravity, being neither vertical nor horizontal, they are either about to fall, or are already in motion. The same designer might transform Pentheus's palace into a façade with diagonally placed objects to show that Pentheus struggles to maintain order as Bacchus's power overtakes the *populus*. Different types of lines are used to create set pieces that can be crafted to support the themes of the production. In a two-dimensional composition, diagonal lines are also used to indicate depth, as Renaissance designers used perspective to pull the viewer into the picture, creating an illusion of a space that one could move within. A designer may integrate diagonal lines if they want to convey a feeling of movement or speed, or a feeling of activity. On the other hand, horizontal and vertical lines in combination communicate stability and solidity. Rectilinear forms stay put in relation to gravity, and are not likely to tip over. This stability suggests permanence, reliability, and safety, such as with the castle in *Shrek*.

Sharp curves, on the other hand, may be discombobulating, turbulent, or frenetic, like waves cresting in a storm or the eclectic lines in the many costume silhouettes in a mass of people. The meanings we associate with **curved lines** are variable.

49

Gentle, shallow curves may suggest comfort, safety, familiarity, or relaxation, as with the human body where we may recall the curves of a baby's face, and associate the lines with a pleasing, sensual quality. Even the exaggerated curves of Shrek's body and head have a pleasing feel. Curved directional forces have meanings associated with encompassment, repetition, or warmth. Eiko Ishioka's designs for *M-Butterfly* include a curved platform leading from center stage to stage left curving around the back to stage right. This curve both recalls the curves of the feminine form as well as the all-encompassing power of sexuality and political ideology. Lines can be combined with other lines to create textures and patterns, such as the patterns of the bricks in the walls of the castle or the design on the chorus's costumes, in *Shrek*'s case. The designer uses line to control the vision of the audience, to create unity and emotional value, and ultimately to develop meaning. Audiences are sensitive to its use and can extract considerable meaning from the kinds of line used, determining the mood of the play, the atmosphere of the location, or the personality of the character wearing the costume.

The simplest definition of **shape** is a closed contour defined by its perimeter. It is a two-dimensional object that has height and width but no depth. As Wilson's thumbnails show, an enclosing line, an area created by color, value or texture, or an area created by surrounding shapes can create a shape. The square, the circle, and the equilateral triangle are the three basic shapes. Similar to line, shape can evoke feelings. A square is associated with dullness, honesty, rigidity and a circle is associated with endlessness, warmth, and protection, while the triangle is associated with action, conflict, and tension. Straight edges and angular corners create rectilinear shapes as seen in Jocelyn Herbert's designs for *Serjeant Musgrave's Dance*. Curves and rounded forms create curvilinear shapes as seen in Posner's designs depicted in Chapter 6. **Geometric shapes** such as circles, squares, triangles, and rectangles are crisp, precise, and mathematical made up of straight edges or consistent curves. **Natural** or **organic shapes** are found in nature in the shape of flowers, tree branches, or leaves. Natural shapes are irregular in outline and cannot accurately be described using Euclidian geometry. The space-filling characteristics of objects are then described as fractal. **Abstract** or **stylized shapes** are natural shapes that have been altered or simplified to reflect the essence rather than the representation of an object. Wilson often uses **non-objective** or **non-representational shapes** created with no reference to subject. He uses them to represent nothing other than the pure shape the audience sees so that he can evoke a feeling or create a mood.

> Pure design is about the manipulation of abstract objects in a space in order to give that space an atmosphere or mood that enhances the nature of what's happening in that space. It's not about pictorial representation but about placing things in such a way that the audience will believe in what is going on.
>
> **John Napier**

The terms **form** and **shape** are often used synonymously. While shape is two-dimensional and appears flat, a mass, volume, or form is perceived as a three-dimensional shape that has height, width, and depth. For example, a square is a shape, while a cube is a form. Form and shape cannot exist without space. Geometric forms are those that correspond to named regular shapes, such as cubes, spheres, and cones. An audience's **perception** of shape and form are affected by several factors. The position or **viewpoint** from which we see an object will emphasize or obscure certain features, and therefore affect the impression it makes. When an audience sees Farquaad from the front he appears like a skinny, short man. However, since his real legs are strapped behind him to create the diminutive frame, if he is seen from the side his cape is bulky and wide and he no longer looks real. Form is also defined by **value**, which is the relative lightness or darkness of a color. Strong contrasts in value within a composition may define the boundaries of forms. Gradations of value, or shading, can also create the illusion of contour and volume. In the same way, **hue**, contrasts, and gradations can also define forms.

Two-dimensional forms can be used to create the illusion of three-dimensional shapes and spaces. These are the techniques that Renaissance designers used to create their painted backdrops. The tools for creating illusions of three-dimensional space are overlapping, changing size and placement, linear perspective, relative hue and value, and atmospheric perspective. The simplest is **overlapping**, which is accomplished by allowing the contour of one form to overlay upon the contour of another shape. **Changing size** and **placement** of elements allows audiences to see multiple perspectives of objects as well as understand their place in space. Linear perspective refers to the illusion that objects appear to grow smaller and converge toward a vanishing point at the horizon line. Paying attention to the shapes of objects in relation to their placement is essential to linear perspective. For example, in *Serjeant Musgrave's Dance*, the rendering of the jail has bars situated in the foreground and then depicts a city in the background. The shapes of the buildings overlap each other and conform to our assumptions about forms depicted through perspective. The rate at which forms appear to change in size and placement is regular. **Atmospheric perspective** is when objects placed in the upper half of the composition lack contrast, detail, or texture. This is also seen in Herbert's design. Three-dimensional form has an expressive vocabulary similar to that of line. For example, **rectilinear** shapes can suggest stability. **Angular** shapes placed diagonally in relation to gravity can suggest instability. Forms that exhibit **curving** surfaces can suggest quiet, comfort, and sensuality.

Even in theatre where designers construct three-dimensional space, they create illusions of depth, volume, and scale. They use both three-dimensional **space** in the form of the volume of the stage space and sometimes create the illusion of space within it. For example, Rae Smith's design for *War Horse* described in Chapter 4 uses a three-dimensional stage platform as well as a two-dimensional space of projection design where her sketches are projected. Like form, the illusion of space in two-dimensional projection has height and width, but no depth. By using visual cues designers create images that are perceived as three-dimensional. In the Renaissance designers used these techniques to create the look of a street stretching into the distance. **Size** is one of the easiest ways to create the illusion of space. A larger image will appear closer than a smaller one because over time we have learned that objects appear to become smaller as they get farther away. Overlapping is another easy way to suggest depth in an image. When objects overlap each other, the viewer perceives one in front and one at the back. **Compositional location** refers to where a form is positioned vertically in the image. The bottom is seen as the **foreground**, the part of the image that is nearest the viewer and the top as the **background**, the part farthest from the audience. The higher an object is placed in the image, the farther back it is perceived to be. Atmospheric perspective uses value, contrast, and color to give the illusion of space. Atmospheric perspective is based on the fact that the farther something is away from us, the more the atmospheric haze may obscure our view of it. By lightening the value, lowering the value contrast, softening the edges, decreasing detail, and muting the color, you can mimic the effect of atmospheric haze and create the illusion of increasing distance. Increasing the bluish cast of an image also creates a sense of depth because cool colors recede and warm colors come forward.

> It was quite tricky [lighting a multi-location – and often non-specific location – play], because it's a big set. It's a five-by-eight metre square of nothing and I really wanted to make sure that the actors weren't too exposed on the set by opening it out too much. Yet Max also wanted to make sure that he used the space as much as possible by having people walk in and out and make long journeys from the back of the stage down to centre-stage. So I decided that the only way to do that would be to use colour (something that I use an awful lot as a designer anyway) to say, "Right, this is the mood of this section, now it's getting a bit sadder" or "This is a bit more funny". So I tried to use colour washes to change each one of those main sections of the play, and from that to close down and open out the space depending on how each section worked.
>
> **Johanna Town**

Color is one of the most important elements because designers harness its expressive quality to communicate emotion in an immediate way. Color is a property of light that is visible when it is emitted or reflected. How a color appears is determined by the way in which the human eye responds to characteristic wavelengths of radiation within the visible spectrum. Hue, value, and saturation are the three main components used to describe color. Hue is the pure state of a color, and it is the name of a color. Terms such as red, blue-green, and brown all define the hue of a given color. **Value** is how light or dark the color is, for example a light blue compared to a navy blue. In other words value is how close to black or white the color is. Adding white to a hue creates a lighter value, or **tint**. Adding white to red creates pink. Adding black to a hue creates a darker value, or **shade**. Adding black to red creates maroon. **Saturation** is the **intensity** of a color, that is to say how bright or dull it is. Is it neon green or forest green? **High saturation** colors are close to the pure hue of a color. For example, they are bright and vivid like pure red or pure yellow. The more gray a color has in it, the less intensity it has, thus mixing pure colors with either gray or the color's **complement** creates **low saturation** colors, referred to as neutrals. Complements are colors that are opposite one another on the color wheel, and also can be compared by their relative temperature. Combining two primary colors yields a secondary color, though additive and subtractive primaries are different. For example in subtractive color mixing brown is derived from red and green paints, while in additive color mixing yellow is derived from red and green. Shining stage lights of red, green, and blue in the same area creates a white spotlight, whereas the absence of all additive primaries, in other words no light, yields black.

Temperature is the psychological property of heat or coolness that a color creates. Warm colors such as red, orange, and yellow are said to remind us of fire and sunlight so they endow an image with a sense of warmth. Cool colors such as blue and green are said to remind us of water and plants so they endow an image with a feeling of coolness. Warm colors tend to feel brighter and more energetic, while cool colors tend to seem calmer and more relaxed. Designers use color because it has the ability to affect feelings and moods. As the image of Fiona, Shrek, and Donkey shows us, the muted palette of greens and browns is calm and relaxed. The color conveys the message that this group of characters is comfortable, like-minded, and down to earth. Color combinations can attract or distract. The right color combinations can be as important as the individual colors. As the image of Lord Farquaad and the chorus from Duloc shows us, though the world is colorful, the designer chose a narrow range of colors to create his sense of character and environment. The world is one of high energy, but also regimented and disciplined. Its inhabitants are always putting on a show to make obvious their support of the Lord. Color has a significant impact on visual communication. If too many colors are used the audience will become visually confused and will reject the image. If not enough color is used the audience will get bored.

Although colour does not really exist apart from light, we tend to connect colour with paint, inks, or dyes and yet we can only establish constant colour values when we have "constants" in light. The general assumption that blue is blue and remains so is soon dispersed when the "blue" dress suddenly appears quite a different hue in the street than it appeared in the shop when it was tried on. The pigment itself may not change its properties, but the colour that we perceive does change. Each object is acting as a reflective filter: white light contains the full range of colours available in the spectrum; so the object, depending upon its pigment, accepts and reflects part of the white light spectrum and ignores the rest of it, giving us the experience of surface colour. If the 'white' light sources vary (as the difference between interior and exterior light) then the reflected colour of the object changes.

Peter Mumford

Color harmonies serve to describe the relationships certain colors have to one another and how they can be combined to create a palette of color. **Color schemes** have been developed to help designers choose colors that work well together. The most typical representation of this is the color wheel, which is a visual representation of the subtractive primary, secondary, and tertiary colors. A **monochromatic color scheme** involves variations, usually in value, of a single hue. Monochromatic schemes are highly unified, but may lack variety. An **analogous color scheme** uses adjacent colors on the color wheel, as well as their tints and shades. Analogous colors tend to be families of colors such as blues (blue, blue-violet, blue-green) and yellows (yellow, yellow-orange, yellow-green). Analogous color relationships are also unified, but have more variety than monochromatic schemes. A **complementary color scheme** is created with colors that are opposite to each other on the color wheel. When complements are mixed together, as when you mix yellow and purple paint, they neutralize each other, but when they are placed next to each other they increase each other's intensity. A **triadic color scheme** involves using three colors equidistant from each other on the color wheel. Triadic color schemes are lively and can be used where a strong impact is needed. Primary and secondary colors are examples of color triads. There are three **primary** hues that can be mixed to form all other hues. When pigment primaries are all mixed together, the theoretical result is black. This is referred to as a **subtractive color space**, which is the traditional color space like in the mixing of paint. The **primary colors** for subtractive colors are red, yellow, and blue, and the **secondary colors** are orange, green, and violet. The **light primaries** or **additive color space** are red, blue, and green, and all other colors are derived from them. Additive color space is when theatrical spotlights overlap on a white wall. If all three primaries are mixed, the theoretical result is white light. Light mixture is sometimes referred to as **additive mixture**.

Colors change under light and a lovely green in daylight or incandescent light can look a muddy gray under certain colors of gels on theatre lamps.

Deborah Dennison

An audience's emotional responses to color can be culturally biased. For example, in Europe and the United States black is the color of mourning, while in many tropical countries and in Asian brides white is the color of death. On the other hand, American brides wear white, while Asians wear red. However, we know that the following associations are generally true in European-based societies. Red is associated with blood, a point that is made in *Red* when Rothko's assistant finds him in a pool of paint and thinks it is blood, however, the play also plays with red's other connotation of feelings that are energetic, exciting, passionate, or erotic. Most colors carry both positive and negative connotations. The downside of red evokes aggressive feelings that may suggest anger or violence. Yellow is the most visible of all the colors. It is considered the most cheerful of the spectrum. It is the color of sunshine, and may suggest optimistic or upbeat connotations; however, yellow can become over-whelming. Pure bright lemon yellow is the most fatiguing color, because yellow is an eye irritant. For example, babies cry more in yellow rooms and couples fight more in yellow kitchens. In its positive mode, green may suggest nature, life, stability, restfulness, and naturalness as with Shrek's skin. On the other hand, green in some tones or certain contexts, such as Elphaba's green skin in *Wicked*, might instead suggest decay, toxicity, nausea, or artificiality. Blue may suggest coolness, distance, spirituality, or perhaps reserved elegance. Its negative connotations suggest blue as being sad, passive, or depressed. Color influences our perception of the objects that we see on the stage.

> My palette came from the steel-work of the set, so it's all very rustic, dirty blues, dirty lavenders, all those sort of material type colours. Industrial lighting green, which looks like the light in factories, is actually what we use for the Scottish Literary Editor. That creates a sort of blend between him being in the middle of a field and in an industrial area. So all the colours are quite industrial and specifically chosen to go in that metal-like environment.
>
> **Johanna Town**

Value or **tone** is the relative lightness or darkness of a color. It is an important tool for the designer because of the way that it defines form and creates spatial illusions. **Value contrast** refers to the degree of variation between light and dark, and it separates objects in space, while **value gradation** suggests mass and contour of a contiguous surface. When contrasting hues are made similar in value, the spatial effects are flattened out. The highest value contrast is obtained just using white and black. The narrower the range of values it has is referred to as **high key**; a limited range of dark values is called **low key**. Value is also used to create the illusion of space, since areas with high value contrast come forward while those with low value contrast recede into the distance. Hue and value are very important cues which tell us whether an object is near or far. In general, we tend to interpret warm hues as being closer than cool hues. We also see colors that are close in value as being close to each other in space, but colors that have strong contrast in value appear to separate in space. In terms of visual weight, darker values feel heavier than lighter values. Value can add emphasis with areas of high contrast standing out in low contrast. Value can evoke feelings or moods. For example, low value contrast creates a subtle, restrained effect that feels calm and quiet, whereas high value contrast evokes drama and conflict. The light values of high key images may convey the sense of happiness and lightness, mid-range values may evoke sadness and depression, and the dark values of low key images may create feelings of fear and mystery.

> Lighting designers are completely keyed in to what the materials and colors the set designers use and it defines so much of where we go . . . The great thing about the floor is that it could take color so well, as could the portals which served as a projection surface for each of the fantasy sequences . . . I could make the curtain red with one circuit and while it was red I could change the other circuit to another color so I was able to get crossfades from any color to any color. Sometimes you don't realize it's lighting that's changing the same piece of scenery, but that curtain was crucial to changing the mood and going into the fantasy sequences.
>
> **Natasha Katz**

Texture is the surface quality of a shape, such as rough, smooth, soft, hard, glossy, or slippery. It is how something feels when it is touched or looks like it would feel if touched. Does it look rough and bristly like stubble; smooth and warm like a baby's bottom; soft like gelatin; or hard and cold like a rock? All surfaces can be described in terms of texture. It can be imaginary, suggested to the eye from our memories of surfaces that we once touched. As a result, designers exploit this in theatre making and use texture as a dominant element in their work. For example, in the production photograph from *Shrek* the brickwork of Farquaad's castle shows how reproducing the value and color patterns of actual textures can create visual textures. Darks and lights can be used to suggest the furrows in a brick or the three-dimensional roughness of a stone surface. Repeating marks or shapes can also create visual texture. It is used to create a surface appearance in design. Surface texture is a tool for creating visual variety and interest.

Movement is the design element that occurs in a visual image when objects seem to be moving through space over time. It comes from the kinds of shapes, forms, lines, and curves that are used. Diagonal lines tend to create the illusion of movement or motion. Changes in direction, or change in the darkness or lightness of an image can also create a sense of motion. Similar shapes connected with each other or overlapping each other can imply movement or restlessness. A series of images shown as individual frames, like Wilson's thumbnail sketches, can provide a sense of movement through time. Movement is often described as either literal or compositional. **Literal movement** is physical movement, such as an actor moving across the stage. **Compositional movement** is the movement of the audience's eye through a composition. The designer in that case is concerned instead with how the attendant perceives the composition. That is to say, how the components relate and lead the attendant's attention. Compositional movement can be either static or dynamic. **Static movement** jumps between isolated parts of a composition, attracted by similarities, and simply shifting to shapes with related shape or color.

Dynamic movement flows smoothly from one part of the composition to another, guided by continuations of line or form, and by gradations of color or form. All compositions can be described in these terms. Theatre is the ultimate expressive use of the aesthetic element of movement of objects through space in time.

The principles of design

The elements of design on their own do not create successful designs, but it is the ways in which the elements are arranged that creates meaningful compositions. To understand this we must be familiar with a few basic design principles. The principles of design are the guidelines used for putting elements together to create effective communication. While the elements are the "what" of a design, the principles are the "how" of a design. The five different principle of design are proportion, balance, rhythm, emphasis, and unity. We can identify the characteristics of a designer's work based on the stylistic ways that it combines the elements and principles giving the design an individual personality.

Proportion or **scale** refer to the **size** of one object or part relating to the size of another object or part, or between a whole object and one of its parts in the design, and have the capacity to modify and define each other. A part of a design is never too large or too small in itself, but only in relation to other parts of the design. In other words, there can be no large without small, but even when large is established through small, the entire scale can be changed with the addition of another element. The most vital aspect of scale is the measurement of its relation to human proportion. In other words, we judge the appropriateness of the size of objects by the measure of the human body. For example, architectural spaces intended to impress are usually scaled to a size that dwarfs the human viewer. This is a device often used in public spaces, such as churches or centers of government. If you make a visit to the Supreme Court of the United States, you will find that your feet barely touch the floor as you sit on a bench looking up at the judge's dais. You are made to feel as you did as a child sitting in your father's chair. In contrast, the proportions of a private home are usually more in scale with human measure, and as a result it appears more inviting, comfortable, and less intimidating. Most important to scale is juxtaposition, what is alongside the visual subject, and what setting it is in. For example in *Shrek*, when the audience sees Lord Farquaad standing next to Fiona they know that he is vertically challenged.

Balance is the equal distribution of visual weight in a design. When elements are not balanced around a vertical axis, the effect is disturbing and makes us feel unsettled. Balance is an equilibrium that results from looking at images and judging them against our ideas of physical structure, such as mass, gravity, or the edges of a frame. Balance in a three-dimensional object is straightforward, if balance is not achieved the object topples over. For example in the image Lord Farquaad's body is unbalanced; he looks as if he will tip back if his cape was not there to balance him.

A balanced object is like the popular toy – the Weeble – "It weebles, it wobbles, but it doesn't fall down." A successful composition will be visually stabile through **symmetry** or **asymmetry. Symmetrical balance** is also known as bilateral symmetry, or when each side is the mirror image of the other. It occurs when the weight of a composition is evenly distributed around a central vertical or horizontal axis. Symmetrical balance is considered formal, ordered, or stable, but it can also be considered boring because it is monotonous. While symmetry achieves balance through repetition, asymmetry achieves balance through contrast. **Asymmetrical balance** is considered informal balance, occurring when the weight of a composition is not evenly distributed around a central axis. It involves the arranging of objects of differing size in a composition such that they balance one another with their respective visual weights. In general, asymmetrical compositions tend to have a greater sense of visual tension. This can be best imagined by envisioning a see-saw that can represent the visual "weights" that can be imagined in a two-dimensional composition. For example, it is possible to balance a parent who weighs more than a child by placing several children on one end to balance the weight of the parent. On a stage, this might be thought of as a cluster of small objects balanced by a large object. It is also possible to imagine objects of equal weight but different mass such as a large mass of cotton candy versus a small mass of gold bricks on equal sides of a fulcrum.

There are a variety of tactics that can be employed to influence visual weight. For example, **position** affects balance. While designers can adjust size making an object larger so that it feels heavier to the audience, position affects the way the audience perceives weight. The further away an element is from the center, the heavier it will feel. A smaller object placed near the lip of the stage can balance a large object placed near the center. An isolated element has more visual weight, a darker value feels heavier, a larger quantity of small objects can balance one larger object, and a diagonal orientation carries more visual weight than a horizontal or vertical one. For example, the image from *Alceste* (p. 66) shows how the rectangular bar of white is balanced with the human figures. The figure in purple looks heavier than the massive light bar and central figures. Asymmetrical balance is described as casual, interesting, and more dynamic than symmetrical balance.

Rhythm leads the eye from one part of a design to another part, creating movement through repetition of pattern or color. Just like the choreographed moves of a dancer, it can be described as timed movement through space. Its presence creates predictability and order in a composition. A designer can achieve rhythm in a design through repetition of lines, colors, shapes, forms, and/or texture. Rhythm does not have to have a regular beat; it can also have an irregular beat. There are many different kinds of rhythm, often defined by the feeling it evokes when looking at it. **Linear rhythm** refers to the characteristic flow of the individual line. Linear rhythm is not as dependent on pattern, but is more dependent on timed movement of the audience's eye. For example in the image for "What's up Duloc?" various forms of visual rhythm are evident. The audience's eye moves from costume to costume of the chorus and sees that same repetition repeated in Lord Farquaad's costume and also alternated in the lines of the castle. **Repetition** involves the use of patterning to achieve timed movement and a visual pulse. This may be a clear repetition of elements in a composition, or it may be a more subtle kind of repetition that can be observed in the underlying structure of the image. **Alternation** is a specific instance of patterning in which a sequence of repeating motifs is presented in turn, for example, short/long, fat/thin, red/blue, or dark/light as seen in the set design, while **gradation** employs a series of motifs patterned to relate to one another through a regular progression of steps. This may be a gradation of shape or color. Some shape gradations may in fact create a sequence of events, not unlike the changes that take place in a setting over the duration of a scene.

Without getting the viewer to look at the image, communication cannot occur. Since Lord Farquaad is at the center forming the fulcrum for visual balance he is immediately given a sense of importance. This shows how **emphasis** is what catches the eye and makes the viewer pay attention to a certain part of the design first. It is also referred to as point of focus. It creates a focal point in a design and is how we bring attention to what is most important. Usually there is a primary, or main, point of emphasis, with perhaps secondary emphases in other parts of the composition. The emphasis is usually an interruption in the fundamental pattern or movement of the viewer's eye through the composition, or a break in the rhythm. The designer uses emphasis to call attention to something, or to vary the composition to hold the viewer's interest by providing visual surprises.

There are a variety of ways to create emphasis. One way is by contrast, because an element in contrast with something else is more easily seen and understood. For example, in the *Alceste* image the contrast between the rectangular bars and the open background calls attention to the figures lit with spotlights. **Contrast** achieves emphasis by setting the point of emphasis apart from the rest of its background. Various kinds of contrasts are possible. The use of a **neutral background** isolates the point of emphasis as seen in the dark blue background. Contrast of color, texture, or shape will call attention to a specific point. Contrast of size or scale will as well. Strategically placing objects in prominent locations such as center stage will call attention to a particular element of a design. Any of the elements can be contrasted: line (a curve in the midst of straight lines), shape (a circle in a field of squares), color (one white box on a background of blues and blacks) or value (a light or dark area in the middle of its opposite), and texture (a rough compared to a smooth). Contrast can also be created by contrasting orientation in space (horizontal, vertical, diagonal), style (a geometric shape in an otherwise naturalistic image) and size. Wilson uses linear contrast to create a changing mood in his compositions. An anomaly, or something that departs from the norm, will also stand out and grab our attention, for example a large swan amidst uniformed soldiers. Another way that emphasis can be created is by position. Implied lines all directed toward the same place can create a focal point there. Isolating an element from the others by its position in space will also create emphasis. An important thing to remember about emphasis is that if everything is emphasized then nothing will stand out, nothing will be emphasized, nothing will grab the viewer's attention.

Unity is the sense that all of the parts of a design are working together to achieve a common result, one whose components appear to come together holistically. Their costumes and their choreographed movements unify Lord Farquaad's people. When things look right together, or harmonious, you have created unity. Lines and shapes that repeat each other show unity, for example the use of curved lines and curved shapes. Colors that have a common hue create unity, and texture also helps create unity. Unity can be achieved through the effective and consistent use of any of the elements, but **pattern** is the most fundamental element for a strong sense of unity. Pattern is an underlying structure that organizes surfaces or structures in a consistent, regular manner underlying structure. Patterns, shapes, or forms can help achieve **harmony.** By repeating patterns in an interesting arrangement, the overall visual image comes together.

Consistency of **form** and **color** are also powerful tools that can pull a composition together. However, *unity also exists in variety.* It is not necessary for all of the elements to be identical in form providing they have a common quality of meaning or style. For example, fashions from a specific period share common features of silhouette, materials, and color that identify the style of the day, or the look of a particular designer. Unity can also be a matter of **concept**. The elements and principles can be selected to support the intended function of the designed object, where the purpose of the object unifies the design. The viewer looks for a connection between the elements, for some sort of organization, for unity in the design. Unity creates an integrated image in which all the elements are working together to support the design as a whole. A unified design is greater than the sum of its parts; the design is seen as a whole first, before the individual elements are noticed.

Understanding how the mind groups elements by proximity, similarity, continuation, and alignment helps us understand how unity can be achieved. **Proximity** is one of the easiest ways to achieve unity, and is based on grouping by closeness. The closer elements are to each other, the more likely we will see them as a group. Repetition is based on grouping by similarity. Elements that visually are similar are perceived as related. Line, shape, color, value, or texture can be repeated, as well as direction, angle, or size. For example in *Shrek* the mice characters all share the same costume elements, as well as being depicted with the same bends to the elbow and curls to the tail. Fiona mirrors this through direction, angle, and texture, but differs in position and color. She is given emphasis despite the variety of elements used. The image is unified but variation makes it interesting. Repetition is one of the most effective ways to unify a design, which it does by creating similar elements. **Alignment** consists of arranging elements so that their edges are lined up. The common alignment allows the eye to group those elements together. **Continuation**

© Jack Vartoogian/FrontRowPhotos

means that something like a line, an edge, a curve, or a direction continues from one element to another. The viewer's eye will follow the continuing line or edge smoothly from one element to other and the mind will group the elements because of this connection. Implied lines are one example of continuation. If we choose to use the form, colors, or other elements that appear out of synch with each other then they do not seem natural.

To make use of **variety** the designer changes the character of an element to make it different and thereby to create visual interest. Without unity an image is chaotic and unreadable, and without variety it is dull and uninteresting. Good design is achieved through the balance of unity and variety. The elements need to be alike enough so the audience perceives them as belonging together and different enough to be interesting. A line of soldiers all the same height, weight, and body type looks artificial. Variety provides contrast to unity and can be achieved by using opposites or strong contrasts. Changing the size, point of view, and angle of a single object can add variety and interest to a visual image. Breaking a repeating pattern can enliven a visual image. A costume designer might vary such things as shape by manipulating its size, color, orientation, and texture, or type. A lighting designer might use variations of hue, value, or saturation to bring interest to color, so darkness, lightness, high key, low key, and value contrast all can be adjusted. While changes from a rough to smooth floor surface might provide contrast for a scenic designer, an effective way to integrate unity and variety is by creating variations on a theme. For example, in an opera such as *Lohengrin* the soldiers might be in the background; though costumed the same they are of different body types and heights. Just as a composer can repeat and vary a musical theme throughout a composition, a designer can repeat and vary an element throughout a design.

How these elements and principles are used is the art of theatrical design. These concepts are descriptive means of characterizing the built environments within theatrical production. The following examples describe how elements and principles were used in production and can be read by an audience and understood.

Suggesting real spaces: *Serjeant Musgrave's Dance* and Jocelyn Herbert's design

Finally, for me, there seems no right way to design a play, only, perhaps, a right approach. One of respecting the text, past or present, and not using it as a peg to advertise your skills, whatever they may be, nor to work out your psychological hang-ups with some fashionable gimmick.

Jocelyn Herbert

Lindsay Anderson directed John Arden's *Serjeant Musgrave's Dance* at the Royal Court Theatre in 1959. Jocelyn Herbert designed the setting and costume. *Serjeant Musgrave's Dance* is a parable about war. Arden poses the simple question, how can a simple soldier make the population back home understand the horrors of war? Serjeant Musgrave and his men, Hurst, Sparky, and Attercliffe, come to a northern English coal-mining town in the mid to late nineteenth century on a seemingly innocuous recruiting tour. Over the course of the play the audience learns that these men were involved in a horrible massacre and they mean to bring back the terror to home by massacring this small village. Arden tells us that this is a realistic, not a naturalistic play. The play is written in eight scenes, moving from a canal wharf to the bar of a public house, a churchyard, a street, a pub stable and

Jocelyn Herbert Archive, Wimbledon College of Art. ©Estate of Jocelyn Herbert

bedroom, a market place, and a prison cell. When the director and designer first sat down to discuss the play they were perplexed about how to arrange the setting without bogging it down in naturalistic scenery. According to Cathy Courtney they were more interested in focusing on the actors and their actions. Lindsay Anderson recalled that Herbert liked an empty stage and she did not really think that there should be scenery at all. He described the style of her sets as being integrated with the play in such a way that the décor serves the play and also illuminates its poetic subtext. As such Jocelyn Herbert makes use of the elements and principles to suggest real spaces and endow them with meanings that evoke the central message of the play. These spaces are both practical and aesthetically evocative of a contrast between the bucolic serenity of the English countryside and the gloom of the war fought far away.

Herbert's set uses the basic shapes and forms of a traditional pub to create an enclosed space. The lines and shapes are geometric and manufactured and arranged asymmetrically. The space is unified because of the variations in shape and form. The diagonal lines in the rear form the wall, which make the space a large cube. In that cube are walls. The narrow rectangle of the door is offset by the bisected square of the window. The bar is another rectilinear cube. The shapes are given texture from the silhouettes of the bottles. Ultimately the forms of the benches and tables help balance the jumble of shapes in the rear. This enclosed space will stand in contrast to the open spaces of the village where the soldiers give their demonstration. Insularity as displayed through the community drinking-hole is juxtaposed to the landscape of the countryside. Herbert described that for the pub scene she had just one flat and arranged the tables and chairs so that they created a room. The director wanted to move the actors outside of the imaginary boundaries of the room. The lighting designer had to remind him where the lines of the wall were.

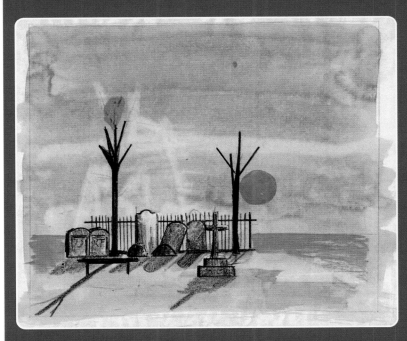

The shape of the sky and earth meet in the background, while the horizontals and verticals of the fence break up the planes. The lines of the trees reach up to the sky, connecting the graves and tombstones to a spiritual reaching up to heaven as seen in the branches. The darker values of the ground contrast with the values of the sky drawing our eyes upward. Death is present, but the trees connect the graveyard to the natural world, and the natural world directs our eyes to heaven.

Jocelyn Herbert Archive, Wimbledon College of Art. ©Estate of Jocelyn Herbert

63

Note the use of line in the prison gate in this image. The regimented rhythm of the lines of the gate contrasts with the shapes of the buildings in the background. The sketch shows that the prison gate is out of scale with the proportions of the figures in the foreground and the city in the background. The shape of the sky and earth meet in the background, while the horizontals and verticals of the jail break up the planes. The lines of the houses reach up to the sky, but are not as high as the prison gate. While the prison is understood to be closer because of its size and overlapping, the hazy background casts the town in pallor. The darker values of the ground contrast with the values of the sky drawing our eyes upward. Death is present, but the prison gate connects the men to the world, and the social and political world is a distant memory. The soldier's experience is lonely, dangerous, and far away from the everyday life of the town. Arden's play wanted to bring this fact home to the audience.

Jocelyn Herbert Archive, Wimbledon College of Art. ©Estate of Jocelyn Herbert

Herbert's costumes are the iconic red and black uniforms of the British army at this time. Note how the shape of each garment is enclosed by line. The red of the jacket is in contrast to the black of the trousers. Where they meet is line. The smear of black along the leg creates atmospheric perspective endowing the shapes with form. These are regimented outfits, where the human form softens the lines. These more delicate lines and curves will stand out against the constructed rigidity of the rest of the setting. The elements and principles are used to create the costumes and settings, but the audience's perception of how these images work in performance conveys the meaning of the play.

Jocelyn Herbert Archive, Wimbledon College of Art. ©Estate of Jocelyn Herbert

Robert Wilson designs *Alceste* with line, movement, and color

Cristoph Willibald Gluck's *Alceste* is the story of Admète King of Thessaly who is gravely ill to the distress of his people, his wife Alceste, and his two children. Ceremonial prayer to Apollo asking for pity elicits the answer that Admète will die that day, unless someone voluntarily sacrifices his life. Alceste offers herself, in the forest at night in a place sacred to the gods. Admète, ignorant of what Alceste has done, recovers. When told that someone has apparently sacrificed themself on his behalf he questions Alceste. The desperate king hurries into the temple to plead with the gods. As she dies, Admète tries to kill himself, but is prevented. The heavens open, Apollo descends and proclaims that the gods have given them their lives as a reward for their steadfast love.

Wilson believes that his scenography needs to leave room for the audience to listen to Gluck's music. Rather than fill the stage with baroque perspectives, he broke the various natural elements of the script into abstract shapes. He suggests locations and uses light to create mood and atmosphere. In this way he lets the music convey the emotional journey of the characters. The conservative crowds at the Lyric Opera who expected to see realistic settings depicting locale condemned Wilson's designs. They missed the sumptuous detail of fairy-tale, period costumes echoing the styles of past centuries. Instead his design team used light, color, line, shape, and form to evoke the feeling of the music. His lighting and setting compositions changed gradually over the course of the opera as an underscoring to the music. Symmetrical shafts of color define the playing areas and a cube rotates in the sky. Their arrangement in the composition led the audience from one emotional state to the next through the elements and principles of design. Shape and color started one mood, then position changes giving it another feeling. Color temperature and intensity was changed to create a new composition. The costumes served to define character and visually organize the characters into recognizable groups. He used contrast to bring focus to Alceste and the purity of her character.

© Robert Wilson, courtesy of the Paula Cooper Gallery

Wilson's thumbnail sketches show the simple use of line to create abstracted representations of trees for the sacred forest. This sketch shows that he will use light and shadow in the background to evoke the mood of the scene. The rigid, rhythmic lines of the trees contrast with the vast expanse in the background. They suggest the constraints under which Alceste lives. As Queen she is beholden to the people and to the priests. However, her expansive love frees her from the rule of law. Her freedom lay within her faith and sacrifice.

65

© Robert Wilson. Photo Johan Jacobs

In production Wilson created a wash of blues and purples as a backlit background. The colors echoed Alceste's mourning as she sacrifices herself to the gods of the underworld in the forest. The contrast between the bright background and the black rectilinear trees calls attention to her environment. She and the other actors are picked out of the bold image with spotlights that brighten their faces, so the audience can see and understand them, and brightens their costumes. Alceste stands out against the background.

© Robert Wilson, courtesy of the Paula Cooper Gallery

The lines and shape tell a story over time. The rhythmic lines transform the space from a civic location to the forest. These spaces are abstract evocations of the changing rhythms and moods captured in Gluck's music. Wilson uses the elements and principles to create a space to listen to the music, where the music is made tangible in three dimensions. From emptiness rises a stable, tranquil force that rises up to meet heaven and connects heaven and earth together. Each change transformed the audience's perception of

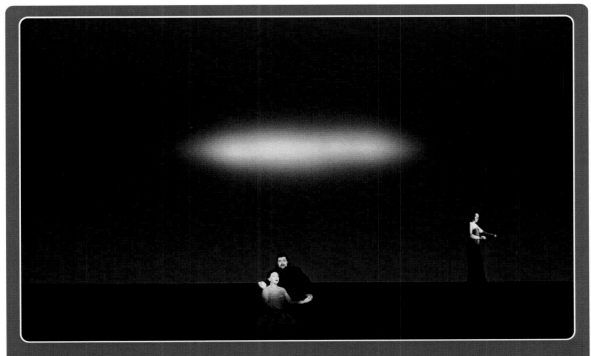

Robert Wilson. Photo Johan Jacobs.

the space and the figures that occupied the space. Space and color worked with the music to create an emotional response within the audience.

Emphasis is the quality that draws your attention to a certain part of the design first. It is the first thing you see when you look at a design. Positive and negative space refers to the juxtaposition of figure and ground in a composition. The objects in the environment represent the positive space, and the environment itself is the negative space. Tension mounts as the horizontal, vertical, and perpendicular merge. Note the use of line to give depth to the image. The black shape of the floor meets the horizontal of the blue background. Each of the light boxes appears to be in different planes, as do the human figures. The implied line of the figures in silhouette creates an implied diagonal line, as well as the meeting of the black ground to the blue background. These lines direct our attention to the depth of the space. The monochromatic palette of the horizon gives us a sense of man's insignificance in the spiritual realm, while the open composition makes the human figures seem small in proportion to the natural environment.

Shrek, The Musical: Color, texture, shape, space, and a large green ogre

Shrek, The Musical is based on William Steig's children's book *Shrek!* as well as the 2001 DreamWorks Animation film *Shrek*. Its book and lyrics are by David Lindsay-Abaire, music by Jeanine Tesori, and it was directed by Jason Moore. Tim Hatley designed the set, costume, and puppets, Hugh Vanstone designed the lighting, and Peter Hylenski designed the sound. Hatley's costume design won a Tony. *Shrek, The Musical* is about a young ogre named Shrek who lives as a hermit in a swamp afraid the world hates him because of his appearance. Upon being invaded by refugee fairy creatures exiled from their kingdom, Shrek must leave his swamp and go on a journey to get Lord Farquaad to stop pushing his citizens into the swamp. Along the way he meets Donkey, gets conned into fighting for the release of a Princess from a dragon, and falls in love. After defeating his foes, wooing his love, and accepting who he is, he marries his princess and lives happily ever after. Sam Mendes, a big fan of the first *Shrek* film, suggested the idea of creating a musical to Jeffrey Katzenberg around the time the second film was in production.

After an initial Seattle tryout at the 5th Avenue Theatre the show opened on Broadway in 2008 at the Broadway Theatre. The design team was brought in even before there was a script, so there was a lot of freedom of how to move forward. Of primary concern was how far they would deviate from the film. Hatley explained to *Live Design* that as part of their research process he interviewed the animators of the film. Because of the complexity and time commitment it would have taken to add texture to the clothing, they made simple choices to costume the characters. As a result the production team decided that they would proceed with a free hand with the cuts, colors, and textures of the costumes. In part this would distinguish the live performance as well as provide a visual vocabulary to build the rest of the elements around. For example Robert Cashill reports that Hatley put Princess Fiona in a bodice made from organza, cut velvet, and a silk base. He chose to tint the material in a range of green hues that complemented the original actress's skin tones. To accentuate the appeal of Donkey's empathetic character he is clad in a bespoke fur costume. The designer describes the handmade fur as having a scale to it. He chose its soft texture to give depth to the character.

One of the major preoccupations for the design team was choosing which green to use

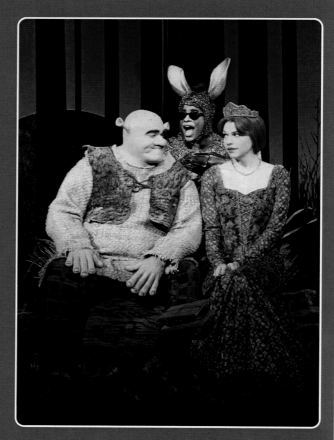

© Joan Marcus

for Shrek. The sets and the costumes provide most of the color in this production. This color choice was difficult for Hatley because of the effects of additive color. Throughout the play the lighting is in constant flux, as well as in what location Shrek is performing in, and what set piece he stands against. Each of these different situations changes the way in which the audience sees Shrek's green complexion. If he is in the green swamp, the white-blue of Farquaad's kingdom, Duloc, or the dark blue of the dragon's keep he would change colors. If they chose a green that worked in one setting it would not work in another. It took a lot of collaboration to make sure the green would not go yellow in the dragon's keep. Vanstone kept the lighting restrained to a white pallet.

Scale was an issue not just for the setting, but also for the size and shape of the costuming. For example, Lord Farquaad is abnormally short with unusual proportions. Hatley made use of a vaudeville trick to achieve the effect. He affixed a pair of shoes on Farquaad's kneecaps. Shrek is encased in an enormous fat suit, made of layered foam with a belly that hangs and sags. It allows Shrek's scale to be larger than the human characters he stands next to. The production also uses puppets. There was a scene from the movie that they felt was important. Gingy the Gingerbread Man is served up on a plate and gets tortured by Farquaad. By using a puppet they could be brutal. They had to decide whether to create a human-scaled costume that would have thrown everything out of scale, or whether they should shrink him down to the scale of a typical gingerbread man cookie. They ultimately decided a puppet would be more fun.

© Joan Marcus

69

The design team chose to use the high value and warm neon green of Shrek's skin and low values and cool of the analogous greens in Princess Fiona's dress. Hatley chose a number of greens that complemented Sutton's skin tones. Each character has a different surface texture. Fiona appears to have silky scales, Donkey has fur and Shrek's smooth, cool skin is contrasted against the coarse brown fibers of his vest. Thus, Fiona is soft and feminine, while Shrek is a little coarse yet still warm and fuzzy.

The use of straight geometric forms for the Duloc scenes that tower over the actors and its symmetrical composition creates a sense of regularity and mundane rigidity within the kingdom. The regular pattern both evokes fairy-tale castles and reinforces the idea that Farquaad is boring and unoriginal. The use of red, blue, and yellow primaries makes these characters larger than life, while Donkey, Shrek, and Fiona are all in natural, soft earth tones making them more human and more sympathetic. As well, the triadic choices for the Court make them stand out in contrast to the analogous colors unifying the hero characters. Repetition creates emphasis by calling attention to the repeated element through sheer force of numbers. The diagonal positioning of the Chorus creates a repeated pattern and form that highlights Farquaad at the apex. The angularity of their body position echoes the lines in their costumes and the rectilinearity of the lines of the castle and its towers in the background. Many of the sets are fairly two-dimensional, however, so the lighting had to give them more depth. To achieve this they projected the scenery on top of itself. Vanstone describes how it gives that depth and allows the designers the ability to control the color of it a bit more, by enriching a pale paint hue, or making it go paler still. The visuals were used as enhancement to enliven the two-dimensionality of the stage.

Hatley manipulates proportion by distorting the human figure through costuming. By making Farquaad one third smaller than Shrek he becomes comic and seems impotent compared to the jolly green fellow. While Farquaad's flashy tights complement Shrek's pale green skin tones, the effect could not be more different. Shrek screams out to be noticed, yet he wears desaturated, muted browns that take focus away from his personality. On the other hand, the pale figure of Farquaad is embellished with the bright, highly saturated reds and shiny metallic boots. He is trying to attract attention to his personality. Repetition is also evident in the

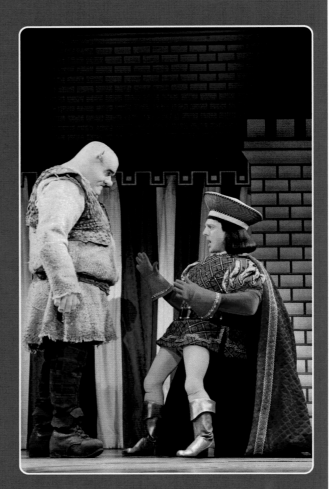
© Joan Marcus

curtains with the alternating blue and white stripes, given variety with the blue and white Greek-key pattern on the awning. Each character has a distinct color scheme and their costumes have a contrasting texture. Shrek's textures are more organic and muted, while Farquaad's are geometric and inorganic. Despite being the human, he is out of proportion and inorganically shaped and proportioned. As well, his off-center stance gives him a sense of movement even when at rest, endowing him with a squirrelly demeanor.

4

The artistry of
the set

Key Topics:

@ The designer's process

- Analysis, research, conceptualizing, concept drawings,
  implementation, evaluation, models, technical drawings

@ The elements and principles in action

Case Studies:

- *Red*: A Lesson on Aesthetics
- Three American Productions of *Mother Courage*
- *War Horse*: Leaving space for collaborative design

Examples:

- *Three Sisters* (1997) / Michael Spencer
- *The Criminals* (1998) / Anthony Lamble
- *Orfeo* (1997) / Sophie Tyrell
- *Twelfth Night* (1996) / Ralph Koltai
- *Sunday in the Park with George* (1984) / Tony Straiges

Scenic designers use the basic principles and elements of design including the characteristics and functions of line, mass, shape, measure, position, color, texture, and the principles of composition such as unity, harmony, contrast, variation, balance, and proportion to organize stage space and create the world of the play. They interpret the play script, through the eyes of the director, and design the physical surroundings of the play to define where the characters are, what is happening, and what the space and setting tell us about the play.

The designer's process

Whether the set designer is working as a scenographer, or designing the set, or the set and costumes, the designer sets the context for all the physical elements of production. The definition of the playing space focuses attention on the actors so that their actions are visible. A design must provide a space for the story conveying information about time, locale, and atmosphere. It provides a context within which to understand character. As well, a good design evokes mood, supports the themes and motifs of the place, and is attractive to the senses. A setting does not encapsulate the play in a single image. Rather it provides a foundation for the other elements of expression to work within. At its core a designer's work is straightforward – to read and interpret plays, and then use that interpretation to build a world that helps the audience make sense of the story. An understanding of how audiences think is important to how the designer chooses the elements of the setting. To create a bridge between production and audience the set designer begins with how the director understands the play. As a result, set designers are the director's earliest collaborator most of the time. However, before speaking with the director the scenic designer must carry out a careful analysis of the play text. Understanding the play is critical and it involves multiple readings of the script. Actors, directors, producers, and designers all read the text for different elements, but their shared goal is to try and make sense of the play in three dimensions. The characters are the heart of the play. Who are they? In what world do they live? With what objects do they interact with each day? When is it? What season is it? Is the world rich or poor? Each question reveals a little more about the characters and the world in which they live. This information is the place where all of the team begins. Designers have their own vision of the script, but they know that ultimately they will work with a director whose vision will guide the choices of the actors and other designers.

I study the script a lot. It is important to me to understand the characters and their humanity. It is also vital to understand how the play works as a storytelling mechanism. I do a lot of research into the period of the play and the living circumstances of the characters, and I look for art and images that resonate with me in ways that are similar to my reaction to the writing. After that, I have no process. What I mean by that is that I let the design evolve in whatever way it wants to. Sometimes I will build a series of models, getting closer to the design with each one. Sometimes the floor plan of the set seems to evolve first. Sometimes it is a sketch or a thumbnail that comes along early in the process. Eventually it all becomes clear. I do know that I get all the design decisions done about eighty percent before I finish anything. That is because every decision [a]ffects every other decision.

Joe Tilford

Furthermore, the set designer also considers the constraints of the theatre space, noting what settings are possible to construct within this theatre. Other influential factors include the ground plans and center-line grounds of the theatre stage configuration, sightlines, general stage equipment, and other physical characteristics of the theatre. At this early stage, to clarify the challenges that will have to be faced in production, the designer will talk to the other members of the production team, and ask questions. Many designers describe this time as exciting as they are trying to figure out what the director is thinking, since at this early point the director does not know what the show is going to be like. Together they conceive of what they want the production to convey to the audience. In the first meetings the director usually just talks. If not, good designers ask lots of questions, such as: What type of stage is the play to be performed on? What are the style, the budget, and the time frame? What does the director want this show to be like? What does he or she imagine the show to be like for the audience? Many designers want to hear what the director imagines the play to be before they begin their thinking, lest they start in a direction that will not resonate with the direction of the rest of the production. Designers listen, question, and probe the director for what the characters are like. For example, on commencing each new production Tony Walton tries to clear his mind completely and absorb the script or score as if it were being delivered by radio. He told William Grimes that he attempts to keep anything visual from popping into his mind until he is clear about the director's take on the material. He claims he wants to let the intrinsic nature of the material, colored by the director's input, incubate in his mind and influence the design.

Unless a director really wants to talk in very visual terms, good designers usually don't need to. You talk about ideas, you talk about action, you talk about why we are doing it, you talk about what's in your mind. Just talk about the play, about the actions.

Ming-Cho Lee

As the analytical process continues research becomes necessary. What elements need extra research? Where is location of the setting? What does it look like? What are its climate and its geography? What is the style of the play? If it is realistic the designer might need to research architecture, sociological, and cultural backgrounds of the environment. If it is non-realistic the designer may need to consider the psychological roots, since a non-realistic setting is a physical extension of the psychological environment of the play. Commonly, research involves trips to the library or museums to look at books, periodicals, paintings, and other sources that provide visual information about homes buildings, furniture, and other details of the period of the play. Increasingly there are more and more image source databases online.

> At every single part of the process, there are hundreds of decisions being made all the time, about colour, about texture, about detail, about light, about where you place something on a stage. For instance, having just done *Phèdre*, there was an empty stage, but into that I had to place chairs. And the process I went through to find the correct chair! The minute you put a chair on stage, it tells you a period, it tells you a culture, it tells you a civilisation – you can place that space instantly by the information that a chair gives you. We went through hundreds of different variations, and I wound up designing them in the end. It's the hardest thing in the world to design a chair!
>
> **Bob Crowley**

Grimes reports that Walton's preparation for his Tony Award-winning design for the revival of *Guys and Dolls* (1992) began by reading all of Damon Runyon's stories, from which the musical is based, researching period details, listening to contemporaneous music to give him a sense of the time period, and studying what other designers had done in previous productions of the play as well as its film version. He kept a research notebook for the play that included detailed information given to him by the archivist at the Salvation Army on what the organization's missions looked like in the 1920s, and what pamphlets its volunteers would probably have had on hand. After absorbing this collection of research he started to explore the ideas of the production on a small scale. Apparently the director Jerry Zaks wanted Walton to have a free hand with color to create a big splash. To accomplish this, Walton began by painting each scene of the play on black cardboard panels joined together to form flip-flop books. Then he constructed what he describes as baby models, three-dimensional versions of the scenes in small boxes somewhat like doll house rooms. His full-color rendering for *Guys and Dolls* showed the color palette, a sense of the playing space, and gave an impression of the lighting effects. Taken as a whole, the symmetrical and balanced setting conveys the stability and grandeur of the city at night. Walton fulfilled Zack's mandate to let the paintbrush rip by using vibrant blues, yellows, and reds. The lit marquees draw focus and set the mood and energy of the scene. The Hot Spot nightclub acts as a siren luring the gambler with its fiery lights. Next he created larger models, 18 inches wide by 13 inches high, with translucent back panels which allowed him to play with lighting effects. Then he drew up technical drawings for every prop and scenic piece. Finally, he produced **paint elevations**, which are poster-size color renderings that scenic artists realize at full scale.

At the start of the design process the designer will use a stockpiling of information to build conceptual research. Conceptualizing is the process of synthesizing and utilizing the gathered information to create as many potential solutions as possible to the design challenges posed. At this point the designer will start producing thumbnail sketches or functional models based on a synthesis of the information. Here the designer begins to experiment with differing combinations of elements from various design concepts that have evolved in discussions with the production team. The designer plays with the combination of existing forms and elements into new arrangements or order. Scenic designers think by drawing. Most designers will read the text several times taking notes, charting character relationships, scenic needs, changes in fortune, time season, and noting anything about character. The first stage of the design process, after absorbing the play and understanding the director's concept of the visual style of the production, is the process of physically making the designs. **Concept drawings** are impressions of the sets drawn with pencil, charcoal, or marker. These drawings put the visual ideas on paper to be shown to the director for discussion and approval. If you consider Rae Smith's preliminary sketches, seen below, for *War Horse*, you can see how her initial sketching led to the ultimate conception of how realistic settings could be combined with distorted and fractured lines to show the journey of the protagonist Joey from pastoral calm to the ravages of war. The preliminary drawings became a seed for the ultimate solution.

> First, we feel that to be designers in the theater, you have to be able to express yourself in visual terms; if you can't draw, it's hopeless. Second, we don't emphasize the finished rendering; in fact we discourage it. My way of thinking, which has evolved over a decade of teaching, is that it's really a collaborative process between directors and designers, so the sketching is not for display; it's a reaction to something that is not visual, an expression of a text in visual terms. You get a visual counterpart without giving the sense that this is the finished product, so that the director can react to it, to see if it has a connection with his perception of the play. Design work is always a constant set of action, reaction, therefore discovery; the hand feeds the mind, the mind feeds the eye, and all the sketching and model making is part of that evolution.
>
> **Ming-Cho Lee**

Beginning with shapes in a sketchy, broad-stroked fashion, the designer is thinking out loud on paper. The working processes of each collaborative production team are different, but conversation is the key. Some designers will come in to the first production meeting with research, images, or movies to show the director, though many want to know what the director thinks the production is about lest they constrain the director's process. For example, Ralph Koltai explains in an exhibition catalog that before he was able to get the rights to put on a production of Bertolt Brecht's *The Rise and Fall of the City of Mahagonny* (1963) he had to convince the heirs of Weil and Brecht, who hold the rights to the work, to release the rights. To do so he prepared a **storyboard** of the production to convince them to authorize it. For example, in one scene, in an effort to shake off the gloom of Joe's death, Jimmy invites everyone to have a drink on him. He dreams of sailing back to Alaska, and he takes down a curtain rod for a mast and climbs on the pool table, pretending it is a ship. Koltai quickly evokes the gloomy atmosphere using the thick lines of shadow. The tables are seen in silhouette and so too is the ship's mast and sail. The mood of the drinking scene is quickly evident. The images show the way in which he set up the initial space and added to it as the play progressed.

> Theatre is very pragmatic. It's no good coming in with a vision and thinking you're going to realise something purely from your own mind, because the process of working with people makes your vision change.
>
> **Nick Ormerod**

The first discussions are almost like the way crime scene investigation teams solve crimes – who are the characters? What happened five minutes before we first meet them? What is their world? Why would that object be there? How you stage the action is as much the designer's concern as the director's. Where are the characters' entrances and exits? Where are they going to stand or sit? How close should the sofa be to the fireplace? A set cannot be laid out or a location chosen if the designer does not have an understanding of the way the actors will move through the space. There are as many techniques as there are designers. Some designers' first drawings are incredibly precise and detailed, even featuring the props. Others' first thoughts might be quite loosely at first about shape and scale and then allow the design to emerge gradually. Some begin by plotting out the movement of the characters in the space, imagining themselves looking down on the scene unfolding in the script and thinking about how characters will enter and exit, where they will sit, what the distances between them might be at any given time in the scene. A designer's first thought might be that the production needs a specific shape and size, before they actually think about what it will look like. This type of thinking leads to sketching out the ground plan that charts the movements of the characters within the space.

> Now designing for outdoors is quite different from designing for indoors. Technically it means that you cannot fly anything because there's no grid overhead, and that controls what you can do. Everything has to be done from the ground up. It's also my personal belief that when you design for outdoors,

especially for the open stage, you cannot fake, because everything out there is real. They're not artificial leaves.

Ming-Cho Lee

Ideas need time to incubate. After playing with solutions to the design challenges the designer puts the design to the side before clarifying ideas. For example, at this stage Joe Tilford explains in an exhibition catalog that he likes the idea of abstracting an environment by keeping its essence of detail, and seeing if unnecessary things can be eliminated. It can be difficult, because the aim is to subtract extraneous elements; what elements remain need still to have vitality. Afterwards, one is better able to consider which solution best fits the parameters of the design challenge set by the director with feedback from the production team, since collaborative ideas transform and clarify the design concept. The implementation phase of the process is where the designer produces plans, drawings, and models that will allow the design ideas to be constructed by the production team. The designer must produce **ren-derings**, a **presentation model**, and ground plan. For example, the images of Michael Spencer's ground plan and rendering of Chekhov's *Three Sisters* (1997) show the various stages that a design will go through. Furthermore the details of the plan will be shown in front elevations, detail drawings, painter elevations, prop dressing lists, prop sketches and other drawings, and notes that will help the shop build the scenery and props.

Throughout, the process is constant evaluation requiring the designer to look objectively at how each choice within the scenic design works in relation to the

Spencer's ground plan for Chekov's *Three Sisters*. Notice that the doors, desks, tables, and shape of the revolve are all indicated. The plan allows the production team to plan the logistics of scenery placement and blocking. The ground defines the space, its scale, and creates the constraints that the other elements must work within. The scenic designer's plan influences where the actors may move, defines the sightlines, provides the objects and surfaces that the lighting designer will work with to project light, and sets up an image that the audience will have an immediate response to.

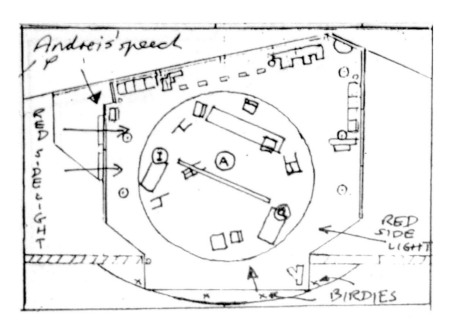

© Michael Spencer

© Michael Spencer

production concept. It is better to make small adjustments as one goes along than to make major adjustments in technical rehearsals, where changes may be expensive. This means money will not be wasted building things that get in the way of the actors or the lighting. For example, the images of Anthony Lamble's design for Adrian Mitchell's adaptation of Jose Triana's *The Criminals* (1998) show how a design created for an end-on scenario would work in the traverse shape. In this way he was able to demonstrate what the sightlines would be and how the blocking might work from a new perspective. What adjustments need to be made as the other designer's work inhabits the stage space? Does the ground plan provide acting spaces appropriate for the movement of the actors? Do the colors of the setting allow for the costumes to achieve their effect? Do the surfaces of the scenery reflect light in a way that is conducive to the lighting design?

> It's cliché to say that Shakespeare paints his own scenes and that he doesn't require scenery, but it is true the word does it in most of the plays that we deal with. Nothing more is needed really than the actor and, say, something to sit on – not even that sometimes. So you start off with an advantage that you don't actually need anything. The essence of the theatre is paring down to the essentials of what you actually need: cutting it back until you discover what you need, and maybe that thing serves many different functions which is theatrical in itself. The visual side springs out of those essentials.
>
> **Nick Ormerod**

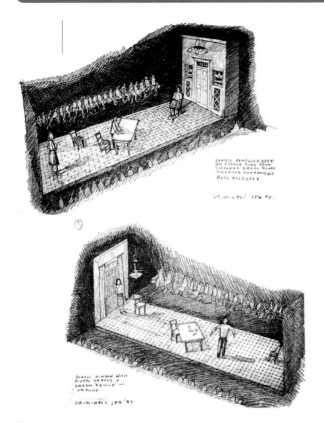

© Anthony Lamble

The design team needed to understand how the setting and blocking would work when the play transferred to a new location. These images show the shift in blocking and lighting that would result in the traverse shape. They needed to work out how equivalent effect could be achieved when the sightlines changed.

One of the most critical functions that the set designer carries out is to clearly define the playing space. **Scale models** are used to demonstrate the relationship between the set, stage, and audience for the director so that he or she can visualize the space in three dimensions. The **functional model** is the equivalent of a thumbnail sketch. These are quickly constructed working models intended to aid in visualizing the basic composition of the scenic design. Set designers make use of models because they give a much clearer impression of the dimensions of a set than a drawing ever can. If the designer has only done a drawing, the director could turn up on the set and declare that she did not know the set was going to be so big, whereas if the designer has built a model, the spatial relationship is clear, and it enables the director to prepare the scene with greater precision. For example, Sophie Tyrrell's models for a production of Claudio Monteverdi's *Orfeo* (1997) show how a gauze canopy above the actors' heads could be used as an opaque projection surface or transparent gauze. They were looking for a solution of how to depict the various settings of heaven and hell in a small concert hall. Poles supported the canopy and the director could see how the action of Orfeo's ascension to heaven could be mirrored in the suddenly transparent sky as he climbed. These models can help the designer verify and solidify their working sketches. They are constructed to provide a clear visualization of the evolving design concept. Furthermore these models can be used as visual aids to the director and technical staff to mock up complicated scene changes or plan out blocking or other technical requirements.

The **production model** shows a more complete visualization of the scenic designer's concept. It is fully painted and decorated with quarter-scale models of furniture, props, and set dressing that will be used during the production. For example, Ralph Koltai's model for *Twelfth Night* (1996) shows the setting of a key moment in the action. It is complete in every detail and provides a method of explaining the full scenic concept to the production team. It can also aid the technical crew in **dressing the set** and choosing the props. The lighting designer can see the types of reflective surfaces and the reflections that might occur. Furthermore, the differences between sculptural scenic elements and painted drops are evident. This model can serve as a discussion point to work out potential problems that might arise as the set is realized at scale.

© Sophie Tyrrell

The problem with that is that we're working with a very tight schedule all the time. I'm usually late. One tries to set a route, like a journey. You know which way you're going but you don't know where you might stop off on the way. I have to design things usually before rehearsals begin. This makes life, for myself and the director and ultimately the actors, quite difficult, because the rehearsal process should be one of discovery. But I'd like to think that the parameters of the design still allow for things to happen. They have to, otherwise one would design game-shows. Things constantly change in rehearsal. It drives everyone mad, but they have to. But the epic, mammoth decisions you make – you've got to be pretty sure that they're not whims and won't backfire on you.

Bob Crowley

Technical drawings, or **mechanical drawings** help the technical director and carpenters understand the details of construction needed to build the set. Drawings called **designer's plans** depict every detail of the set as well as provide exact measurements of its components. These are prepared by the designer or his or her assistant and consist of a ground plan, front elevations, detail drawings, full-scale drawings, sightline drawings, and painter's elevations. The ground plan is a

The model shows the actor climbing to heaven the moment before the black scrim is lit from behind transforming the sky to heaven. The same scenic elements lit differently create two distinct places. The promontory is closed off and the space is claustrophobic. When the lighting changes to a back light, it reveals the heavenly promontory above. Another model, not shown, demonstrates the way in which the volume of the space opens up and a new world is revealed. By working out the potential of these effects the design team can work through potential problems before they occur. These mock-ups are useful in discovering what is possible and where they might improve their concept before the costly expense of building the entire structure.

Koltai's *Twelfth Night* model closely resembles its realization in the production. The model indicates that the floor is of a high gloss, with the ability to reflect the images represented in the backcloth. The reflections add texture and break up the horizontal and vertical planes. He uses a stairway to provide a transition between levels and acting areas. These solutions for creating multiple levels to perform on resemble Appia's designs for creating a harmonious and practical ground plan. The open space allows for many areas to be used as acting areas. The reflection on the floor gives the space interest, while also reflecting the confusing nature of the play. Which is the backdrop, which is the floor? Are they so different from the men posing as women, posing as men? The design makes tangible the controlling metaphors at work in the play.

© Ralph Koltai/Berlin Associates

horizontal section, a view of an object that has been cut through to show the structure, with the cutting plane placed at a level that shows the most characteristic view of the shape of the set as seen from above. Hard lines show the horizontal shape of the set as it sits on the stage floor, the location of all scenic elements on the stage floor, the setting in its assembled state, and the identity and size of all major scenic elements. Thin lines indicate the suggested location of major floor properties and their approximate size. Dashed lines show characteristics such as overhead construction and properties, the swing and arc of all doors, and alternate positions of other moving elements, all backings and draping in position relative to sightlines, and the location of key flying elements, including teasers, curtains, electrics, and cyclorama, if used.

Following the ground plan, the next most important drawings are the **elevations**. An elevation is a drawing of the walls of the set as if facing them, in effect "elevating" the ground plan into three dimensions. Elevations are the framework for detail drawings, painter's elevations, and construction drawings that are produced for the shop. For example, scale elevations of the trap room of the Booth Theatre in New York where Stephen Sondheim's *Sunday in the Park with George* was first produced in 1984, revealed problems the team would face achieving the effects they wanted. The production team wanted to create a stage-scale three-dimensional recreation of the painting. Tony Straiges conceived of a three-dimensional staging of Georges Seurat's *A Sunday Afternoon on the Island of the Grand Jatte*. They devised a concept where the sets roll, fly, and pop up out of the floor. The actors mingle with

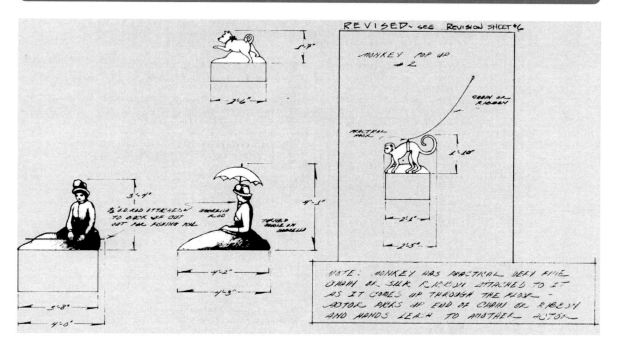

© Ralph Koltai/Berlin Associates

These are Straiges' sketches of the pop-up characters that make up the stage-scale recreation of Seurat's painting. He rendered the pop-up characters with an eye toward Seurat's scale. However, design compromises were unavoidable. For example, the monkey was a problem. He had to conceive of the monkey on a bigger scale so that it was balanced in relation to the whole space. As a result it is too big in relation to the scale of Bernadette.

the two-dimensional cutouts as Seurat arranges the painting's composition. The initial plan was to place the twenty-one pneumatic pop-ups in a way that would avoid architectural obstructions below stage. Unfortunately, the architecture was so restricted that the pop-ups would have been placed in rows. That would have destroyed the illusion of depth in Seurat's recreated painting. By studying the section details they avoided a costly problem. As a result of their discovery, they relocated structural columns to maintain the integrity of the painting.

Elevations are most useful for designs emphasizing two-dimensional scenery. Three-dimensional scenery is illustrated with **orthographic** and **view drawings**. More detailed elevations include **front elevations**, which are scaled mechanical drawings showing the front views of the scenery, where the setting is flattened out and each surface is drawn on a single plane. The ground plan provides the horizontal dimensions, permitting the designer to concentrate in the elevation on designing the vertical proportions and relationships of the various parts of the setting in exact dimensions. For example, Alison Chitty's storyboard, not shown here, working out the staging for a particular moment in Giacomo Puccini's *Turandot* (1997) depicts the metal structure and upper level bridges of the setting that were used by the soldiers for surveillance. It described how the scenery is to transform over the course of the scene. Chitty's designs show how blood is a recurring motif in this production, as it recalls Turandot's bloody reign. The specifications for the placement of the bloody handprints and the blocking call attention to the functioning of the composition. There are three zones. High above, the soldiers watch over the *populus*. They are symmetrically positioned on either side of the round shield. The handprints are a strip in the middle of the horizon and then the population is on the ground. Though there are more citizens than soldiers, the upper regions have more strength in the image. The space is being used to color our perception of the rigid and regimented regular lines. In production, the bloody handprints stand out in contrast to the grey/blue costumes of the *populus* and the gray scaffolding of the structure. The metallic moon hangs over the people. Likewise the population is in the bottom third of the composition while the soldiers' scaffolding and the symbol of the empire are high up dominating two-thirds of the composition. The weight of the rulers bears down upon the *populus*. The designer is concerned with the composition of areas: the size and nature of the decoration, wallpaper patterns, and architectural trim. Elevations include window draperies, wall hangings, set dressings, and furniture or objects placed on or against the walls. **Painter's elevations** are scaled front elevations rendered in color to aid scenic artists as they lay out and paint the scenery. Their details include the proportions, colors, highlight and shadow tones, wall textures, and decoration.

The technical director creates **construction drawings** from the elevations to plan the construction schedule, and provide the building details and specifications of the set pieces for the carpenters and technical crew. **Rear elevations** show the unfinished side of flat walls so that construction details are clear. In other words, they lay out the details, including dimensions, of the materials, hardware, and methods of construction for the crew including instructions for joining, bracing, rigging, and scene shifting. Notes are provided on the drawing describing the specifications of atypical construction methods.

Once the show is sketched and committed to plan, it is time to let technical craft take over once again. The scenery must be drawn with precision, leaving no question of what is expected. Paint elevations offer both feeling and information to the scenic artists, to inspire their own best contribution to the process. The selection of props and dressing must be kept within the established bounds of the concept. Many things can go wrong in the execution of scenery, and from this point until opening, the designer cedes the concept over to the technical crew.

Red: A lesson on aesthetics

John Logan's *Red* is a biographical play about the artist Mark Rothko and the creation of his Seagram Paintings for the Four Seasons restaurant in New York City. *Red* opened at the Donmar Warehouse (2009) directed by Michael Grandage, with sets and costumes by Christopher Oram, lighting by Neil Austin, and music and sound by Adam Cork. It transferred to the John Golden Theatre (2010) on Broadway. The production was nominated for both the Olivier and Tony Awards and won several Tony Awards, including awards for Christopher Oram for sets and costumes, Neil Austin for lighting, and Adam Cork for sound. While Logan takes liberty with the historical accuracy of the biographical event, he explores the contradictory nature of art and commerce. Set in Rothko's studio on the Bowery in the late 1950s, this two-hander depicts the indoctrination of Ken, a newly hired assistant, into Rothko's uncompromising aesthetic. The play unfolds as a Socratic wrestling match where Ken is forced to answer a series of questions about his response to the paintings. Over the course of the play Rothko lectures the young assistant on aesthetics, the act of looking, and the act of creation. Rothko challenges Ken to understand the whole canon of art history both from a formal standpoint and an aesthetic perspective by absorbing Nietzsche, Freud, and Jung. By considering his own works and his rival Jackson Pollock the audience watches artists at work as well as hearing about what drives the act of creation and what makes a masterful painting come alive. Ken discovers that the impulses of the tragic flow through Rothko's work, which is the Apollonian, and Pollock's work, which is the Dionysian. While Rothko steadfastly refuses to acknowledge the new artists such as Jasper Johns, Robert Rauschenberg, and Andy Warhol, because they lack any depth or substance, Ken champions them as depicting the "Now". The two men grapple with the notion of whether paintings are meant to be consumed as a commodity or stand on their own in eternal expression.

According to interviews, Grandage wanted to highlight the mentor/protégé relationship as well as the father/son relationship through the action. The production team saw the play as an emotional and intellectual debate where the paintings are the third party. As the relationship progresses the power shifts between the two men. To show this they wanted the space to be an enclosed and claustrophobic space where the two characters are pushed together. They chose a realistic style, drawing from real spaces, but chose to subtract extraneous details to focus the audience's attention on the work of the painters and the dynamic between the characters. Oram recreated the feel of Rothko's working studio on the stage by referring to photographic documentation, though he did not adhere slavishly to naturalistic details. In London he presented the studio in three-quarter, while in New York he presented a box version. Everything the two would need to create a painting is present and can be used practically. Rothko and Ken create the paintings each night on stage, mixing the paint, building the frames and mounting the canvases. This is a work play, where we watch the work of artists in a studio. It was important to the production team that the audience was a part of the practical art making of the artists. They were to see and experience what goes into making the final product of a painting. While Rothko was concerned that the viewers experience the magic of the final product, the play is about the process of creation. It is about how the final choices are arrived at, how form, composition, and colors come together to create an effect. Like Rothko's paintings, the setting is stripped down to allow the audience to put together the details. For example, the characters often look up at and describe a painting above the sightlines. The painting is present, but only in concept and in the imagination of the audience. It is evoked rather than meticulously reproduced.

Design is a discipline and it covers everything about the piece. These days, there are fewer boundaries to each person's work. The crossover between lighting and projection design affects video designers, which affects set designers. I worked very closely with Red's lighting designer, Neil Austin. The description of Mark Rothko's studio was key about how he controlled life. I knew I had to have close dialogue with Neil about how I would design the space, how he would light the play.

Christopher Oram

The reproduction by the actors of Rothko's paintings in front of the audience served as a constant reminder that the play was about visual art and aesthetics as much as the relationship between the two characters. It was also about the relationship of Rothko and Ken to the paintings and to contemporary art making. Are their interpersonal relationships more intimate than their relationship with the paintings? The compositions of Rothko's work coupled with the staging of two actors within the space were meant to resonate together to create an aesthetic experience between the audience and the art of the production. The studio delineated the parameters of the space and the presence of the paintings, their pigments and lighting crafted a guided tour of Rothko's aesthetic for the audience. The setting was a calm space that allowed the colors and compositions of the paintings to stand out against the action.

Oram's costumes were set in a different palette than the paintings. Note in the figure below the contrast between the neutral palette of the brown, beige, and gray garments against the reds and purples of Rothko's background canvas. Here the costumes and the setting are in contrasting palettes. This allows the actors to stand out from the setting. As well, the characters are more neutral than their artistic output as exemplified by the passionate colors of the canvas. According to Oram the play is a non-costume piece in a Broadway sense. They were designed to be real work clothes that would get dirty over the duration of the play. The actors have physical work to do, mixing paints, wiping hands, and building frames. They must get dirty. As part of the visual palette the costumes were shades of neutral browns, which allowed the characters to fade into the setting and

© Johan Persson

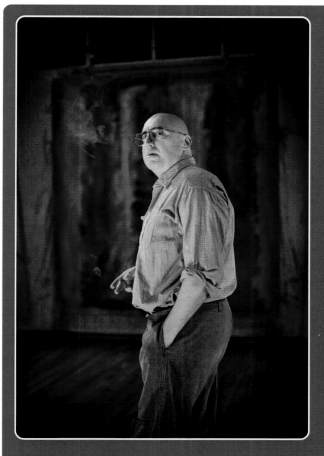

© Johan Persson

the colors of the paintings and the pigments to pop out against the background. It was about the work and the functionality of the space. They are given room for the actions of the characters and their verbal sparring to be the focus of the audience's attention. The pigment red is used here to blur the line between the symbolic evocation of the color and the actual color. Ken enters the studio to see Rothko slumped over with hands and wrists covered in red and mistakes it for blood. Blood is made tangible at the same time as the paint that is being slung up onto the canvas. Like the litany of different hues of red listed in the dialogue the paint and blood come to evoke the emotional content of the text. It is the blood of Ken's parents' murders, the blood of the artist going into the canvas, the mess of work staining the character, and the transformation of the character over time.

The setting was derived from photographs of Rothko's Bowery studio in the 1950s. At the Donmar Warehouse the studio was seen from three sides while in New York the studio was seen behind a proscenium. Oram felt that the frame of the proscenium helped frame the action of the studio. While the studio was modeled after the original the actual footprint did not have to be reproduced. Rather they wanted to give the space a sense of it being hermetically sealed and slightly claustrophobic so that they could allow the audience to focus on the two characters going face to face in a bear pit. Further differences were that in London they could use turpentine and paint, whose scents wafted into the audience, while in New York they had to procure artificial scents of turpentine and paint to offer the audience a similar experience. They wanted the experience of the full sensory range to add to the authenticity of the act of creation. To facilitate being able to see and hear the actors as they scrutinize the painting and discuss it, they looked at an imaginary painting above the heads of the audience. Behind them were other compositions. Thus, the audience was able to see and hear the actors standing center stage as well as be reminded of the effect of Rothko's compositions. The composition behind echoes the experience that the characters describe of the painting they are breaking down.

The painting, seen below, takes on the qualities that Rothko describes through lighting augmentation. As a set piece it takes on life. Furthermore, by rear lighting the canvas we are able to see Rothko's silhouette as he contemplates it. He is positioned against the center line creating a physical reflection of the rhythm of the painter's composition. The setting and the actors work together to make tangible the ideas within the text. The

painting becomes a backdrop for Rothko's behavior. Here the actor's gesture and position makes him look as if he is praying in a chapel that resembles the Rothko chapel built in Houston to house the paintings at a later date. The red pigment behind him and the rhythm of the lines draw our eyes toward the sky, further adding a spiritual dimension to the moment. That spiritual dimension is also an affect of the experience of the composition of Rothko's work.

© Johan Persson

Three American productions of *Mother Courage*

Bertolt Brecht's *Mother Courage* is set during the Thirty Years War and charts a merchant's struggle to survive and keep her family and business intact during the depredations of war. As this is an episodic play, the action takes place in a variety of disparate locations over a long period of time. Mother Courage pulls her cart from battle to battle hoping to find stock and sell her goods. One by one her children are pulled away from her and she is forced to make choices between the survival of her business and the survival of the family. Brecht makes use of a number of epic theatre techniques such as the projection of supertitles, the use of half curtains, and visible musicians, and makes extensive use of all of the practical props. These pose a number of large challenges for a design team.

Jerome Robbins directed *Mother Courage* (1963) at the Martin Beck Theatre with a production team including Ming Cho Lee for scenic design, Motley for costume design, and Tharon Musser for Lighting Design. Brecht was not well understood by Broadway producers in the early 1960s. As the play was both novel in style and politically charged, the production team had to find ways for a commercial audience to understand the material. In a discussion with Gordon Rogoff, Lee describes that the team did not know how to do Brecht in a Broadway context. Since Jerome Robbins understood the commercial reality of Broadway, he feared presenting a piece that was almost journalistic in style, filled with facts. Robbins did not want to use a turntable or a platform as Brecht did in Berlin. Lee claims that the team went through scores of designs to try and find a Broadway idiom, and ended up compromising and committing to a bland solution. At that point they only had a short four-week period to let props age naturally, which is the optimal way to age the props. Instead they were forced to **distress** the materials, and they looked cartoonish and inauthentic. While there were legitimate reasons why they did not use a turntable, the ground plan failed to achieve the desired effect causing critics to comment that they missed the point of the convention. Brecht used a turntable of at least 40 feet with room for actors to walk around it, while the deepest stage in New York was only 40 feet. If you use a turntable that is only 32 feet, it does not work right because the wagon has to have a certain size, and if the turntable is small the wagon just turns on its axle rather than roll across the stage. Also projection was overlaid upon the sets and costumes and it was a visually confusing presentation. The scenic elements did not work together with the costumes to create a cohesive expression. Reviewers panned the production; they were critical of the setting and the use of projecting historical facts on the setting. As well, they questioned why they had not used a turntable as Brecht had done. In addition to the stage itself, the theatre's center and side passageways were used for entrances and exits that the critics felt, at times, made it seem a bit too busy and stagey. They had failed to find a working ground plan that would support the action of the script.

Lee was more successful with his next attempt at *Mother Courage* (1978) when he worked at the American Place Theatre with Alan Schneider directing, Jeanne Button designing the costumes, and David F. Segal designing the lighting. According to Lee, Schneider understood Brecht much better than Robbins, and while this production still did not use a turntable, Lee was able to design a less artificial staging. It was much cleaner. Rather than create phony looking props they picked up an old wagon, cut it down, and patched it together. Robbins had never wanted half-curtains as used at the Berliner Ensemble, which serve a lot of practical functions. However, Schneider wanted to use half-curtains. To construct these, the production team agreed to find material that already had the baggage of history, the feeling of being around, and then put it together. Lee and Button used reclaimed muslin that was once used as backdrops for the Metropolitan Opera. The process of removing the

The wagon wheels make apparent the mixing of eras. At the rear are wagon wheels and at the front rubber tires. The mixing of eras is also seen in Elif's black American Army boots, Swiss Cheese's mountain hiking boots and the soldier's WWI leg wrappings.

© Michal Daniel, 2006

89

paint that once covered the old cloth gave them the authentically aged dirty look they were looking for. It gave the curtains the texture of the fabric and its muted brown values. The same cloth was used for the costumes and props. Likewise the repurposed cart was constructed in the same manner that it might have been in the time of the action. These details carried the weight of the past within them, like the action of the play carries the detritus of the past with it.

Lee designed two different productions of the same play with differing results. The effectiveness of a design is dependent upon the constraints of the production, the interpretation of the director, and the collaboration of the design team. In 1963 the design was a result of a director trying to make the avant-garde more mainstream. Lee was forced to build and distress new materials to construct the scenery and props. This technique highlighted the scenic aspect of the setting rather than blend with the other elements of production to evoke a particular time or place. In the 1978 production the choice of materials added to the underlying themes and concepts that the other elements of production were working toward. The material qualities of the setting added a layer of historical commentary upon the action of the play. It provided a realism to the sets, props, and costumes that was counteracted by the alienation techniques of the text. The next example will show a production that was still different from the previous two.

George Woolfe's production of *Mother Courage* (2006) was performed at the Public Theatre's Delacorte Theatre in the park. Ricardo Hernandez designed the sets, Marina Draghici designed the costumes, and Paul Gallo designed the lighting. Woolfe adopts the familiar trappings of Brecht's dramaturgy using devices that called attention to the production's artifice, such as song titles projected onto the set and the actors delivering the scene announcements in flat voices. The whole set is made of weathered wood, including the revolving platform at center stage. As can be seen in the costumes and props depicted in the images below, Wolfe does not think that alienation is necessary for today's audience, and as a result he has peppered Broadway spectacle on top of the more mechanical devices. Translated by Tony Kushner, the script is filled with profanity, inane humor, and vaudeville jokes that are in stark contrast with earlier translations done by Eric Bentley or Ralph Manheim. His

The residue of history is sprinkled throughout in the costumes. The red scarf Cook wears is Vietnamese from the 1960s, while Courage's jacket and hat evoke WWII and the late 1930s. The colors and textures of the different woods give a timeless feel.

© Michal Daniel, 2006

script embraces the heightened theatricality that matched Woolfe's concept. The artificial devices included spectacular effects such as a bombed-out building bursting into flames, deafening cannon fire exploding to the side, and a jeep clattering into view.

According to the *New York Times* these effects dislocated the action from a singular time and place, evoking instead a range of geographical and chronological locations. The design team was instructed not to make visual references that would attach the action to a specific time and place. Costumes and props crossed the centuries, and are speckled with references to a multiplicity of eras including the Crimean War, World War I and World War II, the American civil war, and the recent conflict in Iraq. To accommodate all the eras evoked by the other visual components, Hernandez constructed a massive wooden framework that acted as a neutral location. Gallo's lights push focus away or pull it in close to control the focus of the audience on the action of the play, lest other movement within the space distract them. Gallo's lighting draws focus onto Mother Courage's emotional state. The environment is obscured in shadow and the audience is free to concentrate on her expression. The earthen floor and the wooden planks of the stage and rear wall serve more as reflective surfaces than architecture or landscape. The regular rhythm of the planks on the wall and stage is broken up with the organic shapes of the shadow. The lighting heats up the focus to draw our eyes in. The setting is a neutral background. While a chair may be new and shiny, a shirt, bucket, jeep, and hat may still be distressed. Likewise the color of the whore's hair stands out as coordinated to her red shoes. In contrast to the intimacy of the general's quarters, the open quality of the outdoor space indicates that this is an exterior camp scene. Focus is limited by lighting. The fluid quality to the open space makes it versatile and convenient for episodic scene changes. In contrast to the Schneider interpretation, Woolfe used the text and acting style to draw audiences into the reality of the circumstances and used theatricality to make overt the dispassionate alienation. Schneider used the setting and costumes to draw in audiences to the action and to make apparent the way history clings to events as dirt to objects. Though Woolfe stuck to Brecht's use of a turntable to allow travel on an open stage, the other scenic elements set the tone of the production as Selected Realism.

Wooden wall units moved in to create more intimate interior settings in the large cavernous space of the open stage. These playing spaces were defined further by the use of light. In this scene, where the general is hosting the hero to dinner, props are used to represent the General's wealth. Campaign chairs and classic war portraiture elevate the simple wooden wall and floors into an elegant residence.

© Michal Daniel, 2006

While the chair is distressed the bucket, clothesline, cannon, and blankets are still crisp and new. Likewise the color of the whore's hair stands out as coordinated to her red shoes. In contrast to the intimacy of the general's quarters, the open quality of the space indicates that this is an exterior camp scene. Focus is limited by lighting. The fluid quality to the open space makes it versatile and convenient for episodic scene changes.

© Michal Daniel, 2006

While all three productions were based on the same play, each had a different look and reception because of the interpretation of the director, the date when it was performed, and the space, materials, and collaborative decisions of the production team. No play has a definitive interpretation, rather the designer works to create a context for the action of the production. He or she uses the principles and elements in different combinations to best deal with the constraints of the particular production situation. Design is a collaborative art, where a team seeks to make the best choices they can at that moment to bring to life a particular interpretation.

War Horse: Leaving space for collaborative design

War Horse was adapted by Nick Stafford from the novel by Michael Morpurgo, devised by the South African puppet company Handspring, and directed by Marianne Elliott and Tom Morris. Rae Smith designed the sets and costumes and worked collaboratively with Leo Warner and Mark Grimmer to design the video projections. Paule Constable designed the lighting, and Christopher Shutt designed the sound. The production opened in the Olivier Theatre at the National Theatre in 2007 and transferred to the New London Theatre in the West End. Its Vivian Beaumont Theatre production won the Tony for Best Play in 2011 and Best Direction, with Smith, Constable, and Shutt winning awards for their designs.

War Horse depicts the story of World War I through the eyes of a horse, Joey, and Albert Narracott, the young boy who raised him. When the war begins Joey is sold to a cavalry division and shipped off to France. He first serves with the British until he is captured and sequestered into German service. Eventually he is wounded and ends up wandering in the no-man's-land and the carnage of the trenches. Albert enlists before he is old enough at the age of sixteen to pursue his beloved horse. Joey journeys from English meadows with his young master to wandering alone in the nightmarish battlefield scenes of rolling tanks, horses, and sword-brandishing soldiers charging out of the trenches through snarled barbed wire. The contrast between idyllic beauty and the broken, wheezing horses stumbling into great blasts of machine gun fire makes tangible the horrors of combat. Their struggle for survival encapsulates the futility of the conflict.

The production team describes the project as madness trying to transform a dense novel told from a horse's perspective into a play. The design team was charged with the task of evoking the imagery of the sprawling prose and keeping the story alive and interesting to the audience. Stafford had to remove Joey's inner narrative voice that was a key feature of the novel. The designers and actors represented this narrative viewpoint through the expressiveness of the horse, where a tossed head, a swishing tail, a whinny of terror, or flailing hooves became the theatrical equivalent of Joey's inner narrative. Its early white card model gives a sense of the scale of the projection screen, stage surface, and scale of the horse puppet. These early mock-ups did not indicate the gray,

© Simon Annand

Here is the model realized. The rip of paper becomes the no-man's-land of the battle-torn landscape. The designers do not disguise that these are man-made contraptions; its three human operators are clearly visible. The puppet conveys the feelings of the horses by the tilting of the head or the shaking of the body. The horse's life is not in the surface reality of its construction. Its bamboo, nylon, bicycle chain, and leather are apparent, though the puppeteers' costumes allow them to blend in with horses. The horse's character comes through in their coloring as much as in the idiosyncratic way each puppeteer team moves their bodies. Smith began the design process by sketching the locations of the play without reference to her research. These images are a part of a large book of designs. They later became the images used as projections to indicate locale. Recurring images were black and white charcoal drawings of poppies. This motif recurs throughout the action. As the casualty list increases, red ink is introduced into the image to represent blood. At first it is very light swirls, as if a watercolor paint mixing with water. Later it becomes large crimson ink stains that fill the petals of the drawings.

brown, and blue palette later used. The armature of the horse puppet is apparent. In effect this scenic design project had two design teams — one for the development and functioning of the puppets and the other for the setting, video, costume, and lighting. It is difficult to untangle the two.

Smith's design needed to accommodate the movement patterns of the large-scale puppets as well as facilitate the rapidly changing scenic needs. This episodic play needed a cinematic flow to accommodate a ground plan that moved between multiple locations, consisting of battlefields, buildings, and farmland. As well, the design had to leave space for the episodic narrative reflected in the original. Smith's design moves quickly from a naturalistic backdrop of the bucolic English countryside to explosive, Vorticist spirals of the Western front. As a result, she designed an open, round dirt promontory in the foreground. A key element of Smith's design is a 25-meter wide, irregular projection screen, resembling a strip of paper that looks as if it has been torn from a sketchbook. The screen serves a number of purposes. The production team projected hundreds of images onto this backdrop. These images are a link to Captain Nicholls, who sketches his experiences in Devon and in France. The shape of the screen also resembles a belly wound or a gash in a landscape that has been torn apart by explosions. Nicholls' drawings reflect a psychological atmosphere. As well, the drawings contextualize the live action battle scenes. The projections establish location, show the passing of time, and are used to create moving scenery. For example, when the locale moves from a Devon landscape to the no-man's-land, the projection created a sinking horizon, which had the effect of the movement of a ship across water.

These thumbnail sketches are part of a storyboard that works out the setting and projections scene by scene throughout the play. Each frame depicts one transition. Notice the notes and specifications added for the rest of the production team. Adding the radiating lines across the sky and changing the focal point of the image transform the composition. In the first, the sketching character is off-center creating an asymmetrical composition, while in the second the charging horse is in the center, thus creating a symmetrical composition. The first image is balanced and harmonious, the character is calm and gentle. The second radiates power and abrupt movement, and is jagged and splintered like a windshield exploding. Smith knew that the narrative needed more than physical scenery to convey its message.

© Rae Smith

© Rae Smith

Smith devised a simple solution to establish where the action was taking place. There were two three-dimensional scenic devices that helped distinguish location. First, rural scenes used wood materials to define location, for example in the paddock scenes in Devon actors used poles to create fences. Second, the war scenes in France used metallic materials such as black metal struts that resembled shrapnel or the remnants of destroyed buildings. Simple objects were used to define more specific space, for example, a door is used to suggest Paulette's farm, and drab military netting placed over a plough created a trench. Since the scenic indicators were so simple, they could be removed and the setting could transform quickly. There is little scenery; the designers tell the story using simple shifts of palette. One moment it might be sound, the next video, and the next light. Constable carved out location from the darkness. Light is incredibly important to the setting because it quickly can shift the locale. Also, offstage locations were used consistently to denote a particular place, such as using stage right for the Narracott farm door and stage left for Paulette's farm door.

Furthermore, study guide material outlines how other two-dimensional scenic devices are used to distinguish the location of action. First, the Devon scenes that are projected are drawn in pencil. Second, the French scenes are drawn in charcoal. Sepia tones are used to convey much of the subject matter for the pastoral Devon scenes. By contrast Vorticist war artists, augmented by stark shadow puppetry, influence the French scenes. Beyond research at such places as the Imperial War Museum, Smith made use of the visual styles of the art of the period. For example such images as *Bursting Shell* by Christopher Nevinson (1915) and *Void of War* by Paul Nash (1918) were influential in her drawings. The fragmented compositions helped convey the effects of explosions and the confusing nature of perception during a battle. This shift in palette came about through close collaboration between Smith, Constable, Warner, and Grimmer. Production materials indicate Warner and Grimmer developed the production imagery during rehearsals as the stage action was worked out. They were careful to make

© Simon Annand

This image depicts the animation of soldiers going over the top of a trench. In time with the sound effects of explosions, shadows of individual soldiers disappeared, marking their death as they advanced towards the enemy. The illusion of battle and of the scale of the number of men involved is made larger by way of the animation. The images above show the same stage space in three different moods. The changes in projection, lighting, and blocking change the location and mood of the action. By changing the quality of line, the contrast between light and dark, and the addition of hue radically changed the mood with little movement of three-dimensional scenery.

clear the journey from bucolic countryside to the horror of war. In a manner similar to the scenic designer's archival research Warner and Grimmer then incorporated Smith's concept drawings, by manipulating Smith's monochrome drawings, turning them into multi-layered images. As well, they worked to create a sense of movement by tracking and panning 'camera-style' across sketches of a galloping horse and rider. They also created special effects like water, blood, smoke, and explosions to accentuate the action. Textures were also created on the screen, moving from sepia and faded-out paper, through various stages of stained and battered surfaces.

> I think I can describe what I am interested in as a designer and how that influences my design decisions. I love how humans interact with, and relate to, objects and environments. People see an object on stage and they instantly know all kinds of things because of their experience and understanding of the objects. I spend most of my design time pondering how the audience will interpret, or "read," or try to "get," what they see on stage. I also love natural objects and the human reaction to nature.
>
> **Joe Tilford**

The final and most spectacular scenic elements were the life-size horses designed by Basil Jones and Adrian Kohler. They developed the apparatus over the course of several years, experimenting with the functionality of the puppets and their aesthetic look. To make the horses expressive they concentrated on five emotional indicators: the tail to show interest in the world, skin to give life to the horse when touched, eyes to provide a focal point for audiences to look at, ears to show fear, anger and interest, and the ribs to show the movement of breath. Each one of these parts was able to move to convey a sense of emotion from the horse. These puppets are not realistic, but their wooden framework, translucent fabric skins, and mobility endow them with a sense of life. The open, round stage gave them a landscape to move through like a corral or circus ring, to show off their expressive capabilities.

This image depicts the Night Time Crossing. Angular and choppy waves and thick and heavy clouds provide a strong contrast with the lighter pencil sketches drawn in Devon. Nicholls' sketches in the projections often had handwritten dates in the bottom left-hand corner to establish the passage of time for the audience.

© Simon Annand

The production team used the projections to organize the stage space. They were able to move the characters through time and change the atmosphere of the location easily. Abstract images were used to show the effects of the bombing upon the landscape, as well as indicate the moods of each scene. The scenic design and projection design worked together to coordinate the elements and principles of composition over time to insure the audience knew when and where the characters were at each moment of the action. Furthermore, the puppets brought to life the formal elements of line and form to become evocative living creatures. There are all manner of ways of creating stage settings. The aim is to serve the material by providing a context for the action and to help the audience understand what they are watching.

The elements and principles in action

In collaboration with the director, scenic designers organize the stage setting to set the context for the action. They define the color palette and set the scale of the environment. The costume designer and lighting designer join the team and further contribute to the visible world by using complementary color and texture palettes. The addition of further elements causes the scenic designer to reassess and modify the design to coordinate effects. Design is a collaborative art where each member of the team contributes to the stage picture, and they must work together to create a unified composition. If a costume does not appear to have the right color, the scenic designer may have to change the color of a floor or a wall, and the lighting designer may have to adjust the temperature of a lighting instrument. Are the lines of the props working with the lines of the character's silhouette? Are the lines of the setting rectilinear and precise and the focus of the light diffuse and indistinct? Are the effects of these choices appropriate to lead the audience to understand the concepts? Together they discuss, analyze, and problem solve to achieve the effects that will best suit the director's interpretation of the production.

The next chapter examines the most basic processes that a costume designer will follow to conceive of the costumes of the production, collaborate with the design team, and coordinate effects to create a unified composition. While in the United Kingdom the set designer is also responsible for the costume design, this is another's responsibility in the United States. In either case, the costumes are conceived once the visual organization of the setting has been arrived at. Setting establishes the physical organization of the location and the movement patterns within that location, the costumes define character, and lighting ties it all together by revealing those elements. There are as many ways to accomplish this, as there are designers.

5 The artistry of the costume

Key Topics:

@ The functions of costume

- Creating characters
- Visual composition

@ The costume designer's process

- The script, sketches, corseting, silhouettes, colors

@ Reading the script

- The costume bible, textile artists, the scene breakdown, visual language

@ The journey from sketch to stage
@ Costume and collaboration

Case Studies:

- Imagining what objects would wear: *Beauty and the Beast*
- *Cabaret:* Two interpretations
- Paying attention to what clothing tells us: *The Miracle Worker*

Costumers shape the clothing a play's characters wear, establishing age, historical period, gender, psychological state, and social status. They use the basic principles and elements of design, including color, form, silhouette, and style to help audiences understand the production's themes, concept, and mood. Like their other colleagues on the production team, costumers begin their work by seeking to understand the script or other source material the production will be based upon. Effective costumes are the result of careful observation, analysis, and imagination. Regardless of whether the play is in period or is contemporary, costume designers begin to conceptualize their part in the production through research. Costumes need to be practical while also looking right. They do not have to look pretty close up on the street, but from a distance under the glare of stage lighting. The following is a broad overview of some of the ways in which costume designers approach their job.

The functions of costume

Costumes serve two important purposes for a production, to support the narrative by creating characters that can be distinguished from each other, and to provide balance within the visual composition by using color, texture, and silhouette. All clothing used on stage is considered costume. Costumes are so much more than the clothes a character wears; they reveal the nature of each character embodying the psychological, social, and emotional condition of the character at a particular moment in time. Costumes allow audiences to recognize characters even before the actor utters a line. Costumers work to know the character as intimately as the actor in the role. A costume designer strives to conceptualize and design garments that capture and define the personalities of the fictional characters in the play. The embodiment of the character comes to life through the actor and reciprocally the costume reinforces that life. Thus, costumes can shape and augment bodies, and the restrictions or characteristics of the materials of the costume influence the particular ways in which actors are able to move while wearing it.

> The thing about research is that any meeting I have, whether it's with a theatre director or a musical artist, it's all about generating ideas and research is the fuel that stokes the whole process. Sitting on the bus, going to an exhibition, watching TV with my children, whatever it is, it all comes out somewhere. Some of it comes from a long time ago, from travelling I did in my twenties or books I read when I was at university – thank God I crammed so much into all that time or otherwise I wouldn't be able to keep all the ideas coming.
>
> **Es Devlin**

99

Costume design in contemporary plays is often thought to be invisible. Contemporary costumes are considered successful if audiences do not notice them at all; however, they must be intimately connected to the characters. Furthermore, a designer must have a thorough knowledge of materials used to make costumes. Like the lighting designer who must understand lighting technology, the costume designer needs to learn the qualities of the fabrics, paints, and printing processes to understand how to achieve effects. How can the fabric catch the light, move, and flow? For example in *Red*, discussed in Chapter 4, though dressed in period clothing, the artist and his assistant are seen in working clothes that are indistinguishable from our own street clothes. Their costumes are not meant to be the focus of the audience's attention. Rather they blend in with the studio, leaving us to look at the paintings that the artist creates. The clothes look natural, as if the character got up and put them on for work. Designing contemporary clothing is a subtle art where a designer can manipulate a **silhouette** to emphasize or understate a characteristic, such as color for example, to make a point. The goal is that the audience must be able to immediately recognize the character. Nothing that appears on stage is casual. Every **accessory** and costume is the result of a deliberate choice made by a designer. Whether you make the clothing or shop for it, the choices are made in the context of the dramatic moment depicted.

A costume can be made from as simple and strange a material as a cardboard box to as complicated a construction as the many layers of a kimono, or even as little covering as a nude body. It can be the distinctive style of a people, class, location or period. Clothing on stage has an influence over the audience. If it works against character the actor will have a difficult time convincing the audience. Take for instance an actress trying to portray purity and innocence wearing a low-cut red dress and patent-leather high-heeled shoes. An actor wearing cut-off jeans with bare feet is going to have trouble effectively convincing an audience he is the chairman of the board at a company meeting.

> I think one of the most important things when you're working with colleagues is to respect them and understand how difficult their jobs are. You have to be a collaborator, and that is one of the most exciting things, one of the most difficult and in some ways one of the things I love the most. You work alongside a whole gang of people and when you start working on it you have to help them feel that it's more important than any other show they happen to be working on or any other show they are going to work on in the future; this is the one, so let's all work together to make this fantastic. You could say that's manipulative, but you could also say how fantastic to excite people to think this is going to be something really special, and enthuse them to do their best work.
>
> **Alison Chitty**

The challenge of a costume design is to design garments that can easily convey information about sex, age, occupation, social status, geography, season, time of day, action, and period. Audiences constantly make subjective judgments about personality and attitudes of the wearer of a costume. Anything the audience sees and reacts to consciously or unconsciously will need to be accounted for by the designer. In a fitting the designer is making adjustments by looking into the mirror to see the garment on the actor from the perspective of the audience. What we wear and how we wear it expresses our personal attitudes and our view of our place in society. On an emotional level, a person in a depressed state of mind might deliberately choose clothes that appear more cheerful, while another might select clothing that reinforces their gloom. Stage costumes work with the other elements to reinforce the mood and style of the production, help distinguish between major groups of characters, and suggest relationships between characters. Costume designs also include any accessories a character uses such as hats, gloves, shoes, jewelry, or handbags. The costume designer must conceive and organize these elements to allow the audience to make judgments about these characters and help distinguish the characters from one another.

> I couldn't light my own show, I wouldn't want to. I want the expertise and knowledge and experience of a really marvelous lighting designer. I love the input of a colleague who knows much more about it than I do. In every area the more experience you have the better you are as a person to work with other people. I have made many costumes in my life but I am not a costume maker and never will be. I have painted many sets in my life but I am not a great scene painter. There are many, many, many wonderful talented people who work in all these different areas who are fantastically skilled; I want to work with them.
>
> **Alison Chitty**

The costume designer's process

Unless the scenic designer is also creating the costumes, the costume designer is the second member of the design team hired. As the scenic designer creates the context within which the costumes are seen, the costume designer quickly seeks to understand what the director and set designer have conceptualized. When the costume designer receives a script, the process of developing visual shorthand for each character begins. Costume sketches, fashion (or more broadly clothing) research, and garments are used to help designers, directors, and actors develop a language to build each character. As the process continues, the director and the costume designer share ideas, which may take the form of costume sketches, photographs, sample costumes, or costume mock-ups, then meet with the scenic designer, lighting designer, and actors. Only after that process takes place does the director give final approval regarding the costume shop manufacture, rent, and/or purchases of the costumes.

When I'm given an assignment, I do a lot of browsing. I'll spend at least two weeks just looking through different sources before I do any drawing. I need to absorb it all, put it through the strainer of my mind. Also, because I didn't know the play very well, I read it a couple of times, as well as different commentaries on the play. Then, after a couple of weeks, I started drawing. I do a series of rough sketches that I generally don't show to anybody. As I develop those drawings, I start having meetings with the director, and then it's kind of a give-and-take of ideas . . . Some people feel that the sketching is the designing, and that the sketches are the final product. But it's so much more about the fittings, the dress rehearsals – that's where the refining really happens. For a costume designer, unlike a set designer, so much of the design is informed by the actor. When I go to the first fitting, the actor's body, the way they react, even the way they look at themselves in the mirror, informs my design. For me, the hardest part is going to my drawing table, because I'm by myself, and that's not really what's natural to theater, which is truly a collaborative art.

Tamar Cohen

A costume designer's first read of the script is to look for its emotional impact or its overall mood that may suggest colors, textures, fabrics, and silhouette. Specific scenes will have their own emotional requirements, as will the specific characters. Once discussions with the director have begun the designer clarifies basic concepts and settles upon an interpretation. Preliminary design meetings are about coordination between the scenery, costumes, lighting, and sound. Here shapes and colors will be discussed to establish specific moods and what the director's conceptual focus will be. Will the sets and costumes use the same colors or will they contrast ground and background? What types of details will be emphasized? How is the stage set organized? What types of textures and fabrics will be considered? Is it realist or expressionist? Does the production call for heavy nubby textures, deep rich piles, or shiny sleek silks? What types of textures will be chosen for effect? Only once basic coordination guidelines have been established is it possible to move forward.

There is no such thing as good costume design separated from a good production. You can't have good costumes and a bad production. It's not possible – that's what I say. As a costume designer, you don't get credit for a great performance, but rarely do you have a great performance with a terrible costume. It's been done, but I really believe that it's got to feel as if it's all coming from the same place.

Susan Hilferty

The journey for the costume designer usually starts with sketches. At each stage of the design process the designer articulates thought through drawing, painting, or collage. Different types of visual display include drawings of particular moments of action and preliminary costume sketches. A costume designer probes the script to figure out the character in the way that an actor does, because the more specific and articulate a costume is, the more effectively it will communicate to the audience. The minute details of costume are often relished by actors and can enhance their performances in imperceptible ways. For example, when Kevin Klein played the role of the Cook in the Public Theatre production of *Mother Courage and her Children* discussed in Chapter 4, the costume designer Marina Draghici gave him a scarf riddled with bullet holes that was once worn by a Vietnamese soldier. A documentary on the making of the production showed how its texture and its smell were a means for him to awaken his senses and discover something about the cook who lived through a war. Many actors credit their costume as a guide to the discovery of their character. Designs will shape the character's silhouette. Like everyone else, actors often need tactful designing for less than perfect bodies. Flattering figures, camouflaging flaws, and rebalancing proportions is often part of the designer's job. Beyond making the actor look good the designer is crafting the look of the character. By flattening a figure an attractive actress can be made to look more tomboyish to suit a particular role. The designer manipulates silhouette to convey information about the character to the audience.

Costumes are an added element of the setting. They add a layer of color or balance and symmetry to the stage set. Since actors wear costumes, they dominate the foreground action, providing a focal point for the audience's eyes. Each theatre space or stage setting provides a foreground and background for the action. The production team collaborates to fill the space and integrate the setting, lights, costume, and actors together into a unified composition, according to the universe of the script as interpreted by the director. To do this they must also deliberate on the overall mood and color palate of the production. **Color** is a powerful tool used to underscore the narrative and create a cohesive fictional space. The dialogue may be the driving force shaping the action, but color provides the balance to the composition. It is imperative that there is a strong reference point from which the production team works. The clothing will work in balance with the colors of the setting and the light will tie all the elements together.

> Color brings my ideas to life, and I don't like to show sketches to a director without color. I'm always surprised when I go to costume shops and see other designers' sketches without color. It expresses as much character and emotion as the silhouette, and I find it's often what actors will have the strongest reaction to when they're looking at their sketch.
>
> **Tamar Cohen**

Even undergarments, which are unseen by the audience, serve a role in helping actors bring to life character. They are like the armature of a sculpture providing the foundation for it to be able to stand up. **Corseting** alters an actor's gait, posture, and vocal delivery while providing a distinct and readily identifiable silhouette. For example, Epheba in *Wicked* is immediately recognizable simply by her iconic shadow shaped by her hat and it shows that silhouette is a powerful tool to make use of. Epheba is recognizable by her black hat and dress. Furthermore, her green skin is a dead giveaway as to her identity. Her friend Glenda is recognizable because of her contrasting white dress, tiara, and wand. The contrasting silhouettes and colors reinforce the theme that morality is neither black nor white and perhaps appearances can be deceiving. Costumes are never clothes. What is pretty in person may not be pretty on stage, because under the glare of lights costuming needs enhancement to convey mood and personality. The designer will add color, texture, or silhouette to make the costume visible from the back row of the theatre. Likewise the lighting designer's collaboration will affect those colors and visibility. Costumes do not have to feel good to wear, they must look right to an audience from the distance of the house. If it looks right, hangs right, and conveys the effect that is desired it is right. To look elegant one does not have to wear silk – just appear to be wearing silk.

> Clothing is the medium in which I work. But it's not just clothes that I like. It's the idea of working collaboratively when creating theatre. It's like having four musicians creating the same piece of music. You can't do it by yourself.
>
> **Susan Hilferty**

Reading the script

Costume starts in the script. If the design is for an opera the designer reads the libretto and listens to the music, or for dance the designer asks for music or any other material available to help understand the shape of the piece. Designers interpret the script to find ways to enhance characterization. William Ivey Long says that costume defines character. It helps someone become someone else. What is the character wearing? Why is she wearing it? A dress can alter the line of a body. High-heeled shoes can pitch a woman forward and change the actor's attitude as she walks. A corset affects performance when it is put on. Though there are rarely explicit instructions from the playwright about costuming, the text serves as the basis for the design. In the first meeting with the director the designer will start with a clean slate. What does the director think the play is about? The designer does not want to be too determined to present his or her own ideas because they might not merge well with the director's vision or the setting. If the play is set in a specific historical era the designer examines books, pictures, and garments from that period. They may create a collage using bits of the information that they dig up. Once the play is cast then sketching can begin. Long believes that one must observe the actor's body type to create a plan for one's approach for getting this body to support the character within the director's vision. To stimulate the flow of ideas at the first meeting with the production team, the costume designer often presents a few rough costume sketches. Once the costumes are designed, he shows photos of the garments to the actors so they know what to expect. In the fitting room he looks into the mirror to see how the garment looks from afar. He works with the actor to try things out first. Once the technical costume parade comes then further adjustments under the lights on the set will have to be made. The costume designer seeks to understand the characters and their interrelationships.

The individuality of the costume grows out of the interpretation of the dramatic elements present in a certain role. The characters' costumes develop from what the characters say and do and what others say about them. Just as we dress according to the daily tasks we have ahead of us, whether we are going to the grocery store or a party, so too characters dress according to the multiple functions that they will engage in. Characters change over the course of the play, and the costumes will change accordingly. Changes may indicate differences in locations or time, emotional states, or mood variations. A garment supports the character but does not try to encapsulate the whole character. It is just one part of that symbolic evocation. Costumes help create a reality for a specific situation. Following these conversations with the director about characterization the designer will consider the impact of each individual costume and all the costumes seen as a whole, maintaining a balance between the two. The scale of the stage space affects the details of the costume. Different types of costumes are suitable for the opera than for a small studio space. You cannot see the detail on the stage of the Royal Opera House as you can at the Lyttleton. As well, the budget for each of those venues shapes the choices that the designer will make.

In each production some sort of **costume bible** is kept. What constitutes a costume bible is different depending on the person. It can contain research and renderings, but often it is not simply used for research and preparation. It can also contain actors' measurements, catalogs that clothes are ordered from, production calendars, contact lists for performers and production team, and so on. The costume shop keeps this as a guide to building and maintaining the costumes. For example, it may contain a rough sketch depicting the ways a ruffle is meant to fall and the manner in which it is to be affixed. It may also contain a sample of the cloth, information on where the cloth was purchased or manufactured, its cost, and the details of elements. In other words, it contains all the information one would need to reproduce the costume if the show has a good run and a costume wears out. For example, costumes for Broadway shows need to be durable enough to stand eight performances a week for a year. That can be difficult if the costume is worn extensively. The costume designer also collaborates with specialized artists to bring the look of the character to life. The costume bible guides those collaborators as they create their part of the design. A **textile artist** works to realize the costumer's effects by printing fabric designs. While costuming is an artisanal craft done by hand, there have been advancements in textile design that make fabric production more readily available. Where once all fabric had to be hand painted, silk screened or dyed, computer technologies and digital printing have made the process slightly faster.

There are a number of practical details that have to be organized and determined, such as the number of costumes per characters, the number of scenes there are, the type of accoutrements necessary, and how many costume changes there will be. A **costume scene breakdown** needs to be done. What factors need to be considered? Are there time considerations to take into account for quick changes? Are roles double cast? How much budget? How long does the costume team have to make or find costumes? Will they be drawn from stock, rented, or built costumes? Who are the actors cast in each role? How heavy, tall, or pale are they? The total costume needs to be considered in terms of effects it will have upon the look of the character. How will the costumes emphasize or deemphasize certain traits? Does the designer need to manipulate the shape of the actor to look more like the character? How will the costume affect movement, sitting, and standing?

Characters are established through costume by considering age, physical stature, occupation, and social position. Psychological motivations are important. In characterization designers do not try to replicate a period authentically by mimicking the lines and silhouettes and random eccentricities of a time. Rather the designer tries to unify the look of the production by choosing the most typical styles that are representative of a period and serve the needs of the script. The aim is to evoke the silhouettes of a period and distinguish characters. Colors and fabrics are considered. The lighting designer is an important collaborator because lighting affects how audiences perceive color and the ways the brain begins to process form and texture. A **color scheme** can help delineate characters or groups of characters by hue or a range of hues suitable to evoke the mood of the play and the characters. Body must also be considered. Costume can be used to enhance or detract from an actor's form.

Costume sketches reveal physical and psychological attributes of a character. How do the characters present themselves to the world? What do their bodies look like? Are they introspective or extroverted? Do they stand in a particular way? How do the clothes shape the form of the character? Are they dressed differently according to mood or psychology? While aesthetic concerns are at the forefront, the designer must also ensure that the designs allow the actor to move freely in a way that is consistent with the historical period and allows the actor to perform the actions required by the role. Also, the designer needs to be sensitive to the creative direction in which the performer wants to take his or her character.

Designers consider how characters can be dressed similarly to allow for immediate recognition of identity, class, and alliance. They will make clear the **power relationships** in the script by creating a visual language that will make immediately understandable to contemporary audiences which character is subservient and which character is in control. Costumes are always influenced by the period in which they are created. However, even the most faithful and accurate picture needs to be

THE ARTISTRY OF THE COSTUME

understood by an audience that belongs to the twenty-first century. Everything a designer puts on stage is for the audience to help them to imagine and relate to the lives of the characters. The principles of design (rhythm, emphasis, proportion, balance, and unity) are how we use the tools (elements) to create looks (whole outfits, accessories, and shoes) that are different or unique. Design affects different performances different ways. Bad designs are those that detract from a performance by looking inappropriate on a character, thus making an actor's work more difficult. A designer can draw pointless attention by including confusing combinations of color that pull audience focus to the wrong place on stage. Also a design can force an actor to move in an inappropriate way, by not making the most of the actor's body type in an intelligent way.

Good costume design on the other hand can help actors to better feel in character, and show their character's traits more advantageously to the audience. Costume designers can provide spectacle that makes musical numbers visually interesting, distracts from poor sections of script giving the audience something to look at, and amplifies scripts that need strong visuals to match the heightened emotion and language. Good design provides needed visual shorthand and coding that can direct attention to the right place on stage, depict **character types** faster than dialogue or an actor's portrayal can, and thus speed up the audience's understanding of the action. Designers help actors to blend their body type harmoniously with that of their character, making the person look sexy or frumpy, young or old, regardless of what they normally look like. They can provide cues, restrictions and/or opportunities for movement that can appropriately limit, or enhance the actor's movements in keeping with the script. A good design helps let audiences know which people belong to which groups in potentially confusing scripts, as in *Coast of Utopia* (2002) where the dozens of writers need to be distinguished from the dozens of politicos. They can communicate information to the audience about period, social circumstances, time of day, weather, socioeconomic status, and a host of other details without needing to waste script time on exposition.

The journey from sketch to stage

Sometimes it takes two or three meetings before we know what we're going to end up doing. But generally after that first meeting we may have decided to go in a direction for which I have no images and need to do a lot of new research. In which case, that will happen next and we'll probably have an intermediate meeting, where people can look at that research and see if it's heading in the right direction. And it might be after that that I start sketching. In general, after we sit with these images that we've gathered and talked about, and come up with an approach that we all feel excited by, that's the impetus for drawing. That's when I imagine a world in which to design, and I start drawing.

Constance Hoffman

The foundation of design preparation is drawing or collage. Usually designers begin sketching out ideas as a means of thinking, and then meet as a team with material that they have found, or interesting images or things that they think are pertinent. Together they look at those sketches and start to choose a direction. This is a gradual process. After the broad strokes of the concept are agreed upon, the next step is to trawl through the piece moment by moment, work out what is happening, what is the story, and in what way the story is going to be told. A designer may then begin to draw more than one character on a page together to show how costumes relate to one another. From the initial drawings the costumer will render the costumes for each scene, and add fabric swatches and pattern templates to show to the scenic designer. The team takes the sketches and models to start to work out how the textures and colors work together. They move things around and see whether the effects that they were thinking about are right. Following this the costume drawings are drawn up. The design team submits this work to the company they are working with for approval.

In an interview with the American Theatre Wing Catherine Zuber describes how after she reads the script, she starts thinking about a production working off the excitement of the director who gets the ideas flowing. By the first meeting she will have some images, ideas or references to start a dialogue with. She likes the director to tell her how he sees each character. She will interview the director about each character in the play. Zuber believes that the costume designer needs to see how the director understands and sees the character so that she can honor what the director sees. Though she will have her own different views from her reading, they need to work off the same point since the other designers and the actors will be guided from the director's perspective. Zuber begins with a slow dialogue with the director over dinner or in an hour-and-a-half meeting. At the next meeting she will come back with sketches to work from. She first sketches out characters in concert with the director. However, once casting takes place the ideas will transform again. Actors are also a factor she considers, because she aims to honor how each collaborator sees the characters. Change happens with each added collaborator. One must understand how the team visualizes the scenes.

Scenic designers are hired first because they need to submit bids to build the set the earliest. Directors prefer to understand the environment and play before they add the costume element. They want to know how the characters live within that environment before envisioning what the characters wear. For the recent Broadway revival of *South Pacific* (2008) the team worked with black and white models and Zuber created silhouettes of costume first. Then they came back and talked about the color palette. They then tested wall color against fabric swatches. Lighting was the element that tied it all together. If everyone is communicating then the lighting designer will know what needs to be done to pull all the elements together. For *Coast of Utopia* there were six hundred costumes. She sketched them all so that she could understand where they were going with the play. The designer chooses the fabrics, supervises construction and fitting. Zuber started with a white muslin fitting and moved to fashion fabric and trims. In particular she had to account for a number of quick changes. For example, there were zippers sown into the back of many costumes to accommodate these. A lot of costumes are necessary to show changing circumstances of characters as the years fly by in this play. Change will show up with time, temperature, season, or age variations. All of these have to be reflected in what the characters are wearing.

To chart the many costume changes in this particularly large costume piece Zuber drew up a **costume plot**. This list or chart shows which characters appear in each scene, what they are wearing, and their overall movement throughout the play. In this way she was able to track the specific costume needs of every character as they move through time. A costume plot is also used to identify any potential costume challenges, such as **quick changes** between scenes or difficult transitions. Once the director and production team approved her preliminary sketches, she drew up the final designs in color, showing the style, silhouette, textures, accessories, and unique features of each costume.

Only in the technical rehearsals do all the elements of design come together on the stage under the lights so that the production team can look at them. Often it is the first time the director has seen many of the elements at full scale, and certainly it is the first time the actors have seen the finished set. At this point work with the lighting designer begins, adjusting color and visibility. Sometimes the costume designer gets notes from the directors who often cannot articulate why something does not look right. Part of the collaborative process is to ask questions to figure out what is not right. This final stage is the most intense, all the ingredients are on stage, all the performers are there, and the production team must look at everything and try and manipulate it, tweak it, and turn it into the best it can possibly be before opening.

Imagining what objects would wear: *Beauty and the Beast*

Beauty and the Beast opened at the Palace Theatre on April 18, 1994. Based on the animated film, this stage version of Walt Disney's *Beauty and the Beast* re-imagined its story, songs, and action to work as a two-and-a-half-hour Broadway show. It is the story of a Prince who is transformed by a witch into a Beast. For the enchantment to be broken he must learn to love and be loved. Adapting the movie into a musical began when Disney's Michael Eisner hired Robert Roth to direct the musical and Stan Meyer to design the set. With the help of costume designer Ann Hould-Ward, they worked to find a way to translate *Beauty and the Beast* to the Broadway stage. According to Disney, their biggest challenge was to find a way to make the objects come to life. They conceived of a way to make the enchanted objects instantly recognizable and allow the actors freedom of movement, to be able to sing and dance. Next they had to find a way to make the film's most spectacular moments work live on the stage. However, it took time to solve how to go about recreating onstage effects such as the Beast's transformation back into his Princely human form. For this, they turned to experts in creating onstage illusion and hired John Gaughan and Jim Steinmeyer who had designed illusions for magicians David Copperfield and Siegfried & Roy.

The musical went into production and the team presented costume sketches, stage designs, and storyboards to Eisner and Katzenberg to demonstrate that the project could be done. Once approval came, Roth emphasized that he did not want the production team to recreate the movie, but rather find theatrical choices that would evoke its many settings and emotional feel. His emphasis was on portraying the true love between Belle and the Beast, as well as the desire of the enchanted objects to be

© Joan Marcus

human again. Myer collaborated with Roth to create spaces for the characters to inhabit, charting the changes in location by including different props in each palace. Each environment reflects the personality of the characters. This provided Hould-Ward with a context within which to place her dressed characters. Only through collaboration can Belle's dress, as she enters the library, have the effect of creating a feeling of warmth. Her pink dress and the lighting combine with the textures of the set to create a small space of warmth and love within the cold environment of the Beast's castle. It is through this color mixing that the mood of the story comes through in the visual world of the play.

In comparison with the Belle who seems innocent and naive in the blue dress above we see a different side of Belle in her yellow gown seen below. Her elegant gown for the ball differs and shows a maturation of character. The shapes are more elaborate and the textures a delicate combination of flowing silks and rippling ribbons. The inspirational images are of older women with much deeper comfort with their sexuality. The shapes are full and the yellow and pinks feminine and ripe. Her two yellow gowns recall the splendor of Fragonard's paintings and the clothing of the French court in the mid to late eighteenth century. Here we see the ball gown on the actress. Note the change of silhouette for her shape. In the simple blue pinafore dress with a white blouse underneath it seen in the first image, with straight lines and angled harmonies, she looked virginal and sweet showing a simple frame. Below the line of the dress is a curved harmony that uses the ruffles and yellow taffeta to fill out her hips, accentuate her bosoms making her an elegant, mature woman.

That's what the rehearsal room is all about. You have to allow yourself the freedom to develop this language. It's terrifying for a designer, because what we do has to be concretized at some point. Actors themselves have much more flexibility in that they change their accents from one day to the next. But once you start to build the set, or once you start to build the clothes, your ability to change is different – especially for a costume designer, who has to work so closely with actors. I have to watch what actors are doing to develop their vocabulary, in order to know that what I am doing is supporting it, and I have to look constantly to where I can make changes.

Susan Hilferty

A large discussion that Hould-Ward had with her team was how to bring to life the tiny teacups and candlesticks on the stage. The production team had to work out what the costume designer was responsible for in this process. She had to give a sense of the rigid structure of the objects while being conscious of the comfort of the actor within the costume at all times. The team grappled with the question of how to make the enchanted objects believable in performance and how to retain the magic of the Beast's transformation. The vision for the live performance was for the enchanted objects such as Cogsworth, Lumiere, Mrs. Potts, and the other enchanted characters to become progressively more like objects. This gave them a stake in having Belle and the Beast coming together, because they wanted to be free from the enchantment as well. They felt that this humanization allows the audience to empathize with them. In particular the Lumiere, a candlestick man, was a concern because his human element had to become evident during the second act to propel the story forward. The team worked to make his humanity obvious through the inanimate structure of his costume. It is the responsibility of the designer to help the action of the play, always keeping in mind that the actor must wear the costume. For example there is a song and dance routine where the candle wears a hat and cane and does kicks up and down a stack of dishes. The designer and the actor collaborated to figure out how constrained the candle had to be. The actor felt that the objectness of the costume was important because it helped him move like an object. They had to hire on a number of experts to handle the pyrotechnics, the prosthesis, and the butane pack that they placed on his back. Meyer's scenery is in an ornate, slightly sinister German Gothic style, giving it an almost sinister feel. To keep the action visually interesting the special-effects engineers conceived of, among other things, apparitions, disappearances, thunderstorms, and atmospheric fog. At one point, the carcass of the Beast rises up from the castle floor, floats ten feet or so into space, and then starts to spin round and round. As he spun he mysteriously sheds all his beastly features and transformed into the hero.

For Hould-Ward the design process begins with in-depth research into the period of the show followed by a consideration of the period from the point of view of what can be used to evoke the world of the play. For *Beauty and the Beast* her research focused on teapots, clocks, and kitchen utensils from the mid-to-late eighteenth century. She also examined iconic French rococo paintings by Watteau, Fragonard, and Boucher. This research was placed alongside the aesthetic choices seen in the animated film from which the production was being conceived. Once she settled on style and period she then needed to consider the bodies of the cast. All the period research in the world is useless without the human frame to hang the clothing upon. The performer's body and the choices of how to portray the characters help shape the form of the costume. For example, she claims that the essential qualities of the Beast's costume emerged from watching the movements of the original actor who played the Beast in rehearsal. As the development of the production progressed it emerged that over

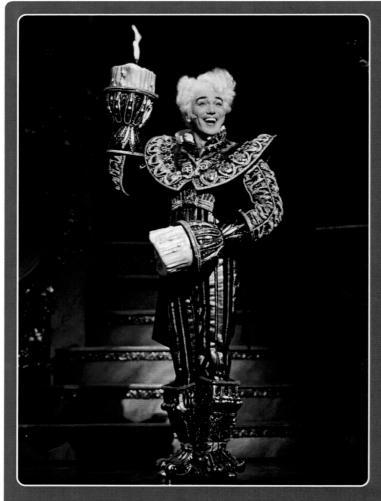

© Joan Marcus

Lumiere's torches light up from a butane pack on his back. The designers determined the stubs looked best, as the character has been around a while and is worn down. Lumiere's costume uses vertical lines to help square off his frame to make him appear to be a rigid candlestick. The gold of his costume helps make him appear like a gold candlestick, but since it is broken up with black fabric he has a vertical line elongating his frame. He is balanced vertically and the lines move the audience's focus to his face and to the curve of his arms and the candleholder that will be lit. As we saw above, the object chorus is in contrast to Belle in her blue. Furthermore you can see the saturated reds and purples that the team assigned the show to bring out the fairy-tale quality to the palace. Color families make the characters easily identifiable by type. The contrast in colors also helps the main characters draw focus even in a large crowd. The palette of the setting, costume, and lights is balanced here. Balance can be achieved with color, line, shape, and/or texture. There are two different types of balance: symmetrical (formal) and asymmetrical (informal). Symmetrical means having all elements equal on both sides of a design. This image shows the balancing of forms, mass, and colors on opposite sides of the centerline or vertical axis of the design. Designs employing symmetry tend to be stable, formal, and without much sense of motion.

four hundred sketches of the objects and costumes were needed. She created such a large number of designs so that the team could respond and offer feedback. For example, there were fifty drawings for the candelabra, exploring whether one, two, three or more candles would work best. What style of candle should they be? Would they be fresh, new tapers, or burned down into a stub? While the team argued about the number of candles, she had to keep in mind the presence of the actor in the costume, considering how he would be able to move and whether he was able to wear it over the duration of the evening. In her preparatory sketches the shape of the collar is drawn as a piece of the clock. In development the collar was reduced and allowed the actor more freedom of movement. The shapes were made more organic and the head and torso became more unified. In the first image the head seems cut off from the torso, while in the bottom image the eggplant shape of his face is connected to the eggplant shape of the costume covering his torso. Next the clock hands became a handlebar mustache thus endowing the object with more human expressiveness. Ideas transform slowly over time.

Hould-Ward's choices had to make sense to both adults and children. She had to decide what elements were necessary so that a child could identify the characters and decide how to engage the parents at same time. Designing the Enchanted Objects was a particular challenge for the costume team because the objects are animate. To allow the actors to move the objects and allow them to be expressive the costumes had to be flexible. There was a risk that the costume could get in the way of an actor's performance. Also Hould-Ward had to determine how, visually, a person might transform into a candlestick or a clock, how a collar might represent the sconce of a candlestick or how the front of a jacket could become the face of a clock. How would a spatula move, how can the costume enable that? She had to map out the transformations to maintain a visual through line – Mrs. Pott's cap gradually enlarged until it became a top of a teapot. Cogsworth's epaulets were stiffened so that they became the ornate edging on a clock. At the end, the audience had to recognize that the objects, when they were returned to human shape again wearing their everyday clothes, had once been the teapot, the candlestick, or the clock. To accentuate each object's characteristics, Hould-Ward painted directly onto the fabric as the set designer might add paint to a drop to create more defined shadows and contrast. She brushed shadows into the creases of a jacket to give the costume added dimension. She uses line, shadow, texture, and pattern to intensify the look of the character. Thus the audience's eye keeps its focus on the visual details of the character. It is a way of attracting the audience's attention. Her choices add to the characterizations of the actors' performance. Furthermore, Natasha Katz, the lighting designer, used over six hundred lighting instruments to bring out the fairy-tale qualities of the setting and costume. The design team chose a lot of saturated colors – deep blues and reds – to give the scenes a fairy-tale, otherworldly feel. Katz used the large number of lights to make sure the audience could see the faces beneath the costumes as well as create a mood. Hould-Ward's costume bible shows her sketch for Belle. Around the periphery of her preparatory drawings she placed images taken from art history of the dresses of young maidens that inspired the design. There are swatches of fabric of the different fabric used to create the dress in the shop and details about her accessories and undergarments. You can see the fabric of the shirt on the edge of the page. In performance the flowing white apron was modified into a plain blue skirt. The basket and the colors of its contents are picked up on the book and in performance there was a blue ribbon that hung from the book.

Belle's iconic costuming in the film led Hould-Ward to choose to dress her in the familiar blue outfit but she embellished it for live performance with silky fabrics, delicate patterning, touches of lace, and embroidery. Hould-Ward interprets the character as an intelligent woman who enjoys reading and gets excited by books because they open up a world of adventure and possibility. The scriptwriter wanted her to be a good role model who gets elevated because of her deeds. As Roth cast he looked for an actress who could bring Belle to life and make her believable. Rather than the stereotypical sweet heroine, they looked for a beauty who had some spunk and could portray a sense of adventure and determination since she is the moral conscience of the play. The production team saw Belle as making a transition through the play; though she is strong at the start, she matures during the play, and learns to see beyond the superficial ugliness of the Beast. To reflect this Hould-Ward made Belle's costumes more and more beautiful as her journey progresses. Her costumes reflect her growing love for the Beast.

The initial costume sketch for the Beast was based on the premise that he is like a rock star. He had an open collar to expose his chest and hair, tattered cuffs on the pants to reveal his leg hair, and he had long locks of hair. As the process went on they covered more of the body with hair and prosthetics. At one extreme the costume was subtle with suggestions of beastality in hair length and chest hair, at another it was a full body suit. In the end they kept the body suit and took away some of the masking to allow for the actor's expressive features to come through. This conception of the Beast is far more vertical than the eventual design, which is rounded and squat in shape. The Beast's costume is one of the most significant transformations that take place on the stage. The actor is encased in a hulking, hairy body, with clawed hands and sharply pointed horns. Roth drew inspiration from photographs of rock performers, because he wanted to give the Beast sex appeal. His hairy chest and long hair are meant to evoke an animal magnetism, which would in turn stimulate chemistry between himself and Belle. According to Hould-Ward she conceived the costuming through extensive research of the film plus representations of werewolves and beasts through the ages, and she combined this research with the director's image of the rock musician. She explored different manifestations of the Beast through sketches, but did not finalize her conception until she observed the actor in rehearsal. Terrence Mann saw the character as explosive, because he is a young man who made a horrible mistake when he turned away the beggar woman. If only he had not made the wrong choice, his life might be different. Hould-Ward observed the physicality of the performance and was able to humanize the character even though it was covered up with prosthetics. They began with heavy rubber on his face, which was removed slowly until a balance between prosthetics and facial movement was achieved. He needed control over his facial muscles to allow for the emotion of the role to come through.

Here we see the Beast's mask. Note that they they did not cover his mouth, nose, and eyes beneath the mask. As well, his hand is recognizable beneath the long fur on top. His wig and horns further change the shape of his form and help change his silhouette to that of a hulking beast. The puffy sleeves with a tight cuff further accentuate the mass of his body. In both these elaborate costumes filled with a variety of layered textures, colors, and details our focus still goes to the face of the actors. The costume does not make the character, but augments the actor's expressive performances. The wig maker makes a wig so that a hairstyle stays the same in each performance. It does not react to changing weather conditions and health the same way that hair growing on our body does. It is also a place to mount and hide microphones.

© Joan Marcus

Cabaret: Two interpretations

Cabaret, directed by Harold Prince, premiered on Broadway in 1966 with a production team including Boris Aronson as Scenic Designer, Patricia Zipprodt as Costume Designer, and Jean Rosenthal as Lighting Designer. The musical is based on Christopher Isherwood's *Berlin Stories*, and John Van Druten's *I am a Camera* based on the Isherwood stories. *Cabaret* is set as the Nazis begin their rise to power in Germany in the late 1920s when hatred and anti-Semitism were shaping their political views. Clifford Bradshaw, an American writer, visits Berlin in search of inspiration, and after making a few friends and finding housing, Clifford visits the sleazy Kit Kat Klub and meets an English singer, Sally Bowles. The writer and singer fall in love. Soon, Clifford discovers that he inadvertently has been helping the Nazis by delivering packages to Paris for a German friend of his. After circumstances explode Clifford ends up deciding to return to the United States but Sally, after aborting their baby, decides to remain in Berlin.

Zipprodt's design made the club look shabby-chic. The Emcee wears a tuxedo and the women slinky evening dresses. All the formal wear was made decadent through color choice in the accoutrements. Her daytime wear was the flapper cut of the 1920s. This was in contrast to her long evening gowns. Her skirt flows as she moves. The dress accentuates the movement and creates a mood of excitement. Lotta stands out against the chorus because of the length of her dress. The chorus is unified because they all wear the same shape hats and the same style of dress, yet the visual design has variety because their print-patterns differ. Color, silhouette, and pattern all help make Lotta the focus of the audience's attention. The flow of the dress also allows for dynamic movement, while Lotta's dress is more constrained. In comparison to Ivey Long's sleazy, available chorus girls, this chorus girl retains her composure and teases rather than prostitutes herself.

Photo by Friedman-Abeles/Museum of the City of New York/Getty Images

115

Prince wanted to set the play in period to suggest to the audience that these events could happen today. However, from a visual perspective, Zipprodt had to take liberties with the period to achieve the effect, because the diminutive frame of Jill Haworth, the actress playing Bowles, did not suit those styles. The period hemlines were three inches below the knee and made the character appear as if she was dressed in her mother's clothing. Instead Zipprodt turned to the mid-twenties for daytime wear, using the flapper cut, and for her evening wear the bias cuts of 1932. At first Zipprodt thought Sally was a silly, Lolita-esque, pubescent woman, who along with all the accoutrements of glamor such as long cigarette holders, and long green fingernails, was still carrying around crayons in her purse. To achieve this look Zipprodt put Sally in a simple red mesh dress. When Prince saw this he decided that Haworth's blondness did not work for the character Sally. Instead they decided to put a black wig on her. At this point Zipprodt began to interpret Sally from a different perspective. She described Sally as more of a boisterous, bold, and rude tomboy and a flapper who was out deliberately to shock. She was less Lolita and more a woman with edges who had no place in her life for childish things. They changed the simple red mesh dress into a long, bias-cut red satin dress with metallic threads to put fire in it and 3-inch wide panels swinging from mid-hip.

While the costuming was not precisely true to period, the effect was true to the audience's perception of the mood of the period. The Kit-Kat Klub is populated with slinky seductive dancers and an Emcee who is a slick, sleek, nightclub entertainer wearing a pink vest and a cold-cream face. Zipprodt's preparatory drawings for the *Cabaret* dancers' outfits depict each figure with a physical attitude to the body making it seem alive. She drew them to show the skirts open so the team would be able to see the detail of their stockings, their shoes, and the hang of their skirts.

While the chorus girl outfits depicted here are risqué, they have a different quality than Ivey Long's chorus girls. Here we have a more classic look with the Emcee in a black tuxedo and the chorus girls in Rocket-like sequins. These outfits accent their legs more than hips and breasts. The variety of colors and textures make each outfit distinctive without stealing focus from the Emcee. Zipprodt used a variety of colors, textures, and lines to achieve the look.

Photo by Friedman-Abeles/Museum of the City of New York/Getty Images

Texture, weave, and silhouette are clear. The director was able to see the type of glamor that the production wanted to convey through the dancers. One review notes that even the pianos seem to have feathers. The look of the club is sophisticated with the men in tuxedos and women dressed in showy sequin-covered dresses that are intended to be stunning. Haworth performs the title song "Cabaret" in a red sequined dress in front of a tinsel backdrop and a red neon sign. The reds mirror each other, as do the shiny, reflective texture of the dress and the backdrop. In comparison with Ivey Long's nearly naked Lotta, Zipprodt's is tame yet sophisticated. This is a world of elegant decadence with a dark side. The landlady and greengrocer are dressed in more conventional middle-class clothing. Though their behavior is far from bourgeois, they are made to look respectable in contrast to the seediness of the dancing nightclub inhabitants.

In contrast to the 1966 production, the anti-erotic outfits of the Kit Kat Klub girls were seedy rather than seductive in the 1998 production. Sam Mendes' revival was set in an actual nightclub. Its set and club design were conceived by Robert Brill, its costume design by William Ivey Long, and its lighting design by Peggy Eisenhauer and Mike Baldassari. Reviewers describe this cabaret as a sleazy dive bar; the girls and transvestites are coarse and crudely available. They wear cheap fishnet tights associated with peep shows and strip clubs. These tights are visibly marred with runs and holes, and it is implied that they wear them until they are in tatters. Ivey-Long had to figure out how to make this flimsy ripped mess durable enough for a long-running Broadway musical with eight shows a week. Accordingly, the Kit Kat Klub girls' fishnets could not simply be allowed to accumulate runs and scores, while merely cutting holes in them would mean having to buy each girl a new pair at least once a week. Newspaper interviews reveal that these tights were elaborately wrought. Long designed them so the holes in each pair were cut so that they would appear in a different place from those in the other girls' tights. Then each hole was hemmed so that it would not widen, and then loose threads were sewn onto the hem so that the holes did not look distressed. For this cabaret Ivey Long purposely began the costume of the perverse emcee as a straightforward tuxedo that he then took away piece by piece, leaving a leather jacketed, shirtless character with cut-off dress pants, retaining only the dangling suspenders, bowtie, and garters – a disheveled costume resembling bondage wear.

I think the most difficult period in the creative process is the period between being asked to work on a show and the first conceptual meeting. Because you don't want your mind to race too fast in any one direction or the other before you figure out where the director wants to go. That's difficult. Also, not only is the costume-design department in the background and in the shadows aging the slips of Sally Bowles, but we're the second person in the design pantheon. The scenic designer is the one who creates the world and is the first on board. This is always the case. It makes sense to me, because the set design defines the physical space. In addition to where are we, when is it, there are things like: How do you come on? Are there door-knobs or is it a scrim? Is it a poetic journey, which I was referring to with the scrim, or are there doorknobs?... Very important to get that figured out.

William Ivey Long

Ivey Long's developmental regime strives to create truthful historical representations while at the same time generating a sense of energizing the process in what he calls "circling the campfire". For each production he assembles, sorts, and edits a range of visual sources, taken from newspapers, magazines, books, and the Internet,

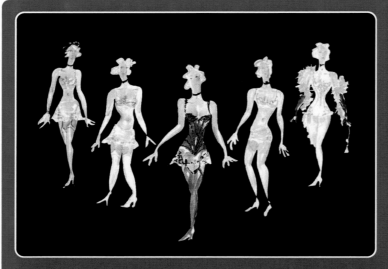

A number of chorus costumes can be presented in one rendering to give the same type of group effect that will be seen on stage. The costumes are unified through the choice of material and their individual silky textures. Despite the varieties of styles between negligee, bra and panty, and corset, the garter straps and detailing of each is unified.

Sketch for Natasha Richardson as Sally Bowles and Kit Kat Klub girls – "Don't Tell Mama." Graphite, watercolor, gouache, and ink on watercolor paper. William Ivey Long

This photo shows the sketch as realized in performance. The violet of Bowles's negligee depicted in the sketch is rendered through lighting effects. Her garter straps are evident as are the variety of negligee styles presented in the chorus. Though the shapes of the dancers were elongated in the sketch, here we see the natural shapes of the dancers' bodies. The sketch illuminated the mood, color scheme, and proposed clothing that would be used in production. Some of that atmosphere came out in the lighting rather than in the fabric or color of the clothes. This is how collaboration manifests itself in performance. When Molly Ringwald and Brooke Shields played Sally Bowles the costumes of each actress changed slightly. Ringwald's costume had lace sleeve and a black strap around her neck, while Shields' exposed her shoulders and neck. When a show goes on tour or runs for a long period the costume designer has to adapt the costume to different actors. It depends on whether the actor fits in with the style. Others you have to start over to fit them in place with the structure of the storytelling. The designer retains intent rather than a literal reproduction of the costume. This could have to do with body type or characterization of actor.

© Joan Marcus

into large cut-and-paste panels. Bouncing ideas off these collages of source materials, he often begins with loose, freehand, preliminary drawings which may consist only of figural shapes or costume particulars. This is followed by a second, more systematic analysis of the production as he develops all the characters and costume changes for each scene in storyboard panels. The multiple panels are decorated with fabric swatches. It is reported that he goes as far as to gesso over the collages, redrawing shapes and details, or introducing final colors and patterns. Finally carefully realized presentation drawings are completed in evocative stylistic and media techniques that advance the atmosphere of the specific dramaturgy in development.

The two productions of the same play have a different feel and effect. Even though both productions begin with the same dramatic script they look different. Each designer chooses elements to emphasize according to the directorial interpretation. Each brings out different nuances of the script. One may emphasize history, while another contemporary life. It is how the designers put together the elements and principles of design to achieve a desired goal that makes each design work. There is no single interpretation of the play, or one way to dress and prop a play.

According to one reviewer a man at his table exclaimed "Good God," when the Emcee displays his naked buttock daubed with a Swastika in the Mendes production. However it made the final moments more potent when he undoes his leather trench coat to reveal a striped concentration camp suit with both pink triangle and yellow star. This evoked such a collective gasp of horror and shock that the audience could barely applaud. These costumes reflect our time more than the 1930s in Germany. While they hint at the mid-century, the clothes reflect what we consider sleazy and risqué, more than what was considered risqué in the 1920s and 1930s. We need to expose more flesh, add tattoos, and use more frilly and skimpy laces and satins.

© Joan Marcus

Paying attention to what clothing tells us: *The Miracle Worker*

First staged in 1959, *The Miracle Worker*, by William Gibson, was directed by Arthur Penn with scenic and lighting design by George Jenkins and costumes by Ruth Morley. Though also winning several other Tony Awards, George Jenkins was nominated for Best Scenic Design. The recent revival in 2010 was directed by Kate Whoriskey with scenic design by Derek McLane, costume design by Paul Tazewell, lighting design by Kenneth Posner, and original music and sound by Rob Milburn and Michael Bodeen. Set in the South in the 1880s, *The Miracle Worker* depicts the characters and events in Helen Keller's *The Story of My Life*. Keller lost her sight and hearing as a toddler, and Annie Sullivan, a twenty-year-old from Boston, was hired by the Keller family in Alabama to serve as her governess. Helen's mother showers the child with unconditional love, while her father, a straight-laced retired Confederate Army officer, believes she is beyond help. As a result, tantrum-prone Helen is a wild, unpredictable child. Her instinctive intelligence means she knows how to get what she wants, delivering a well-aimed kick or punch when she does not. Annie diagnoses Helen's problem as an excess of pity and indulgence in place of communication, so she embarks on a journey to teach her how to communicate.

The revival was staged in the round at the Circle in the Square in New York. McLane suggests a comfortable nineteenth-century Southern home with only a few pieces of furniture and doorframes. The action of the play takes places in numerous locations, so a fluid set works best. Anything else would have blocked sightlines. McLane used a fly system with pieces of furniture descending from the ceiling to indicate location changes. The scenes are set at different corners of the playing area. Reviewers describe how McLane's rising and falling scenery tends to upstage and diminish the emotional power of Annie's story. The overly theatrical solution to multiple settings in a round staging works against the realism of the play script. He created a fluid ground plan, but the play was conceived for the picture frame stage. The round created a boxing ring that focuses the audience's attention on the characters' actions. McLane supplied key props and set pieces to indicate location. For example, a dining room table created the context for the first battle to tame Helen's tantrums, a battle that leaves the Keller dining room a wreck. The two hanging doors at either end of the stage serve as a metaphor for the door being so painstakingly and persistently opened for Helen. It was left to the costumes to anchor the production in a realistic world.

Tazewell's costumes evoke the period, and Posner's lighting defines the space by drawing focus inward to create intimate moments. Changes in costume reinforce the narrative of the story. The differences between the hats with feathers or without, or between which dressing gowns have color and which vests have patterns help the audience distinguish between characters and follow the way the moods and fortunes of the characters change over the duration of the play. Those details are easy to miss, since we take the language of clothing in everyday life for granted. A well-defined costume in a realistic play will seem so natural that the audience often does not think about them as having been designed. However, they affect, subtly shaping our understanding of the characters and the action. Costume was the main way for this visual narrative to come through in this space.

The costumes help to illustrate the social niche of each character. I think that costumes can really help to give the audience a clue as to how the characters relate to each other and what they're thinking . . . how successful are they at appearing the way they want to appear. Sometimes it's fun when someone thinks they're sexy and they're not quite successful at it; it adds to the humor of the situation. Hopefully the costumes are doing all those things.

Catherine Zuber

Gibson's play is often interpreted as focusing only on the relationship between Helen and Anne, charting the story of how Sullivan helped Keller overcome her disabilities and communicate with the world. However, Whoriskey wanted the production to expand the notion of what the play is traditionally understood as. By calling attention to Keller's family – her mother, father, and aunt – the production sought to understand the relationship of the women within the context of the family and the broader society of the time. Tazewell used the costumes to bring attention to the social world in which the action took place as a larger strategy to broaden the show's focus.

© Paul Tazewell

According to Tazewell, the choices the production team made were aimed at defining the nature of the relationship between a mother and a disabled child, and examining what it means when the mother cannot take care of that child on her own. What did it mean for Mrs. Keller to have to pass that child off to someone else? Tazewell wanted his costumes to reflect that theme and made character-driven clothing choices. Kate Keller's dresses were not conceived to be pretty or historically accurate. They were meant to evoke the emotional impact of the actions performed by the actors. For instance, Tazewell establishes that Kate and Arthur Keller have a fairly stable life, and their clothing choices are a reflection of that. When the circumstances of these characters' lives change, so too do the qualities of their costumes. Captain Keller's is stable and conservative and his suit has some stripes or modest pattern. The stripes and muted brown colors reflect that stability. The silhouette of his sack coat accentuates his solid stature and his cigarette holder shows his personal sense of fashion and awareness of his station in life.

In this production the costumes and lighting bring out the muted colors in the fabrics suggesting an emotional response to the events. The costumes reinforce the social, economic, and emotional qualities of the characters as they change during the play. The costumes tell the story of the plays as much as the action. As the audience looks across the group of characters the economic relationships between them are revealed. What do differences in the characters' silhouettes reveal about their class? Is the fabric thick and crisp or flimsy and sloppy? How do clean, curved lines suggest wealth and stability? How do straight, jagged lines suggest poverty? What does a clean white blouse communicate that a stained brown dress does not? Annie Sullivan's costumes are clean and conservative displaying modesty, while Martha's dress is disheveled, dirty and in disrepair. These costumes stand in contrast and reveal socioeconomic relationships. Costume helps the actors show the characters' story.

Tazewell also wants his costumes to elucidate how the characters operate in a larger society. Kate may be dressed fashionably, for instance, but since her family's finances are in trouble, she does not have, say, as many feathers on her hat as characters who are better off. However, in this image Kate's dress is simply embellished with a pattern to the collar and cuffs. These patterns and neutral colors help give her a sense of respectability and stability. When her mental state changes, the color of her clothing and its detail will change. According to Tazewell once Kate loses her ability to control Helen, her costumes become more muted and constraining.

© Paul Tazewell

© Paul Tazewell

However, the audience senses that she is aware of fashion, because her costumes retain some elegance, with bits of ribbon, silk, or embroidery, which he states are an expression of her refusal to stop fighting for her child. He wanted to underscore the emotion of each time she picks herself up and tries again. Once Annie's work changes Helen's behavior, Kate's relief is shown with clothes with brighter colors and more feminine cuts. Her clothing told the story of her journey from frustration and gloom to hope and optimism.

Tazewell began his design process thinking that perhaps it should all be monochromatic and without patterns and so on, but his entryway into design tends to be much more personal. Instead he began to try and think what felt right for each character. The production team especially wanted the costumes to be personal and connected to the family. At this point Annie is established in the family and is in control of the situation. The cool, blue-gray hue accentuates her calm and restrained temper in the face of Helen's tempestuousness. As well, the color and silhouette are solid and disciplined in nature. Later her costumes become more like economical versions of Kate's wardrobe.

© Paul Tazewell

© Paul Tazewell

Early on Helen's costuming is disheveled, dirty and her hair and silhoutte are untamed. Tazewell chose a liliac dress to suggest that she is feminine under all the grime. That she wears no shoes shows how uncivilized she has become. This look will transform as she comes in contact with Annie. Her dress appears asymmetrical, which is when elements on both sides are not equal. Asymmetrical balance is achieved by careful placement of unlike items, and is sometimes referred to as psychological balance. If the two sides are different in some way but still give the same weight, it is asymmetrical balance. Balance refers to how elements are arranged horizontally or vertically in a design. Here the belt and seams break the balance and give her an unstable psychological appearance.

As she is exposed to the discipline and stimulation of Annie's influence, she becomes more in control over her actions and emotions. A pale green accentuates the emotional struggles she faces with each obstacle that she must attempt to overcome. She is wearing shoes now, the lines on her dress are more regimented and symmetrical. Balance makes the right and left side of a garment appear to be equal, even though they may not be exactly the same. If the two sides are the same, it is symmetrical balance. Here it indicates that order is beginning to take hold. Once Helen gains mastery over her ability to communicate, she calms down. Her clothing reflects her control. The shape and pattern of the fabric of her dresses show she has control and echo Annie's long, rose pink quilted dressing gown. Here Annie has the blush of life visible in her appearance. This echoes the journey Helen takes as she gains control and is better able to keep to task. The costumes transform and reinforce what the audience sees and hears from her as she interacts with her teacher and her family. She is seen to transform slowly as she begins to look more and more similar to the other characters. Her disability was echoed in the disheveled qualities of her early outfits that stand out, and then she transforms into another individual within the group who blends in.

Costume and collaboration

Costume design does not exist in a vacuum. The actors wear the costume in the stage setting and can only be seen because of the lighting effects. While the costumer may choose fabrics, colors, and textures for the clothing, the lighting changes the looks of these elements. All design work in the theatre is collaborative and it is through the design and rehearsal process that the team works together to find the best way to bring out the qualities they want to convey to the audience through the visual world of the production. Costuming shapes character, and lighting brings out the character of the clothing that the characters wear. While the lighting designer is hired after the costume designer, lighting is no less important. The following chapter explores the ways in which light adds to set and costumes design to evoke the world of the play.

The artistry of light

6

Once the set and costume designer has been hired then the lighting designer is brought on to the team. First the world of the play is organized spatially, next the characters are defined, and finally lighting reveals those qualities through light. Lighting designers make use of the elements and principles of light to sculpt space and the human form. The basic principles and elements of light design include visibility, naturalism, motivation, composition, atmosphere, and qualities of light. They use composition, line and form, intensity, color, distribution, and movement by harnessing the physical properties of light and their psychological effect on people. Their methods of illumination balance visibility and mood as seen through setting and costume. The lighting design ties together all of the elements of production.

The lighting designer uses light within a setting inhabited by an actor. It is produced live, and changes over the course of the play. Lighting is the last of the elements to be added to the production and as such is done on the spot during the technical rehearsals. Before this the designer chooses which lights to use and chooses the aesthetic and lighting positions, but the actual product is **level-set** in **cueing sessions** with the production team present, the director giving notes and actors standing by. In some sense lighting is the glue that holds the production together. The space itself and the colors of the elements are defined by light and the colors and textures of the sets and costumes come to life underneath light. Emotional and atmospheric qualities also emerge for the audience through light. Lighting designers work in the moment to bring together the work of the design team into a cohesive project during the technical rehearsals.

Physical properties and psychological effects of light

In illuminating the intention of the playwright and director we want to transport the audience to the very being of the characters, make them feel what the character feels. We use the four qualities of light – intensity, color, form, and movement – to allow this magic to occur. To give the audience a time of day, a sense of the heat of the desert, the mist of the sea, the romance of the dusk, the city at night, loneliness, surrealness, other-worldliness, naturalistic interiors or fantastic environments, the engulfing forest, a blank stage bathed in an unrealistic but claustrophobic inducing color, or a million other circumstances in which visual imagery will transport you into a poetic realm. No place, time or emotion is beyond the imagination of the lighting designer. That is part of the art, the "magical" art of the lighting designer.

Jules Fisher

Stage light is defined in two ways, as **general indirect light** such as with an overcast sky, or as **specific direct light** such as with sunlight. Furthermore, these two categories of lighting have **four controllable properties** that can be manipulated by the designer: intensity, color, distribution, and movement. It is by manipulating these properties that the designer evokes mood, defines the setting, and makes visible the action of the play. Without dynamic lighting our eyes accommodate to the visual world and lose interest in what is transpiring in front of us.

Intensity is defined as the brightness of light. In other words, it is a measure of the strength of a light source in a particular direction, ranging from the flicker of a candle to the blast of an atomic reaction. How bright you can get in the theatre depends upon the technology available in tools such as the lighting instruments and dimmers. Brightness is subjective and relative. In absolute darkness a candle can seem so bright it is blinding, whereas 1,000 watts channeled onto an already bright stage does little to change an audience's perception of intensity. Other factors such as costumes, props, scenery, and the actor's skill also have variable effects upon perception. To keep the audience's eyes from adapting to brightness, it is in constant motion over the course of the production. As brightness changes, our eyes adapt, especially if it is in strong contrast to what came before. Regardless of the light level, as time goes on our eyes adapt to the light and it affects how we perceive it. A bright scene will appear brighter by contrast if it follows a dim one, thus contrast and change attract the audience's attention and direct them to where the director wants them to look. Generally, our eyes tend to follow the brightest area on stage. As time goes on our eyes become fatigued, because too much or too little light exhaust the audience's ability to sustain focus. Visual perception is dependent upon how much illumination is needed to allow our eyes to perceive an object clearly, and depends upon its color, reflective quality, and its size and distance from the observer. One large variable in the theatre is that all the audience is not at the same distance from the stage; those in the back of the house need to see as clearly as those in the front of the house. Intensity and mood are associated with the brightness of the space. The brighter the light, the more alert the audience becomes. There are two ways to adjust focus through brightness: (1) Bring the intensity up in a specific area, or (2) Lower all of the other areas on the stage.

The lighting designer can make use of all the colors of the visible spectrum. Our eyes perceive objects because objects reflect light. **Color** on the stage is a result of the color of light, the color of the object, and the result of reflected impression on the eye. To create primary colors the lighting designer places a gel in front of the lens, the resulting colored light is reflected off the surface of a costume with its own color, and then the audience sees a color that is a mix of all those colored lights. Thus the designer's choice of color defines the colors used by the set and costume designer and can help highlight or adjust the audience's perception of the image upon the stage. The two types of color mixing for lighting designers are additive and subtractive. **Additive color mixing** is when two or more lights, each with a different colored gel, are focused on the same object to produce a third color. **Subtractive color mixing** is when two or more gels are put in front of the same lighting instrument to produce another color, for example with a **color scroller**. As choices mount the designers use color to enrich the visual and emotional atmosphere of the stage. Color is the best tool that the lighting designer has to affect mood. Our eyes see the yellow-green zones of the spectrum more clearly than the red-blue ends of the spectrum. Warm colors and tints are associated with comedy and cool strong colors with tragedy. Color is a potent tool to affect the imagination. Natural outdoor light is predominately white, but the white is modulated by the time of day, weather, and atmospheric conditions. Designers also use the color spectrum on the stage to mimic daytime to nighttime perceptions.

Light has form and direction, ranging from **soft diffusion** without shadow to **hard distribution** with stark shafts of light. **Distribution** is the way in which illumination of any color or quantity is spread over a particular background. A designer has control over where lanterns/lighting instruments are positioned, thus the angle of beam and resulting shadows are limitless. The eye is invariably attracted to the brightest object in the field of vision and shadows and movement attract attention and capture its focus.

The fourth controllable property is movement, which refers to the changes in the light from moment to moment. The intensity and distribution of light may be altered. The rate of change from quick to slow is perceived in distinct ways. A room may grow gradually darker as the sun goes down across the horizon and color and shadow change until light becomes the soft diffuse light of dusk. With automated lighting the lighting fixture can move and point light in different directions on stage to guide the audience to notice different elements. Movement creates visual interest by keeping the eye scanning. Lighting designers arrange lighting effects to force the audience to focus at different parts of the stage, different objects on the stage or on different actors. Colors may shift or transform on an object, changing the feel of the atmosphere. In musicals, designers might increase the intensity of the lighting to increase the energy of the moment. Audiences often do not notice how much the lighting in a production changes from moment to moment, however, they might notice if it did not because the image would seem dull and boring.

Intensity, color, distribution, and movement are properties that the design manipulates to create effects, establish time, place, and mood. It is through **specific cueing** that the lighting designer is able to shape the way in which the audience perceives the setting, costume, properties, and actors over the course of the production. Lighting design is as much about understanding the physiology of the perception of the audience as it is about understanding the collaborative concepts of the design team. The following section discusses the ways in which lighting designers harness the elements and principles of design to contribute to the expression of the play.

What does stage lighting do for a production?

Light is used to reveal an object or a setting. Lighting designers combine and modify the controllable qualities of light to produce the varied functions that we find within lighting. Visibility is important. Whether it is to create a bright space or to select what the audience is able to see, light is used for dramatic effect. For example, the angle of light might help an object either blend in with the setting or pop out from its background. Lighting can help in establishing a scene, by indicating time of day, season, and geographical location. These cues will blend with the setting, costume, and sound to create a cohesive environment that creates the world of the play.

> The basic concern in theatre lighting is with the *dramatic intention* of a particular moment. The visibility, or the kind of light, in which you see the actors and the scenery, the place, must have a logic. The logic is based on tying all of these in with the idea of being there, in the scene, in the first place.
>
> **Jean Rosenthal**

Modeling or **sculpting** is another common function that refers to using light for enhancing the three-dimensional qualities of an object. This can be seen in the ways in which highlights and shadowing create form. **Highlights** represent the flashes of reflected light from areas that are directly illuminated by a light source, while **shadows** may be represented by either the area of an object that is not lit or the area of darkness or shadow that is cast by a lit object. Areas that are raised are prone to highlights while recessed surfaces usually fall into the shadow areas. Revealing shadow and highlight is dependent upon both the angle and number of lights that strike an object. Furthermore, **mood** refers to a given emotional response to the lighting by an observer. Lighting can be crafted to be foreboding or inviting, carefree and light, or moody and oppressive. The light provides an atmosphere or ambience for the environment.

Focus relates to drawing attention to various elements within an environment. One role of the designer is to help point out where a viewer or an audience member's attention should be directed at any given time. For example one could black out an entire stage except for the areas where the focus must be directed, as seen in the *Bacchai* example below. The designer could highlight an actor delivering a monologue with a spotlight, or pull the lighting down to direct focus on a single prop. One also might raise the intensity of lighting an area, such as around a couch or a table for a long conversation. Changes in contrast work both ways; the designer can lower the intensity around an area to heighten attention to the area. The eye will usually focus on the element within its vision that is different from the rest of the objects.

Composition is a function of lighting that relates to the combining of all the elements of the stage into a complete visual package. What and how much is revealed is the task of the lighting designer. While the production team gives us the

129

primary objects of composition, the scenery, costume, actors, props, and furniture, the lighting designer can use his or her tools to reveal and define those objects within the space. The lighting also determines how all of the individual objects and designs tie together as a whole and becomes a unifying element for most design projects. **Rhythm** in lighting relates to movements and transitions of light that allow an audience to follow the action. Do changes between scenes occur in a natural fluid manner, or are they disruptive to the flow of the show? Lighting's rhythms underscore the mood and action of the show. How designers decide which elements to work with comes from the ways in which they interpret the play and what the director wants to evoke in the production.

The lighting designer's process

Each director has his own way. Preproduction – in trying to find out if we're on the same wavelength, I use art books a lot and show pictures in terms of texture or color. In the theatre, I have very little to say other than yes or no. It's all been discussed. You're bare assed up there. Whether I agree or disagree, I'm good at letting people know that. If it's something I have a note on and I'm going to fix, I tell them. If it's something I don't agree on at all, I say, "let's talk about it later." It depends so much on who the person is. If the director has changed his mind, you have to assume the playwright and composer go along with him, so best you do that.

Tharon Musser

As with all design practice, there are diverse methods to achieve the same effect. However, one thing that designers all share in common is their intense scrutiny of the script or source material of the production. When lighting designers read a play for the first time they try to stay aware of the part that directors, set designers, and costume designers will play in development of the landscape of the production. Script analysis is key and multiple reads of the script are necessary to look for the feel of the atmosphere, breakdown of the scenes, references to light, time of day, weather, and to analyze the atmospheres.

Early on lighting designers tend not to be too specific about their ideas; the rest of the team might have ideas that would block the implementation of these initial thoughts. Ideally the lighting designer is included at a meeting of the director, set designer, and costume designer early enough to throw ideas back and forth freely before any design has been developed. However, this is a luxury in the professional world. Listening to the director allows the designer to understand what style the production will be and what the director thinks the play is about. As conversations occur, the designer can produce thumbnail sketches as a means of illustrating ideas about possible lighting tactics. Storyboards are pictorial representations of all the stage components, including the lighting, for a specific moment of a production.

These images are based on a perspective sketch of the stage and often take on qualities that are similar to a miniature rendering. A smart set designer will meet with the lighting designer, to ensure that the lighting designer knows as much as possible about the light in the space, and the set designer understands the angles available for a lighting designer to light the setting. The setting needs to leave room to hang lights and for light to reach the surfaces of the setting. Much of the information the lighting designer will have about the approach to a production before going into the theatre is from the set designer.

The designer's beginning work with the script is the basis of a **lighting scheme**. As the production process progresses, attending rehearsals and design meetings allows the designer to understand the approach the director is taking. Rehearsals allow a designer to observe blocking relationships, character associations, and specific interpretations that the director has brought to a production. This additional work is done alongside further script analysis to determine the details that emerge and shape the unique qualities of the show. Several tasks associated with the second reading of a script involve responding to a specific image that might be imagined while reading the script and creating a scenic breakdown that lists the interior or exterior locations and time frames such as seasons or time of day for each scene. Further readings will refer to specific references to light. The designer needs to identify specific staging requirements such as **motivational lighting** needs, lighting effects, and character associations for more specific lighting demands. The designer will be sensitive to mood or emotional events to create conditions that provide clues to lighting.

Discussions about the scenery need to happen before the set is completed so that space for light can be accommodated in the final design. The lighting designer examines the working drawings from the shop to understand the hidden spaces in a set that a plan and section alone do not reveal. The lighting designer's paperwork begins only after the designer has a clear idea of the director's interpretation of the play and how the lighting can help the ideas of his or her colleagues. At this point the designer begins the task of doing worksheets to determine where lights can be hung and what **beam width** and color they should be to create the desired effects. Ideas are condensed into plans and plots. The preparation of the physical aspects of the equipment allows the freedom of creation during technical rehearsals.

In lectures Jennifer Tipton describes her process as largely intuitive. She begins with a list of front, side, and back light for the whole space. One of her guiding principles is that there is only one good place for a light for any given purpose. If there is a need for two colors for any purpose and there must be two lights in that place, then it is necessary for her to compromise. Early in her process she decides where it is essential to have two colors from any given angle. Once she determines the front, side, and back light for the whole space she then makes more specific choices that work toward creating the effects. These choices determine how the space is divided, how it is colored, how it is made to seem larger, smaller, unified, intimate, or fractured.

131

Is lighting necessary to move quickly from one place to another, or to show one place relying on other things for its change of dynamics? At this point the lighting ideas relate to a way of thinking about the play from the perspective of the director's interpretation. Tipton tries to balance her final list of ideas to ensure that the distinctive ideas part of the list is longer than the general illumination part.

> Lighting design derives its validity from the answer to the fundamental question *Why who is where* in the first place. In the answer is the logic of lighting. This is logic of lighting. This logic applies equally to lighting in the theatre or to street lighting or to lighting in the interiors of buildings or to the light by which you read a book in a corner.
>
> **Jean Rosenthal**

Lighting is something that is hard to show to directors. Directors sometimes feel they have to take a leap of faith with the lighting designer. Though a storyboard can be created, no drawing captures the quality of light or the audience's response to what effect the light will produce. Designers can only provide snippets of moving images of compositions they will try to create. The quality of the light and the emotional response to the lighting effects cannot be captured in any substantial way, so the designer draws up technical plans to lay out the position of the lighting instruments and show light angles. Drawings, models, sets, and costumes are made, but how they look on stage will not be clear until lighting illuminates these objects. Tests may be done using the models to show what the space is like. The lighting designer must understand where there are walls, reflective surfaces, and where there is room for lighting instruments. Also there are practical considerations such as the budget. Lighting is getting more and more expensive because of the cost of digital technologies that are being developed. Thus, how much equipment is available in the space, how much power, and how many circuits will affect what is possible in the lighting design. Since the lighting designer's work is the last to be added it cannot be finalized until the technical rehearsals, because as the play moves through rehearsal all design concepts have to remain fluid so they can be modified if necessary.

> We're not in a field where any one part of the show can live on its own without the others, especially lighting. We get credited for lighting, when what we really do is just edit and reflect what's naturally there. A beautiful stage look is not on a bare stage. It's a combination of all the ingredients of scenery, costumes, and lighting to create the place for the actor. I really don't like people who dictate. As a young designer, a director will tell you exactly what to do: "oh no, no . . . a little brighter, a little dimmer." That's no fun. I have to believe that — for myself, my sanity, and livelihood — it's much richer to collaborate than to have it dictated. The more cross-pollination you have, the healthier the art form is

going to be. I would rather recreate my own personal dream than someone else's.

Brian MacDevitt

The most creative part in the process begins in the technical rehearsals where the artist experiments with lighting effects that are continually evaluated by an impatient audience of technical staff. Lighting design is a live process delivered upon demand. That is why it is often referred to as painting with light. The designer has ideas to start with and then crafts the light while everyone waits. Some designers make a preliminary **cue synopsis**, with the **cue number**, the count of the time needed to bring **light levels** up or down, when the cue starts, what the aim of the cue is in terms of atmosphere and effect, and specific lighting elements to be used. At the start of the technical rehearsal this will be limited to bringing the lights up slowly or quickly, but as the rehearsal progresses it will become refined, and the counts will become more precise. These preliminary cues indicate the feeling and atmosphere, as well as lighting instruments that will be used for the cue. The cue sheet is only a starting point. As the rehearsal progresses, some elements that were planned will not work, so the original cue sheet will help point to the original goal. The lighting rehearsals are a process of refining and reworking this cue synopsis for use later during plotting of the lights.

> Once the focus is finished the good part begins. Now is the time to start using the words of the "light language" to create sentences and paragraphs. I NEVER create cues before the actors are on the stage. In the early days of my life before the time of computer boards the practice was to sit with the director and the set designer while the stage manager walked the stage holding up costumes making the light without actors, setting cues usually late into the night. I found in those times that I was always unhappy with the way the light looked once the actors got into it and I had no idea which particular elements were making it look so terrible. Now I love the way a computer board allows me to work in real time, sketching in the light as the actors work through the play. This first time through the play with the actors allows me to see the shape of the piece with light. The computer allows me to make lighting cues as the actors go through the play; I make a lighting cue where I feel there needs to be a change in the light, even though perhaps this time through nothing does change in that cue.
>
> **Jennifer Tipton**

There is a pressure of the moment to be creative and solve problems as they arise. Lighting must satisfy all of the designer's needs. For example, if a costume is green, the light has to work to bring that quality out. Questions such as how much reflection there needs to be on the set must be addressed. As well, light must create the emotional connections that the director is trying to bring out in the performances.

The director may not be articulate about what he or she wants in a moment, so the lighting designer must experiment by continually adjusting intensity and level until the team agrees that the effect is appropriate. Next we will discuss the basic tactics for arranging the lighting to achieve the effects desired.

Kevin Adams prepares the lighting for *Spring Awakening*

Spring Awakening opened on Broadway in 2006 at the Eugene O'Neill Theatre directed by Michael Mayer. This musical adaptation of Frank Wedekind's *Spring's Awakening* (1890) had music composed by Duncan Sheik with books and lyrics by Steven Sater. Its set design was by Christine Jones, costume design by Susan Hilferty, lighting design by Kevin Adams, and sound design by Brian Ronan. Set in late-nineteenth-century Germany, the story follows a group of adolescents, Wendla Bergmann, Moritz Stiefel, Melchior Gabor, and their cohort as they struggle to understand their blossoming sexuality and all the good or bad that comes along with it in an oppressive and repressed society where adults are too embarrassed or too prudish to discuss the questions that are most important to these adolescents. It depicts a variety of taboo subjects including rape, abortion, masturbation, and homosexuality.

> Not that everything has to be a big light show . . . but you can drive a discourse of space that can tell a story. People often say my work is like another character in the show – and not in an overwhelming way. It's another narrative element. For me, it's all about looking at the different ways you can light a space within a text. I'll follow a logical path in creating a vocabulary, then I'll go back to square one and create another that subverts the first. Then I'll create a third, and possibly more. After establishing several different modes of lighting, the fun really begins by overlapping them and mixing them up.
>
> **Kevin Adams**

According to Adams in an interview with Strand Lighting, *Spring Awakening* contains two independent narratives, the nineteenth-century play and the twenty-first-century rock concert. He needed to find a way to organize the action so that the lighting would provide visual punctuation to the transitions between rock-concert antics and storytelling. For the book scenes, he conceived of the real space of the characters as done in the style of a contemporary small classic play. Adams explained that he wanted the hardness of white work light to work in contrast with the sincerity of the language and the vulnerability of the performers. Spoken scenes were simple, nondescript, and without any pretense of an illusion of place. It appears more like a workspace than the realistic spaces where the scenes take place. Adams also wanted the rules that define the lighting to shift and become more complicated as the show progresses. The show begins with the actors entering into the white work light of the preset. An adolescent girl in a white slip steps onto a chair, and one hundred clear light bulbs pop on to announce the beginning of the show.

The parallel twenty-first-century rock'n'roll narrative expresses the interior world of the youths. Adams designed this world to be brimming with abstracted environmental details, saturated color, and complicated cueing. His use of different types of light bulbs, fluorescent fixtures, and neon framed this part of the show as an environment that contained sculptural light objects. The production team collaborated to surround the

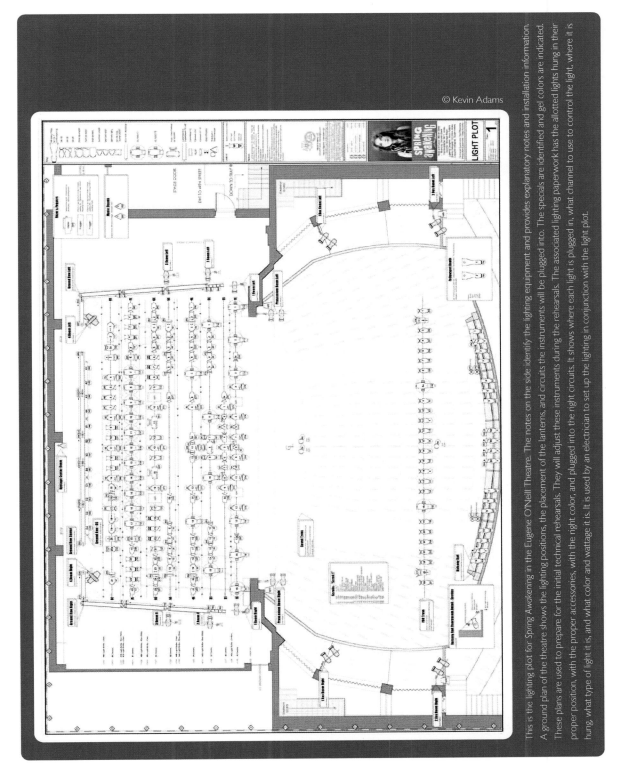

© Kevin Adams

This is the lighting plot for *Spring Awakening* in the Eugene O'Neill Theatre. The notes on the side identify the lighting equipment and provides explanatory notes and installation information. A ground plan of the theatre shows the lighting positions, the placement of the lanterns, and circuits the instruments will be plugged into. The specials are identified and gel colors are indicated. These plans are used to prepare for the initial technical rehearsals. They will adjust these instruments during the rehearsals. The associated lighting paperwork has the allotted lights hung in their proper position, with the proper accessories, with the right color, and plugged into the right circuits. It shows where each light is plugged in, what channel to use to control the light, where it is hung, what type of light it is, and what color and wattage it is. It is used by an electrician to set up the lighting in conjunction with the light plot.

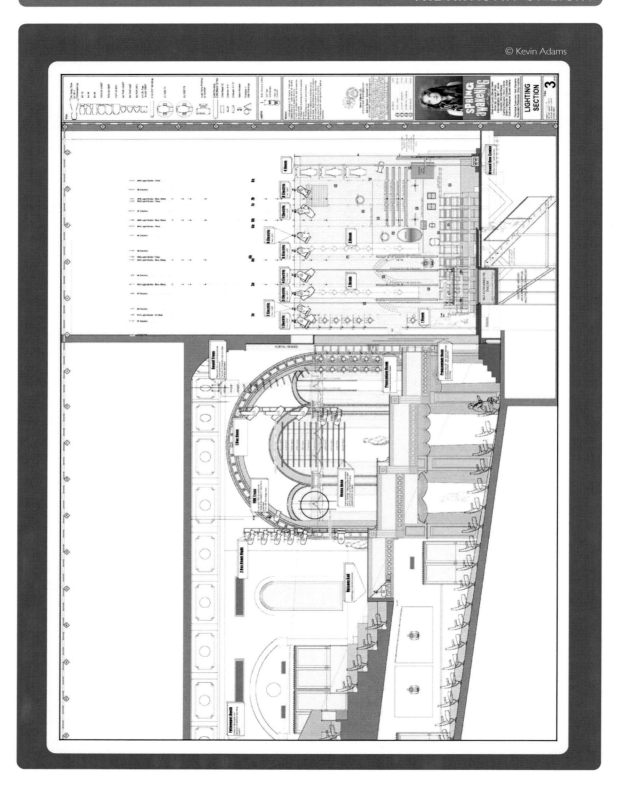

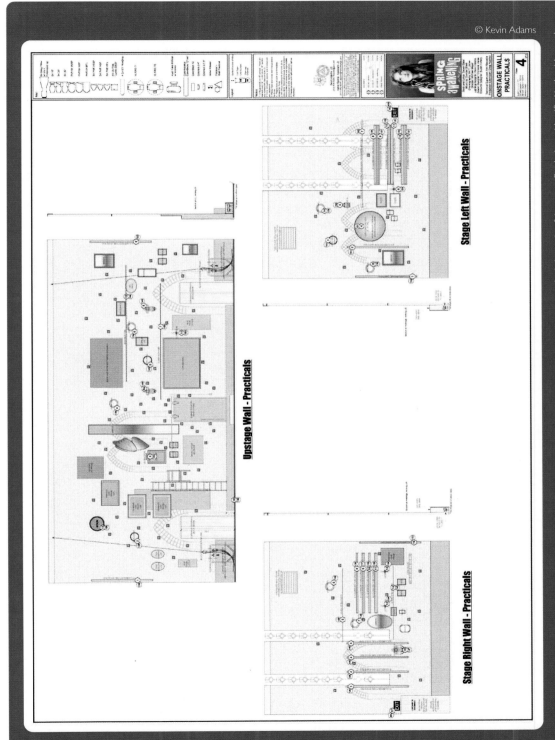

© Kevin Adams

This is the lighting plot section of the O'Neill Theatre. This drafting shows the height of the lighting booms, the traps, and relative scale of the space. Symbols are identified in the side panel, notes are listed, and specials are identified.

actors and audience with colored fluorescent tubes, neon lines, and circles, and hanging fluorescent blue light bulbs, as well as light boxes and vertically mounted ceiling fixtures. These sculptural objects, as well as LED strips that illuminate the walls, were used to create a moving palette of brightly colored bubble patterns, dots, and lines of light that flash and blink like abstracted signs and signals. He used miniature deeply saturated audience blinders to transform suddenly the simple white scene space of one frame into a variety of spectacular concert spaces. These two parallel narratives run separately until late in Act II, as the narrative turns to montage and real space overlaps with interior space, and they intertwine and eventually become a single visual narrative mimicking the action of the book.

The production uses contrasting styles of lighting to define the real world from the emotional expression of the music. Rather than slavishly create realistic settings lit with realistic light, Adams found visual styles that capture the stark emotional content of the dialogue and the ecstatic celebration of the musical expression. He re-imagines what the distorted elements of expressionism look like so that contemporary audiences could relate to the action of the play. The rhythm of the lighting set the parameters of the different worlds and gave the audience a means to understand what the characters were experiencing.

photo © Doug Hamilton

This production photo shows the lighting rig and where the instruments were placed for production. It also shows where the fluorescent specials were located. The smoke effect reveals the beams of light and shows angle and focus. Shadows in front of the actors show they are backlit. The lighting intensity and color was in a constant state of flux during the musical sections providing variety and interest. As well, the rhythm of the movement created mood and reflected the discombobulated emotional atmosphere of the adolescent characters. The special fluorescents are apparent. They create vibrant lines across the background. The multiple directions of horizontal and perpendicular reflect the disorder of the characters' sexual emotions. The lighting helped make the late-nineteenth-century play accessible to the twenty-first-century teen audience it was geared toward. Lighting punctuated the music and generated a contemporary feel to the action.

Arranging the lighting effects, lighting angles, and light qualities

A designer may light a subject from almost any direction, with each angle creating a characteristic effect on the subject. Light distribution affects how we perceive that light. For example, **backlight** produces a different image than **sidelight**, while an **up-light** creates a different mood than light coming from a steep angle. As designers become skilled at using light distribution they learn how to associate each angle with the audience's perception and create different moods and effects by using various combinations of angle and other lighting properties. Distribution not only plays a role in the shadow and highlight patterns that are found on a subject, but also reveals which surfaces are illuminated and the amount of color mixing and revelation of texture that occurs on a particular surface. It plays a significant role in how a subject is perceived by an audience.

> Controlled light is something more than a medium to promote visibility. It affects the appearance of all the elements of the stage and by this power becomes a determining element in the composition of a stage picture.
>
> **Stanley McCandless**

Light for the performances and for the set come from various directions, in other words from a combination of different lighting angles and intensities. **Front lighting** is the most common angle from which to light a space, an object, or an actor's face. **Side lighting** whether used horizontally or diagonally from above creates a great sense of depth. Most times one main source of light will set the principal direction of the lighting. A single direction, also known as realistic lighting, is chosen for dramatic effect. One of the main concerns for determining the effect of a technique is deciding upon angles. This is limited by what equipment and rig positions are available. **Spotlights** are used because they give the lighting designer more control over the light. **Wash light** generally supplies color and atmosphere. Projecting light from different positions in combination with color filters of varying degrees of intensity creates a moving composition that keeps the audience interested. Does the designer use cold or warm light, moving lights, or make visible color changes?

In developing a lighting concept the designer considers different light types. Does the designer craft **bold light** to have a monochrome or regular general light, without any outlines or noteworthy shadows, with incandescent or daylight, or did the designer craft it to have a strong color and distinct shadows? Other tactics include a lighting design with directional light, light from a main lighting source, or non-realistic backlight. The same space can be changed visually by deciding that its limits are symbolic and lighting the whole stage generally. This sort of lighting is chosen when the image presented is supposed to be blatant, lucid, and informative, but without details. It makes a superficial statement about the scene, conveying weak outlines and no atmosphere like the example above of *Spring Awakening*. **Realistic light** recreates the look of a real lighting situation. Realistic light is created if the space contains realistic shapes that are possible to light as if from nature. Doorways and windows can be lit to suggest that it is bright outside. If we use those natural openings in an inside room it is identified as natural lighting. This is the tactic that Neil Austin used in *Red*. The designer can add visual interest using **mixed lights** by differing qualities to enhance the contrast. A color mixing system, additive or subtractive lighting, or color filter mixing accomplishes this. **Accent light** picks out details to call attention to structures and outlines. **Moving light** or moving color changes are also means to add accent light. All of these tactics are can be mixed and matched.

The lighting designer uses the set design and its qualities and colors as a guide and uses light to complement or enhance the overall design concept. However, to achieve the director's concept the designer must weigh what actually can be done given the equipment available for use in the venue. What choices of fixtures are available? Are there floods, general cover, or open face lanterns? Are there spotlights with lenses, prism lenses, Fresnel lenses, profile spots, fluorescent lighting, or neon lighting? Are there PAR and moving lights? The right fixtures must be chosen to light the stage from the right positions, and with the correct color to achieve the desired effects. The characteristics of the technology define what is possible in a given space. Decisions about light and dark contrast become an issue when choosing which fixture to use, since the characteristics of the lighting instrument determine how much intensity can be achieved. Furthermore, in the choice of gels, whether to use color mixing systems, or the use of color perspectives, the designer sets the **color quality**, or **temperature** of the light. The designer determines what the light will look like for the performers or the stage by considering the color in combination with color filters as subtractive, intervention, and additive combinations for the elements such as set pieces, costumes, or skin color. Finally, the designer considers the small detailed accents by choosing accessories such as neon light, fiber optics, fog, smoke, or projection video. The design of a space depends not only upon the set designer, but also on the audience's visual impression of the physical space rendered by light.

Once the preliminary work of developing the light plot starts the next step is drafting the light plot. A **light plot** uses symbols to indicate what equipment will be hung from what position on the **rig**. To do this the designer refers to the ground plan of the theatre as well as the ground plan for the set design and the sections and painting elevations to understand the volume of space to be lit, the reflective surfaces and color schemes that are in play with the design as situated in the particular theatre. For the initial plans the designer determines the best lighting positions for the lighting instruments. The equipment is hung and the settings are adjusted and worked through at the technical rehearsals. There the designer fine-tunes the adjustments as he or she focuses the lighting, adjusting the lights so they are pointing as precisely as possible. Generally speaking some designers choose to adjust groups of lights in sequence. Typically the designer will focus general and directional lighting first, then background and outline light, and finally effects light. In this way you become more and more precise as the focusing goes on. When color is added a similar sequence with color filters is followed. It is often easier to focus the unfiltered light first before adding the color or diffusion, which might make sharp focuses more difficult.

> My least favorite part of the process is the focus. This is the time when I must direct someone to point and shape each light. I see at this time how each light hits the floor or the set as well as imagining how it will hit people. I go back and forth from the stage to the audience to check the way that it looks as well as how it feels in it. I know from long experience that it matters where the heat of the light is put. It will show to the audience if only subliminally if it is in the wrong place. The lines of light in the air help make the three-dimensional composition that is the end result of any lighting. The focus is critical; I know how important it is to "get it right". There will be the time to make corrections later but not again will it be possible to get to each light.
>
> **Jennifer Tipton**

The designer will adjust the lighting angles to create the desired effects. **Direct light** refers to the angle of light that falls directly on the space or the object from the lighting source. Each lighting instrument is positioned at a certain angle and its beam travels unimpeded to the reflective surface. However, if an angle is changed or deflected by an object or surface, the light is called an **indirect light** or **reflected light**. Indirect light can be attractive because it makes the illuminated materials look soft and diffuse; shadows can also be made softer or removed completely in this type of lighting.

   Footlights or up-lights light the space and the object from below. Lighting from below seems unnatural and is used to create unrealistic, fantastic moods that are slightly exaggerated. Front lighting is when the source is beside or behind the observer and lights the space from the front. It is needed to illuminate faces. There is less constraint between object and space than with any other light. Front lighting is the flattest kind of light as the shadows are wholly or partly behind the object and scarcely visible from front. The space loses its effective depth. Despite these disadvantages, front lighting cannot be discarded altogether as it makes all the action directly visible. With **back lighting** the light source is behind the object, lights it from the back and casts shadows towards the spectators. This light creates the most convincing spatial depth. **Side lighting**, light illuminating the space from the side, is the most frequently used direction for light and is useful for creating a particularly strong sense of space, and gives the actor the best three-dimensional quality.

   Color quality and **color rendering** are the quality of any particular light, which has to be decided along with the choice of angle and direction. It is important to exploit the potential characteristics of the various light sources. The lighting designer chooses light types and direction. **General and main lighting** is the kind of light created from strong, focused sources. **Accents** are used to enliven an objects with points of light and highlights, or used as brighteners. Accents are made up of sharply focused beams of light.

Brightening is used to make dark zones lighter. **Background lighting**, or horizontal lighting, is used to establish correct brightness levels in the background. It creates spatial depth. Backlighting is a technique that detaches the performer from the surrounding space and pulls the performer away from the scenery. By reversing the effects of light and shadow for the spectator, it plunges concrete objects into darkness or silhouette if nothing else is on. Back lighting can create a bizarre, ghostly effect if no other lights are on. It is not necessary to use only one quality of light or another. Often an excellent effect can be achieved with a mixture of different color temperatures. The contrasting behavior of different light sources makes a strong and colorful impression.

The addition of color gels in front of the beam of light colors the whole beam. Filtering light in this way becomes an essential technique for creating harmonious color impressions. For example, among the effects possible, warm colors can be used to enhance other warm colors and absorb colder ones. Cold colors can be used to enhance other cold colors and absorb warmer ones. Cold pure shades of blue in various color grades are often desired without a greenish cast. The most suitable blue filters are conversion filters intended to give incandescent light the feeling of daylight or more light. Pale violet and pale pink are pleasing and flattering to facial colors but are still relatively neutral. They can enhance make-up without changing the lighting in the space. Over time, designers learn which color combinations work best. It is always the particular production that guides the designer's choices. The following are examples of some of these concepts in practice.

Hairspray experiments with new technology

Based on the John Waters film of the same name, the original Broadway production of *Hairspray* was directed by Jack O'Brien in 2003 with a production team including scenic designer David Rockwell, costume designer William Ivey Long, lighting designer Kenneth Posner, sound designer Steve Canyon Kennedy, with wig and hair designer Paul Huntley. Among its award nominations were Best Scenic, Costume, and Lighting Tony Awards. Ivey Long won for his costume designs. *Hairspray* is set in Baltimore in 1962 and depicts the adventures of Tracy Turnblad, who is obsessed with *The Corny Collins Show* and its star dancer Link Larkin. Though rejected by producer Velma Von Tussle at auditions, when Tracy shows off her moves at the Sophomore Sock-Hop, Corny Collins gives her a place on the show. Tracy is soon launched to stardom. Her escapades lead her to fight with Amber and Velma Von Tussle, to seduce Link Larkin, become a model, and get arrested. By the end she ends up integrating the first national Corny Collins broadcast.

There are a number of spectacular scenic effects that punctuate the action, which captured the attention of critics. For example, in the opening scene, they depicted an overhead view of Tracy's bedroom. At another point during the song "Welcome to the 60s" a poster of the Dynamites comes to life. This playful tone emerged out of close collaboration between the designers. Early research and development for the production included the participation of John Waters, who guided Rockwell on a research tour of Baltimore. They thought it was important to recreate the characteristic Formstone decorations of the façade of townhouses in the Pigstown neighborhood. Rockwell used that emblematic look on rows of townhouse set pieces for several scenes. Although the design team did voluminous research into the Baltimore of 1962, they filtered that research through Waters' eccentric aesthetic seen in his movies. Close collaboration allowed the design team to coordinate the color scheme for the set, the costumes, and the lighting where each overlapped to create their compositions. O'Brien and Rockwell came up with a color scheme based on the orange, lemon, lime, clove, chocolate, cinnamon, licorice, and wintergreen colors of Necco Wafers popular in the 1960s that worked from the point of view of the set. Next, Ivey Long looked at the color scheme, and came back with costumes that coordinated, and then Posner discussed elements as detailed as gobo patterns with the director, to make sure there was a relationship between everything. Their big challenge was creating a set that complemented and enhanced, yet did not compete with, the action on stage.

Keeping in tone with Water's pop-filled camp send-up of 1960s extravagances, the designs incorporate spectacular references to contemporaneous musicals, such as a women's prison right out of *Chicago* and a jungle gym that pays homage to *Bye Bye Birdie*. Rockwell's early discussions with O'Brien and Mitchell led them to decide that they did not want the music and pace to be interrupted by heavy transitions or scenery changes. A simple fluid setting used lighting to define and set the pace. Lighting effects were present from the preset, where audiences see a curtain made of quarter-inch red silicon tubing hand-stitched to a blue Austrian velour backing that looks like a beehive hairdo from the audience's perspective. When the curtain opens viewed as if from

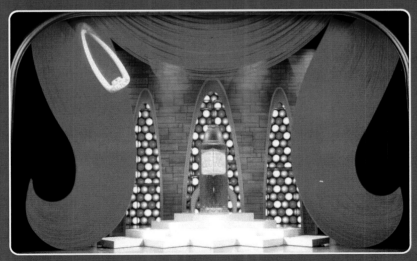

© Rockwell Group

The opening curtain is made out of lighting material to look like a curtain. The silhouette resembles a giant bouffant hairdo. The LED lighting has a red face with black slits as eyes and yellow and green ribbon programmed into it. The lighting was refashioned to make a cute curtain. This pre-set immediately set the tone for the playful quality of the production. Rather than attempt to create realistic settings, the scenic effects support the tone and atmosphere of the piece and get the audience ready for the jokes and spectacular effects.

143

above, Tracy wakes up in a vertically positioned bed at center stage, and sings the Brenda Lee-style "Oh, oh, oh" opening strains of "Good Morning, Baltimore" establishing the tone of the production. Though the show uses almost minimal scenery, by the end of the first act, the audience has seen dozens of different settings fluidly moving from the bed, the prologue drop behind Tracy with people appearing in her dream, all of Baltimore, *The Corny Collins Show* studio, several versions of the Turnblad house, and Motormouth Maybelle's record shop. Among other tactics, Rockwell devised automated scenery for keeping the sets moving, allowing the lighting to unify the visual with the aural elements.

Posner bumped up the level of theatricality of *Hairspray* by defining the setting and scene changes keeping pace with the musical score. Each lighting choice followed the tempo of the show's musical numbers that push the action along, often flowing between multiple locations and time frames. Posner's lighting served as a visual guide to organize the action so the audience would not be confused. The number "Welcome to the 60s" and "Good Morning Baltimore" follow Tracy through the streets of Baltimore. Another number, "Mama, I'm a Big Girl Now," is a sextet featuring three mother–daughter combinations simultaneously arguing in each of their

© Paul Kolnik

In the scene "Welcome to the Sixties," the audience sees Posner's lighting design feature that is a wall of LED units that pulses, chases, and runs brightly colored patterns. Critics described it as a proto-Pop Art effect. The movement, brightness, and intensity add to the energy onstage. Intensity is important in musical theatre. The more energy the musical number has, the more intensity the lighting must have. Posner raised the light levels during the number to subtly affect the audience's perception of the energy of the number. Low light during a high-energy song will drain the number of its intensity.

homes. Posner used Shaiman's early-Motown-style music as a guide for his lighting aesthetic. Lighting keeps the action moving, providing shifts of scale and focusing timing changes according to the music's insistent beat, and directing the eye to exactly the right place to keep the action straight. Though invisible to the audience, light kept them clear on when, where, and who they were.

One of the most noted features of the lighting design is a backdrop that is reminiscent of the Lite-Brite toy popular in the late 1960s. Its points of light could change to create designs. Posner used close to six hundred fixtures to create those points of colored light. He programmed the fixtures to generate continually morphing and changing light, transforming the backdrop into different patterns and shapes of richly colored light distinct to each scene. It emphasized the playful tone and atmosphere of the action. According to reviewers Posner's most dazzling effect comes during "Welcome to the 60s," when a pulsating wall of light is revealed following the tempo of the music. Toward the end, The Dynamites perform in front of the hundreds of LED units placed in white translucent circular housings. The effects in the light wall perform colorful chases, wipes, and pulses. The wall's color scheme splits into quarters, chevrons, and at one point reveals a pair of intertwined hearts. During

© Paul Kolnik

For "You Can't Stop The Beat," Posner brightened the general lighting to heighten the energy of the full company number. The center of the stage is the brightest and the background lighting recedes to the back to allow the audience to focus on the dancing. This adds excitement to the audience's experience. The lights seem to explode upwards for the finale as he intensified the brightness. The scenic rhythms, lighting rhythms, and musical rhythms worked together to create a high-energy tempo that grew to the climax of the spectacular ending. It was rather like the tempo of a fireworks display. Color was used as an accent for the setting, wash light and front light made the actors' faces visible, and the intensity of the light increased as the energy of the song built. The lighting helped the actors and musicians build their energy.

the finale, the entire cast is in a frenzy intensified by the pulsing wall. This bright, high intensity, moving light show ends the production with a bang.

In interviews with David Barbour Posner describes how Rockwell developed the concept of the wall of light. Apparently, during an early production meeting with the producers, Rockwell saw a piece of art that inspired them to think about a light wall. Even though the light wall was a scenic element, it fell to Posner to find a technological solution to how to create the effect. Conventional units would have been difficult to use. Power usage, wiring, and maintenance issues made it unfeasible. Neon would have been too costly and troublesome, and finally he considered fiber optics but felt that it was not really workable because of the technology's limitations. Posner instead decided to experiment with LEDs. These units had numerous advantages since they are programmable, energy-efficient, and do not produce much heat or draw much power. Posner's team pre-programmed the light wall during pre-production, continually updating the images and tempos as they learned to use the technology. They began with a simple palette of eight colors, and then expanded into more, as they figured out what the LEDs could do. The entire team started having fun making suggestions. Exhausted and in a silly mood, the design team decided to program the image of a pair of hearts into the wall as a joke. They turned it on to punctuate the end of the song "Without Love." This playful accident worked so well it was used in production.

Musicals need to be bright, but our eyes grow accustomed to static lighting levels. Posner worked to balance his effects highlighting the actors in one scene, and then after a few minutes increasing the intensity and washing the environment with color. It is important to constantly modulate the audience's experience. To accomplish this, Posner says he is guided by three principles. First is a respect for the cast, where the designer is careful not to block out the actors. He used the spectacular light wall mostly for large-scale numbers, where they would not upstage the actors. Second, he chose a restrained color palette that fits in with the Necco Wafer colors favored by Rockwell in the setting and Ivey Long in the costumes. The team chose this low-saturation range of colors because they were right for the period. High-saturation colors are more appropriate for shows such as *American Idiot* set later in later decades. Finally, there is a sense of musicality in the cueing. Posner's cueing is closely tied to the music, picking up on its driving rhythms, meshing the two together to make a fabric of light and sound that is specific and particular to the production of the play.

Lighting as visual organization: Peter Hall's *The Bacchae*

Peter Hall's *The Bacchae* premiered at the Olivier Theatre, London in 2002 and then transferred to the Ancient Theatre of Epidaurus, Athens. Its Set and Costume Design were by Alison Chitty, and Lighting Design was by Peter Mumford. Colin Teevan adapted the text, with music by Sir Harrison Birtwistle. Set in Thebes, *The Bacchae* is about Dionysus' arrival at Thebes with his band of women supporters, from the East, called the Bacchae, intent on winning converts to their new religion. However, Thebes' young, dictator Pentheus, a follower of Apollonian order, denies Dionysus's claim of divinity and attempts to suppress his religious rites. In return, Dionysus persuades all its women, including Agave, Pentheus's mother, to go up into the mountains and indulge in ecstatic secret female rituals that are sexual and animalistic. Pentheus's edicts are resisted and eventually Dionysus

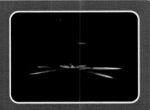

Here the Chorus of female devotees is lit from below and from the side with side light accents. The sharp contrast between the darkness of the space and the sliver of light intensifies the mood. When Bacchus appears later, back light and color accents accentuate the otherworldly power of the god. Spotlights brighten focus. The background recedes and only the god remains.

National Theatre production of *The Bacchae* at Epidavros, photo Peter Mumford — lighting design by Peter Mumford and design Alison Chitty

persuades him to go and watch. Dionysus humiliates him by convincing him to pose as a woman. Pentheus's eagerness to peep leads to his discovery by the women and, still entranced, they tear the flesh off his bones. Agave comes back to the city bearing what she believes to be the head of a young lion but realizes in the light of day that it is the head of her son.

The production was developed during an extended rehearsal period at the National Theatre. Hall wanted to begin with nothing predetermined to let the production grow out of the desire to tell the story clearly. He pares it back to basics, with three actors playing three roles apiece, fifteen actors as a chorus, and no scenery. Hall believes the important thing to evoke the play is the words, what the characters say, what they are, and what they make the audience feel. Hall's choices as a director spring from his desire to concentrate on the text, so the production team chose not to use scenic units. All the designers were present in the rehearsal room from the start collaborating in the discovery process with the actors. Hall accentuates the focus on the text in the slow movements of the Chorus and their rapid speech. The setting was bare and costume and lighting were the predominant scenographic tools used to organize the piece visually. Furthermore, Hall used masks as scenic props and felt that it was important the chorus's voices not be recognized individually. He believes this conveys that the sentiment of the chorus is representative of the voice of the city. Masks, he explained to the team, help us imagine the events that usually occur offstage in Greek drama. To reinforce this, the chorus appears mainly in the shadows giving the impression that the chorus is a single character that witnesses the action. Principal characters were highlighted with an accent light. According to Hall, the play resonates with the horrors that are going on in our contemporary world. He believes that a production does not start or end with a concept, but rather the production elements work together to allow the concepts to come out of it. Overstating a single

The round makes it difficult to light the space evenly from a single direction without multiple instruments. The light hits the figures and leaves shadows. Mumford embraced this to add emotional texture to the action. Here the cool blue of the ground is in contrast to the hot red of the chorus of bacchant revelers. In contrast to a setting with scenery and many reflective surfaces, this setting is the choruses of red-cloaked Bacchanalian followers.

National Theatre production of *The Bacchae* at Epidavros, photo Peter Mumford – lighting design by Peter Mumford and design Alison Chitty

theme can unbalance the production. If Pentheus, who is in certain respects an authoritarian fascist, is portrayed solely as an authoritarian fascist, the complexity of the play is dissipated.

The production opens with an unmasked figure standing, with the house lights up, at the center of Alison Chitty's wooden disk of a stage that serves as a fluid setting, instantly transporting the action from one location to the next. The figure puts on the golden, horned mask of Dionysus, a deity devoted, he tells us, to "the transformation from the humdrum/ To the wild abandon of the play." A large, raked, saucer-like disk marks the central playing area similar to an angled Greek orchestra. Across the back of the stage sweeps a ramp, rising in

The footlight lanterns are visible framing the circumference of the circular playing space. As you can see with the shadows, spotlights accent and brighten the characters that we are meant to focus on. General lighting washes the playing space in red light. In other scenes the designer used white accents as a contrast between the red of the chorus and the white clothing of the principles. The red fades the chorus into the background.

National Theatre production of *The Bacchae* at Epidavros, photo Peter Mumford – lighting design by Peter Mumford and design Alison Chitty

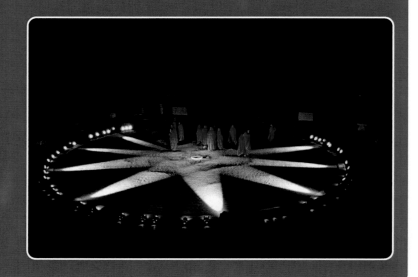

a curve from stage right to stage left, leading from Thebes to Mount Kithairon. Spectacular images are evoked on this simple stage. When Dionysus assaults Thebes with an earthquake, Pentheus's palace burns, the disk splits in half, and ferocious blasts of fire erupt from flamethrowers beneath the stage. Dionysus makes his final appearance upon a small, circular platform that magically rises from the mutilated remains of Pentheus's body 40 feet above the stage and then vanishes through the floor at precisely the moment he speaks his final line.

Lighting defines this open stage. The volume of the stage can be expanded and contracted as needed through lighting techniques. For example, Agave, who awakes from her savage, divinely fomented delusion to perceive that the bloody head she carries like a trophy is that not of a lion, but of her own son. Houston's Agave, soaked by slaughtered animals' and her son's blood, looks like a butcher's carcass. The shape of the space has changed from the previous example. The intersecting sidelights add depth to the stage, and the addition of a red spot upstage accentuates the blood of the carcass. Furthermore, color creates an emotional narrative that underscores the dialogue and action. Lighting angle differentiates the different classes of character from each other. Red light bathes the chorus of Bacchants, and white and green light bathes the nobility. It appears that the god is able to change the environmental lighting because of his powers. The general lighting mimics natural sunlight, but when the god is angered darkness envelopes the space and shrinks the volume of the stage space. Lighting is central in the definition of time, location, and mood. Visual interest is from the changing dynamic of the lighting score, as well as from the details of the costumes and masks. The playing space leaves room for the audience to listen to the words and watch the action. The audience has a place to witness the triumph of Dionysus and his followers.

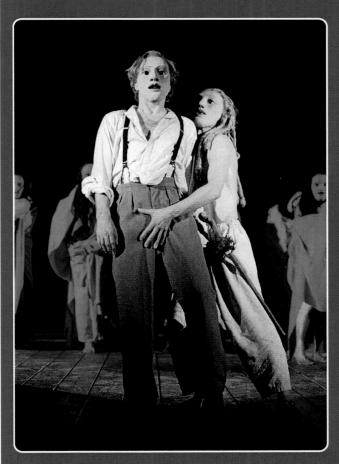

The white lighting on the main characters sets them apart from the red chorus. The tangled black braids of the chorus's wigs and their coverings of old-blood-colored rags, and mud-besmeared semi-nudity of the actors show their devotion to the rites of Dionysus. Peter Mumford's lighting score is composed of un-muddied reds and greens, plus one striking moment of purple as Pentheus's royal palace implodes. Accent light highlights the two characters' masks and physical gestures. The Dionysus mask is peeled off to reveal the false-face human mask he assumes to wreak havoc in the locality. The image depicts the moment when Bacchus puts a disastrous spell on the priggish Pentheus, prompting him to put on a frock and head off to the mountains to spy on the women's rites.

© Manuel Harlan

Stephen Sondheim's *Sunday in the Park with George*

Stephen Sondheim's *Sunday in the Park with George* has had multiple award-winning productions since its original Off-Broadway opening in 1983. Each of these productions uses lighting and projection technology in different ways to evoke the creation of a diorama or two-dimensional reproduction of a painting. In doing so, they reveal different interpretations of Sondheim's creation. In its New York Playwrights Horizons incarnation, only the first act in development was performed with work on the second act only begun during that time. The original finished Broadway production opened in 1984 at the Booth Theatre directed by James Lapine, with scenic design by Tony Straiges, costume design by Patricia Zipprodt and Ann Hould-Ward, lighting by Richard Nelson, and sound by Tom Morse. Among other awards given to the show, the designers were nominated for Tony Awards, with Straiges and Nelson winning for their contributions.

The plot of *Sunday in the Park with George* revolves around the relationship between the late-nineteenth-century pointillist painter Georges Seurat and his model, Dot, who appears in his famous painting *A Sunday*

Photo: Martha Swope

The production combines live actors and painted characters. Straiges' sets pop up through the floor as Seurat creates his masterpiece in front of the audience's eyes. The apron allows for the "real characters" to be distinguished from the "painted" characters that fill the upstage volume of the space. Straiges rendered the perspective by placing two-dimensional pop-ups to create a sense of perspective in the painting. The scale of the upstage is proportional to the live actors downstage. By combining the two-dimensional pop-ups with the three-dimensional actors the whole "painted" image is flattened out.

Afternoon on the Island of Le Grande Jatte. It is broken into two interlocking parts, the first of which tells an imagined story of how the Parisian painter created his masterpiece while ignoring his mistress Dot. Painting for Sondheim's Seurat is a process that transforms the chaotic ugliness of reality, by rearranging and improving upon the world, to create a work of art that incorporates order, design, symmetry, balance, and harmony. Dot, pregnant with his child, but knowing that she cannot get what she wants from Seurat, marries a baker and moves to the United States. The second act is set in 1984 where another George, the grandson of the daughter Dot bore to Georges in Act One, has been commissioned to create a new multimedia conceptual art piece to celebrate the one-hundredth anniversary of his great-grandfather's painting.

The scenic design recreates the two-year process that Seurat went through creating his masterpiece, showing the process of how he conceived and executed the painting. Seurat paints on the apron with three-dimensional actors and two-dimensional cutouts in the background. Both Straiges and Nelson worked closely with a special effect team to create a three-dimensional setting of the park, his studio, and the stage-size replica of the finished painting. The park setting alternates with scenes in the studio. The second act shows the grandson returning to the twentieth-century version of the park and fantasy sessions in the original painting. Nelson's primary task

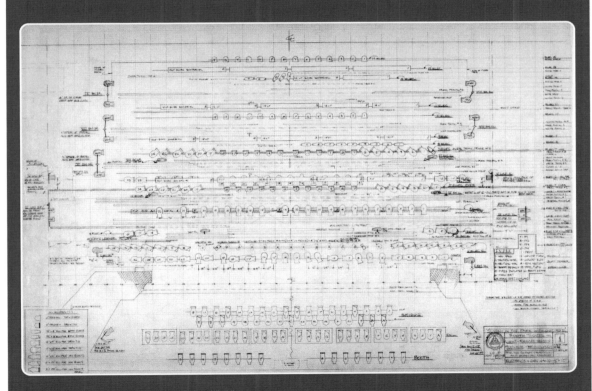

Image courtesy of: Richard Nelson/New York Public Library

This is the hanging plot for the workshop version of *Sunday in the Park with George*. Much of the set lighting and backlighting was done with one kilowatt lighting instruments that were softened with frosts, an open-faced quartz unit that was softened with frosts that had the effect of blending the floor and backdrop into a unified whole.

151

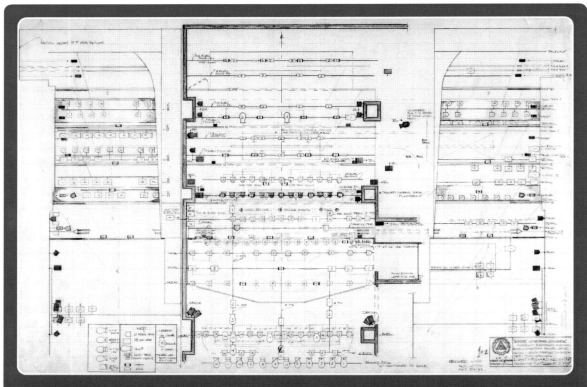

Image courtesy of: Richard Nelson/New York Public Library

This is Richard Nelson's lighting plot depicting the general hang for the electrics. Though the lighting was not hanging in the best configuration to achieve the effects they wanted, the technical rehearsals allowed the designer the time to adjust the lighting focus and brighten the holes with follow spots. The designer's job is to make the lighting work within the constraints of the technology and designs.

outside of the lighting in the studio was to illuminate the park scenes. The stage space is crowded with cutouts and the live characters. Each time an element was added the balance of composition changed and the lighting had to adjust. Live actors enter and exit, trees are moved to the perfect spot, and cutouts pop up out of the floor. The lighting for the workshop was much more constrained because of the intimate space of the stage. This lighting had to change when the production moved to the Booth Theatre. In the original space, the lighting was static, but in the larger space that used more scenery the lighting had to constantly adjust and change.

According to an interview with Steve Pollock, although it seemed that the wing-and-border style set would allow for side lighting to make an even side wash up and down stage, there were too many scenic elements to make this work. As a result Nelson made each side of the stage different. The asymmetrical composition gave the stage a lighting quality similar to the multiple sources of direct and indirect light that are found outdoors in nature. As well, taking a cue from Seurat, Nelson used color in the park setting to reflect the interplay between fantasy and reality. He exaggerated the fantasy elements so that even what was supposed to be naturalistic seemed bizarre. Color and scale were manipulated to make clear what lay beneath the seemingly naturalistic portraits. The whole composition has a purple glow that became more dominant as the play progressed.

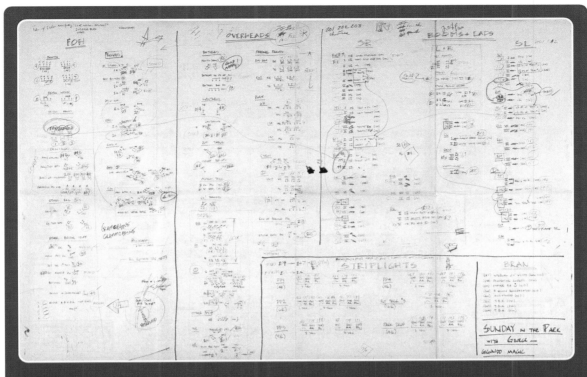

Image courtesy of: Richard Nelson/New York Public Library

Here is Nelson's magic sheet. The magic sheet is a practical tool used by designers during technical rehearsals. It allows them to group the types of lighting and their positions into an easily recognizable cheat sheet. In this way they can quickly determine what angles, colors, and type of lights are available at any given moment to create an effect. This is rather like the palette a painter will use. He can arrange colors on the palette to pick from and mix to achieve an effect as he works on the composition of the painting. Much of the lighting designer's problem solving is done on the spot in rehearsal.

Seurat's dialogue is filled with references to violet and the mixing of red and blue, so Nelson decided that violet was the key to lighting the show. Nelson used purple washes to create a saturated wash. He had been saving a discontinued purple gel stock for just such a purpose. He created a crude wash of four lekos mounted on a bridge and deliberately placed without symmetry. Seurat's aesthetic relies on our eye's way of perceiving color. This interest in light and color and the ways in which the eye perceives multiple points of color as a new hue poses a particular problem for the lighting designer. He considered using a pointillist technique with additive color to recreate Seurat's original. In the end, Nelson chose to use the technique sparingly. He used pinhole lights to make the patterns layer over the templates for foliage. He also washes the paintings with these pinholes to give it the texture of Seurat's paint strokes. Rather than slavishly recreate what the paint can do, Nelson evokes an atmosphere to suggest the painter's technique. Nelson found an analogy to Seurat's technique, while using light technology to evoke the effect of the paintings. This process echoed the scenic process of finding a three-dimensional equivalent to painting.

153

Sunday's 2005 London revival and its 2008 transfer to Broadway

The musical was revived in London at the Menier Chocolate Factory. Directed by Sam Buntrock, its setting and costumes were designed by David Farley, and its lighting was designed by Natasha Chivers and Mike Robertson. The production transferred in 2006 to Wyndham's Theatre. It received six Olivier Award nominations, and won five in total including Best Set Design and Best Lighting Design. The production then transferred to Broadway in 2008, where Roundabout Theatre Company and Studio 54 produced it winning even more awards. In New York Ken Billington reworked the lighting, and the projection design was by Timothy Bird and the Knifedge Creative Network.

Reviewers praised the innovative design, describing it as an intimate production where actors talk to projections, scenery darkens as day turns into night, and animation seamlessly blends into the background. Rather than using pop-up cutouts that the original production made use of, this version uses newer technological developments such as three-dimensional animation to create the painting as the painter gradually composes it onstage in front of the audience. At first a sketch emerges, then color is added, and the rest gradually comes into focus, piece by piece as the action progresses.

Projection technology conveys the vision of a nineteenth-century pointillist using two dimensions to render three dimensions in a similar way to the illusion of three dimensions in a painting. Buntrock, who has a background in media, wanted to demonstrate what can be achieved by exploiting special effects by integrating animation. The play is about perception, and Buntrock wanted the audience to see the work the way that Georges perceives it coming to life.

While Buntrock feels that sometimes the effects are made invisible in contemporary practice so they do not intrude upon the action, for this production he wanted to show the progression of the creation of the painting to get into the mind of the artist. That his art comes to immediate and fluid life lends the show a physical

For the London production Chivers and Robertson use neutral colors at the beginning. The sketch emerges at this point and the park begins to take shape. As the painting begins to take shape, and his ideas become clearer, then more vibrant colors are added in. It was important to make sure that the lights brightening the actor's face did not interfere with the quality of light in the projection.

© Tristram Kenton

154

Chivers and Robertson use more vibrant colors to brighten Farley's costumes. In this scene where Seurat is composing the famous painting, we see how the lighting brightens the live actors without washing out the background. He accomplishes this by keeping the facelight tight to the characters.

© Tristram Kenton

seamlessness—as if the artist's process was fluid. In contrast to the 1984 production the actor appears to paint Seurat's painting's image into existence in real time. The audience sees George's vision, with landscapes and people projected on scrims and small canvases. These images are altered as he sketches them. Perspectives and colors alter as George's moods change and time goes on and the perspectives of the images and their colors change. When autumn arrives, a pointillist shower of color falls from the sky. The look of the show feels like thought made visible, like painterly flecks of light and color. It captures the act of creation in real time, as the dialogue questions the nature of perception and the difficulties inherent in mimetic composition.

It is very different working in London and New York. The thing about England is that, by and large, people do what they do because they love doing it. It isn't just about money. I'm not saying that people in America only do it for money, but it's gotten in the way a lot, creating attitudes toward working and penalties for infringing very rigid strictures. Very often, in London, the lighting is allowed to develop and grow and nurture during production process. Exactly the opposite in New York.

David Hersey

For the New York performances all of the projections were created far in advance as compared to the London performances, with the final video approved well before the technical rehearsals began. According to the projection designer the production team spent a long time planning how it would work. Everyone had to understand what would be moving and when it would do so. The music guided the pacing of the images since they were able to time the movement to the beat. The original projections were redesigned to fit the larger venue of Studio 54, which has more scale and height to it, with a bit more space on the stage for the performers. They needed the additional space so that they would not hit performers with projection. The projection designer worked closely with Billington to insure that light did not hit the actors in a way that would cast shadows given how their rig was devised. The technical rehearsals in London were more hurried than in New York where they were described as systematic. There they were able to match the projection with the lighting during a one-week projection tech rehearsal before the actors arrived on the set. The set and costume designer also worked closely with the projections unit. Once costumes for the animated characters were finalized, the designer hand-painted the performers' garbs to reinforce the pointillist patterning. Farley conceived that the surfaces within George's studio would serve as the projection surface. As the park comes together on stage, it is as if George has set up a still life in his studio and is painting from that, as well as from his sketches. Those choices allowed them to hang drapery all over the set. Two trees that are made of heavyweight crème velour descend to the stage deck in a tree shape, complementing the design.

Billington blends the different elements together with the lighting. While it is difficult to come in and adjust an award-winning design, he brought new ideas to the table when the production transferred to the U.S. He wanted to emphasize the "day" in Sunday and make the setting bright. However, the danger with this is that brightness has a tendency to wash out the projections. Billington worked to get the light in the right place and at the right angle. If the set recedes in the projections, the light has to go with it. He did not use the lights on the balcony rail too often. Light does hit the walls, but it was conceived so that the audience would not notice it. These effects had to be adjusted and monitored during technical rehearsals with the actors present. Colors had to be adjusted according to the projection, the setting, the costumes, and the actor's pigment.

The two productions had different feels because of the style of technology that was used to recreate the painting. In the original, the designers made use of traditional stagecraft to create an image behind the proscenium. They used flats to accentuate the perspective and flattened the volume of the space out with front lights. Color was added through reflective lighting techniques. It was a much broader and theatrical style that was matched in the quality of the new cast's performances. In the second production, projections are used to recreate the painting. The projections add indirect lighting sources to the general lighting. The designers had to be careful

Billington explains that once the show was lit he returned to color-match the lighting and the projections, so that the walls are exactly the same color in projection as they are in life. The projections change color with every light cue. As the walls downstage to a ten-point cue, going from stage left to stage right with the light, the projections adjust as well. Two pinspots are used throughout the entire show for visibility, rarely accentuating anything beyond head-and-shoulders.

© Tristram Kenton

156

not to interfere with the technology of the projections. The images could transform in real time with the moving film images. The pop-ups created the image in spurts. This production was more internal in nature, as if the projections were the images we see in our heads. Likewise the actors' performances were more muted. This quiet feel was also emphasized because of the muted color palette used for lighting the live actors.

7 The artistry of sound

Key Topics:

@ The nature of sound

  - Quality, duration, acoustics, material variables

@ The job of the sound designer

  - Technical sound design, the sound system, conceptual design

@ Collaborating with the design team

  - Mixing desks, playback cues, sound reinforcement, sound engineer

@ The designer's process

  - Microphones, loudspeaker systems, underscoring

@ The basic sound system

  - Transducers, microphones, loudspeakers, amplifiers

@ What sound design adds to a production

  - Establishing time and place, enhancing meaning, dramatic impact, reinforcement

Case Study:

- *Wicked*: A fantasy world with a natural sound

Examples:

- The mixing board
- The sound design

158

While sound has been used in some form in performance to create simple effects such as thunder and rain as long as there has been theatre, recent innovations in audio technology have allowed sound to take on a more active role in performance. The role of sound design developed from advancements in the digital recording industry during the twentieth and twenty-first centuries. Audiences now expect sound in the theatre to be as intricately designed as the sets, costumes, and lighting.

The nature of sound

Sound is the movement of air in the form of pressure waves that travel 1,130 feet per second. Whether it is wood, strings, vocal chords, or a croaking frog, sound requires some sort of medium of transmission like a solid, liquid, or gas, because a vacuum will not transmit. Sound is propagated through media by causing adjacent particles to vibrate in a similar fashion – the strings on a cello vibrate at a given frequency and thereby displace air molecules adjacent to them. The most common analogy used to describe sound wave propagation is that of a rock dropped into a pond. When it hits the water the rock produces ripples that originate from the point of contact and then spread out in all directions. Energy is used up in making the water ripple, and thus as the ripples travel further and further away from the rock's point of impact, they lose intensity. As sound travels it loses energy getting softer.

Sound designers use five controllable properties of sound to create the effects or music required by the production. Pitch, volume, quality, direction, and duration can be manipulated and shaped as line, shape, color can be. **Pitch** is the wavelength or frequency of the sound, **volume** is the loudness or quietness of the sound, **quality** is how pitch and volume combine to give each sound its own distinctive effect, **direction** is the location of the sound in space and how sound travels from one location to another, and **duration** is the length of time the sound lasts. The controllable properties of sound allow sound designers to adjust the audibility of a sound for an audience, to use sound to motivate action, to alter the voices of the actors, or to create mood. Some functions are accomplished by the manipulation of processing equipment, and others are designed and programmed. For example a sound can be manipulated to become bright instead of dark to enhance the mood of the scene. A designer can change a sound's intensity or direction to influence how the audience feels about the action. Both musical composition and sound design are processes of building structural relationships through time and calling attention to the moments that the audience needs to pay attention to.

159

Sound designers need to know audio technology well and need to understand hardware and how it is used to control sound. Designers make use of equipment in innovative ways to find solutions to the demands of theatre practice. Also, space affects sound quality, and the designer must understand **acoustics**, the behavior of sound within different spatial configurations. Sound behaves differently in a black box than it does in an amphitheatre. To work around those differences the designer must understand how to use the equipment to connect to audiences within that space. Sound design is grounded aesthetically in the psychology of perception and the development of meaning, and so a designer needs to understand the physical behavior of sound, the characteristics of hearing, and the principles of acoustics.

The basic sound system delivers sufficient sound levels to the audience through the placement of microphones within the listening area. Understanding the acoustic characteristics of the venue allows the designer to find the optimal placement for microphones. Designers will control loudness and adjust for ambient sounds that seep into the auditorium as they propagate sound for the audience. Generally, sound can be altered four ways by its environment as it travels. It can be reflected, absorbed, diffracted, or refracted. These are variables that will have to be controlled in each space. **Reflection** occurs when a surface or other object reflects a sound wave because the object is physically as large as or larger than the sound's wavelength. It will have a different frequency characteristic than the direct sound. Reflection is also the source of echo, reverb, and standing waves. **Echo** occurs when a reflected sound gets delayed and is heard by the listener as a repetition of the direct sound. **Reverberation** is when there are multiple reflections of a sound that maintains it in a reflective space for a time even after the direct sound has ceased. Imagine a man standing in the middle of a black box theatre with cement block walls who claps his hands. The audience hears the direct sound waves from the hands, and hears the sound waves that have been reflected by the cement walls at a lower level. Every venue will have different reverberation characteristics depending upon its size, shape, obstacles, and construction that influence the way sound behaves. **Standing waves** in a room occur for certain frequencies when the original sound and the reflected sound reinforce each other.

Absorption, on the other hand, is a result of a material that absorbs sound rather than reflects it. Carpet affects high frequencies, and drapes and padded furniture affect low frequencies. Adding absorption can control reverberation in a room, since the more absorption there is the less reverberation occurs. Clothed humans absorb mid and high frequencies well, so the presence or absence of an audience has a significant effect on the sound in an otherwise reverberant theatre. However, a sound wave will typically bend around obstacles in its path that are smaller than its wavelength. This is **diffraction**. Since a low frequency sound wave is much longer than a high frequency wave, low frequencies will bend around objects that high frequencies cannot. A similar effect is **refraction**, where the bending of a sound wave takes place as it passes through some change in the density of the environment. It is noticeable outdoors at large distances from loudspeakers as a result of atmospheric disturbances such as wind or temperature changes.

When loud instruments, weak performers, or echoing venues of this sort are encountered and are undesirable, designers adjust the sound source, use a different microphone, reposition the microphone, or possibly add absorption to improve the situation. In most cases acoustic problems are solved with little intervention from electronic devices. There is no one ideal microphone to use on any particular instrument and no ideal way to place a microphone.

The job of the sound designer

First and foremost, the sound designer's goal is to provide intelligible and even reinforcement of the show to every seat in the house. Understanding the interaction of sound within the venue's physical constraints (scenery, lighting instruments, walls, floors, ceilings) and accommodating for variances in the natural acoustic response of the hall are key; in addition to knowing which tools can be used most effectively to provide the best possible solution for the given situation.

Kai Harada

Today sound designers record, mix, filter, reverberate, modulate, and amplify recorded sounds from the world around us or from sound libraries that have preserved sounds such as a horse-drawn cart trotting down a cobblestone street or a steam locomotive that have disappeared from our everyday existence. Their task is to choose and modify sounds that capture the tone of such things as a doorbell chime as a way to indicate social status or to evoke atmosphere. They might also create unique sounds that will add emotion or meaning to a scene. As with other design practices that support the work of actors, auditory practice supports and supplements the sound produced by the actors. Music is used to create a pre-curtain mood, as well as to underscore stretches of dialogue, transitions between scenes, or to enhance emotional response. Sound effects can create narrative – does the action need to conjure up a car driving up a gravel driveway and stopping, a hurricane, gunshot, or ambulance? Sound design conveys shifts in mood, location, time, or place. Also our internal states may be evoked through sound. For example, a throbbing heartbeat may express panic or paranoia. Sound can add a punch to a shocking revelation, a door slam can emphasize an exit, or a storm may indicate an argument. A designer does not simply create a doorbell ringing, but chooses a ring that contributes to the inner life of the play by suggesting what the characters feel about their situation.

Sound designers and projection designers are the most recent additions to the production team. Though their functions are frequently interchangeable, for the most part only one Sound Designer is hired to take on the roles of a Technical Sound

Designer or a Conceptual Sound Designer. This is similar to the dual roles played by a lighting designer who selects the technical equipment as well as creates a conceptualized design. Most Technical or Conceptual Sound Designers simply call themselves Sound Designers no matter which role they fill primarily. **Technical sound design** requires designers to build a **sound system** that will fulfill the needs of the production. That is to say, if there is a sound system already installed in the theatre the designer will adapt it and supplement it with other equipment. A technical sound designer makes sure that the performance can be heard and understood by everyone in the audience. They will spend a lot of time finding the ideal placement for microphones to create a balanced audio environment.

> Sound design in the theater includes designing all the sounds for a show, and designing the system is only part of that. The first thing I have to do is talk to the director and find out what the show is about, what the concepts for the show are, and the type of sound that director wants. That can start with the composer: for example, is it Rogers and Hammerstein or Elton John? To put it simply, you'd need bigger speakers for Elton John. Also, the director may want surround sound to make the audience feel like they are part of something and totally surrounded by an effect. Or, it may be just a straightforward sound reinforcement system without sound effects. After I find out what the director wants, then I go to the theater if it's a Broadway show with one stop. There, I work on the needs of the audience: once I know what the input is going to be, then I need to know how to get the output to every seat in the house. That's where the sound system comes into play.

> **Tony Meola**

Conceptual sound design requires designers to conceive of an abstract soundscape that will complement the themes or atmosphere of a production. The designer, in conjunction with the director, decides what sounds he or she will use to create the mood and setting of the production. This might include choosing or composing music for the play or **ambient beds** under every scene that evoke moods or environments. An obvious example is the music that plays underneath the action of a Victorian melodrama. As well, the conceptual sound designer must build the prop sound effects such as doorbells, car door slams, voice-over announcements, and determine how to fit them into the established themes with regard to when and where the action is supposed to be taking place. Examples of this are the sound of a string breaking that punctuates the action of Anton Chekhov's *The Cherry Orchard* or the door slam at the end of Henrik Ibsen's *A Doll's House* when Nora storms out. Both the technical sound designer and the conceptual sound designer ensure that the sound is in harmony with the work of the actors and other designers. It is similar to the way in which the other designers make sure their colors coordinate and that the surfaces of the setting and costumes reflect light in the desired manner.

Collaborating with the design team

Like much of theatre practice, collaboration, and cooperation is at the heart of sound design practice. A designer must work within the constraints laid out by the director and work to fit their design with the other designers' work. For example, sound designers have to find good loudspeaker positions that do not interfere with scenic elements or lighting instruments. Sometimes this can become frustrating, but it is the most important thing designers do to support or augment the needs of the production. Microphones can be hidden in costumes, speakers hung behind scenery, and musicians relocated. Sound designers also work with actors to show them how to position themselves for the best amplification.

> Learning to deal with the politics of a theatre institution is often the most challenging thing about theatre. That, and learning how to deal with different directors: how to approach a new director for the first time, not knowing their background or how they work with sound designers, or even if they have worked with sound designers. It's like a new marriage every time. It's everything from a director walking in and saying, "I have no idea what I want to do; give me something" to a director walking in with a list of CD tracks that they want to use in the show – those are the ones I hate the most, but at the same time it's all about what you make of it, to find the challenges in it for yourself. That's what makes the design that much better – going out and looking for those little challenges that will make the design yours.
>
> **Garth Hemphill**

Over the past twenty years improvements in sound technology have increased the role of sound designers in the creation of a production. All of the improvements in sound quality at live rock concerts, the capabilities of surround sound in cinema, and other developments have trained theatre audiences to expect more from theatre production. Technical innovation has allowed playwrights to try new ways of writing. Playwrights increasingly use shorter scenes set in multiple locations, which are difficult to stage fluidly using conventional moving scenery but can be done easily using light and sound. Productions are louder, system designs are more technologically complex, and directors expect more creative involvement from sound designers to exploit the potentials of sound within the production. This increased expectation is similar to the pressures on a lighting designer to create more intensity and movement over the course of a production. **Mixing desks** require more inputs, directors require more sound effects, and systems require more loudspeakers.

> Audience perception of how they want a show to sound has changed in the past few years. They have different expectations now: to hear every word as if they are watching TV or at a movie, for it to be exciting but still sound unamplified and invisible. I use more distributed loudspeakers for absolute even gain

163

throughout the auditorium and rely heavily on delay imaging. In *The Woman In White*, the score itself comes back to intimate dialogue on stage then swings to big musical moments, and that makes it more exciting. You have to know how to use the sound judiciously. Not just loud, but big. Also you want people to be able to suspend belief and think they are in Bombay or 19th-century England, so sometimes you have to be very discreet.

Mick Potter

Depending on the type of production, the sound designer's responsibilities range from creating aural soundscapes through the use of **playback cues**, emphasizing moments within a show with sound effects, or amplifying and reinforcing the performers' voices. Sound designers labor to balance the perspectives of the director, music director, orchestrator, producers, and choreographer with the practical demands of the cast who need to hear onstage, and the orchestra who need to hear in the pit. They are also involved with the aesthetic concerns of the visual designers. For example, a costume designer may not like the look of a microphone on one of the characters. If it is a realistic play such as *Red* the costume designer will not want to see a microphone visible on the clothing, whereas in *Spring Awakening* it may be a natural part of the rock concert aesthetic of the production. The needs of the production dictate that the sound designer's ultimate goal is to reinforce the work of the team. **Sound reinforcement** relies in some small part on the natural acoustic sound delivered by a performer from the stage to the audience to provide imaging cues to the listener. In other words, audiences need to see an actor to understand his or her words. Nevertheless, directors have a tendency to stage actors in such a way that may look better but complicates the ability of the sound designer to support the production. Why face upstage when singing a ballad? Why speak lines from behind a prop? Simple adjustments to blocking can help the sound equipment do its job better. Blocking can often solve technical problems such as feedback, reverberation, and poor amplification that occur when actors put on the costume on the set. Sound designers find that during technical rehearsals they must gently educate the production team on the nature of sound and the technical capabilities of the equipment used.

Modern acting styles have altered. Actors used to sing in a more operatic style, but now singing performances are more natural in scale. These performances are quieter, and require more amplification. Musical orchestrations are also much bigger than they used to be and they generally don't reduce that much when somebody is singing. This again drives the voice amplification louder.

Nick Lidster

How much of a role sound designers play is dependent upon the producer or director who hires them. Their function can be defined by the needs of the director or the needs of the theatre space. Basically the sound designer controls everything everyone hears in the theatre. On the technological side the designer decides how much amplification is needed, where the microphones are hung, and what sound effects are chosen. Every single word needs to be heard. On the aesthetic side, the designer aids in telling the story. Sometimes the sound designer needs to consider where emphasis is placed. Will the sound be enhanced by reverb to create an effect to call attention to a plot point? Do voices need to be coming from different places in the theatre? When is an effect needed? Who are the characters talking to? These decisions come only after reading the script multiple times and talking to the director.

The production team works together to figure out how to bring the effects to life. For example, Peter Hylenski describes the difficulty in choosing the right sorts of farts and burps to accompany the action of *Shrek*. Robert Cashill explains that members of the production team sat down and considered the timbre of farts for the song "I Think I Got You Beat." They rated farts one by one. At another point they had to decide on "Shrek roars" and searched for a sound that did not frighten children. The production also uses numerous ambient effects as underscoring to the action. The sound team chose the diverse sounds of Shrek's world, from crickets in the swamp to dungeon noises. Their aim was to create a bridge between Shrek's world and the world that the audience inhabited.

> The day we had burp and fart auditions was the day we were all wondering where our careers had led us. It was me, Jason, the composer, Jeanine Tesori, and the book and lyrics writer, David Lindsay-Abaire, sitting around a table listening to a computer play back numerous recordings. We played them all through, and if something caught someone's ear, they'd say "that's a funny fart," and we'd classify them. They had to fit musically as well. Jeanine had a hard time with the burps and left the table after a while. It did get a little gross.
>
> **Peter Hylenski**

Hylenski's design for the sound systems included choosing the right microphones to fit in the prosthetics used to create the animal costumes for the actors. Microphones had to be placed correctly to pick up the actors' voices without distortion. It took close collaboration with the prosthetics designer to find a solution. As well they transformed part of the backstage space into a studio space for part of the orchestra, and had to design an audiovisual link to the conductor so that the orchestra could act as a unit. The sound designer and composer chose this tactic so that they could give the music a studio precision in a live environment. The system was organized to carry out the conception of the piece.

The designer works with a production **sound engineer**, also called a **mixer** or a **soundboard operator**, who is responsible for the running of the show. Sound quality is not consistent for audiences since there are a variety of factors that influence how sound is heard. Therefore, there is a sound operator present to use the mixing desk to make adjustments to the output. Humidity, temperature, a full house compared to an empty house, overheated electronics, a singer having an off-day all have an effect on the quality of a sound. Live sound engineering is mostly about taking something that exists already and amplifying it. Apart from **playbacks** and **sound effects**, the designer and operator do not create anything. The lighting designer and lighting console operator in comparison create the light. Sound engineering is all about having a responsibility to the original sound sources, and to the audience. The operator is the medium through which the sound flows. Lighting, however, creates its own effects. In this sense, the lighting designer's function is similar to the music composer, and the lighting console operator is similar to a musician.

> There were lots of other shows along the way to *The Woman In White*, but this show was a real challenge. A very natural sound, intimate at times and yet dynamic and cinematic at others. It's also like two different scores: one that is very natural and orchestral, and one that is darker and more synthesized. Again we did a lot of the show in surround, often just subliminally to open up the sound and make it bigger without it getting louder. It was a big job, but *The Woman In White* was the most enjoyable thing I've done. Andrew Lloyd Webber and Trevor Nunn, the director, were very precise and aware of how it should sound. There are big moments that envelop you and help tell the story, yet it never feels overblown, and always comes back to a human level.
>
> **Mick Potter**

Ross Brown explains that sound design is an organization of sound and silence in a framework of time. This philosophy allows the designer to approach sound design as a piece of music. The sound designer asks questions of what the director may have in mind for their production. Reading the text through this filter allows the designer to consciously develop ideas and channel them in the direction of the director's notions, not necessarily the designer's own.

The designer's process

Unlike the sets, costumes, and lights where the design does not change for each performance, sound design relies on inputs that produce variable results night to night. Sound designers must be flexible in their design so that they can adjust the sounds that actors produce. They use **microphones** to pick up sounds and then use loudspeakers to transmit those sounds. Sound design is both a technical component of producing amplification as well as an aesthetic strategy to support production design. As with all design practice, each designer approaches the task his or her own way. Musicals and plays have different requirements, so the processes and the technology the designer employs can differ. Also different projects have a different range of collaborators. Conceptual design is a more immersive aesthetic exchange

This is the mixing board for *Frankenstein*. Here we see the annotated script with notes regarding sound cues as well as details regarding sound levels. Each of the channels can control a different microphone. The operator can make adjustments on the spot during production to make up for variable sound quality, a weak performance, or other interference. The preset cues as well as the live cues are indicated in the script. The soundboard operator plays the soundboard as if it is a musical instrument. Moment to moment variations in the physical sound coming from the stage is adjusted to achieve optimal output.

than a job that only requires amplifying voices. The amplification and recording of the human voice is a function of sound equipment. While a soundboard operator can manipulate the sonic qualities of the actor's voice, designers manipulate these qualities to influence the emotional content of the drama. Why does the ogre's voice need to be so deep? Is this a natural sound used to convince the audience that this is the way he speaks? It is more likely that the director and sound designer understood the ability of the rich low voice to affect the audience emotional response.

I read the script and listen to the music several times – once with the script and a couple of times whilst doing something fairly undemanding in order to see what stands out (and what doesn't). I obtain a cast list, an orchestra line-up and acquaint myself with the theatre if I don't already know it, and after all that I decide first of all, believe it or not, on a speaker system that I feel is appropriate for the job. After that I go about physically designing the show by doing some preliminary drawings of the mixer, listing any special functions and spinning off all the other drawings from it. I'll always try to introduce a new product, but usually only one on any new show.

Andrew Bruce

Similarly to set, costume, and light designers, when sound designers begin they collect as much information about a production and venue as they can. After reading the script and listening to recordings of music from the show they examine the scale drawings of the venue and design the **loudspeaker system** from those. To determine what they need, they consider how big the theatre is, how the seats are laid out, and whether there are hanging positions left on the batons/pipes. They determine what microphones will be needed and what systems are required based on who has been cast. A major consideration of what is chosen is that an audience's perception of what is being said often relies on a visual connection with a performer more than on amplification levels. Audiences often say they cannot hear an actor if they cannot see his or her face, and it may be necessary to amplify the voices louder for the back of the theatre, than in the middle of the stalls/ house where the audience has good visual contact.

When the designer talks with the director about what he or she wants, a good designer will ask questions. Is the show's sound imagined as conceptual, rock'n'roll, live, or realistic? A show like *American Idiot* was a re-imagining of a rock album, so the team had to decide whether the aural experience was meant to be like attending a rock concert. A show like *Equus* was a straight play, and the team had to decide how much of the sound is conceptual or how much is dictated by the script. To achieve the sound of the show the designer must collaborate with a committee of designers and technicians. The director, musical director, the costume designer, and wig master will all have a say in where wires and microphone packs go, the set and lighting designers have a say in where the speakers get hung. Will the speakers obstruct the lighting instruments if they are hung on the same pipe? Decisions have to be made on whether the team is going to try and hide things. Can a speaker be placed in scenery? For example, in *Wicked* vines were hung over the speakers and then painted to integrate them into the scenery.

Blocking also affects sound quality. Part of the sound designer's job is getting people to understand that by blocking in one way the other production team members can create amplification problems, while if blocked in another way they can achieve a similar effect that is conducive to good sound. A change in the distance of a microphone gives a rich sound close up. For example, the sounds of Jerry Herman work well with close up headsets, but that is a different solution than the sounds generated by forehead microphones in *Hairspray*. In the case of designing a musical it is important also to meet with the music director to go through the show, so that notes can be made and the stage directions printed in the libretto can be confirmed. This meeting is often scheduled after the show has been cast and rehearsals have started, since by this time the music director will be able to identify the stronger and weaker voices. When going through the libretto the designer might look out for romantic duets to check with the director about exactly how affectionate the actors will be since it poses a technical problem; feedback can occur when two radio microphones get too close. Both the director and the designer think of things, and the ideas will transform over time. Does the designer have the telephone object ring, have a speaker nearby with the sound, or put the ring in the wings? There is an unspoken rule that good sound design is there but the audience is not aware of it. An audience should not worry about hearing the words over the **underscoring**. Anything that takes away from understanding the actors is a distraction. Once the underscoring in a scene is defined the designer is given license to do more, since sound will underscore every thought of the characters. In a musical a designer may keep the dialogue and underscored scenes subtle and natural, so that when the songs come along they can create a bigger sound. Sound designers scour play texts for any loud scenes that might cause problems, such as fight scenes or shouting matches. Screams are a problem, because a scream is substantially louder than other vocalizations. In general the soundboard operator makes on-the-spot changes to variable voice levels in dialogue, in a song, or where music is played under spoken dialogue.

> The hardest thing in designing sound for theatre is that you have to concep-tualize how a show will take shape. This means designing the sound system, preparing a bid list and most of the scale and line drawings, then putting it out to bid and building and installing the system months before the cast are on stage and the creative team is in the theatre. You have to ask lots of questions that people don't always want to answer at an early stage – because their focus is elsewhere – so that by the time you get into the theatre, you've covered all your bases. By that stage, it's most important to concentrate on the detail and creative aspects of the show without having to worry about achieving complex orchestra monitoring, sound effects spinning around the auditorium, or simply having enough headroom for the vocals.
>
> **Mick Potter**

An example of a designer whose work encompasses both technical and conceptual sound design is Jonathan Deans, who has collaborated with Cirque du Soleil since 1992. There he worked with the company for two and one half years developing their production of *KÀ* for the MGM Grand in Las Vegas. As the production was to take place in a new venue, he designed a sound system for the venue as well as the show. His process began by designing and installing sound, video, and intercom systems. Next he went to work with the production team to create an equipment list for what they would need. These lists are created to convey design approach rather than the nuts and bolts of cable lengths and bolt measurements. Instead he created what he terms "intention drawings." He worked with the team to create a versatile system that could be adjusted. According to John Huntington his most innovative contribution to the show was a custom-made headrest for the audience seats that allows the movement of sound and can manipulate how the audience hears the show. As well it can misdirect perception of where sound originates. Sound became an interactive design element that was as playful as the physical acrobatics of the performers. He developed an aural equivalent to the style and mode of Cirque's expression. His process merged the technical and conceptual roles of the sound designer. He both designed the sound systems as well as manipulated the systems to create conceptual effects that worked in tandem with the performers and other design elements.

Straight plays take less time to design, even if they are no less complicated in their conception. The process is more concerned with sound effects or composing music that may underscore or evoke the world that the production seeks to create. One of the central roles of sound in this situation is to create a sense of where the characters are. In a musical the music accomplishes this with its orchestration. However, in a play sound effects are used to tell the audience where the characters are located. For example the audience may hear rain, honking, and music thumping from a nearby disco. Immediately weather, urban density, and mood are apparent. Sound can also tell the audience what year the characters live in, giving audiences an instant knowledge of the time. An audience will recognize songs or musical logos on the television. Sometimes verisimilitude of sounds is called for, while at other times a designer may compose a sense of a sound to suit the play. For example, a sound designer may think that *The Sound of Music* might have Austrian bells, or the sound of Vespers. Most often a designer does not authentically reproduce a sound, but rather captures a sound that the audience thinks something sounds like. *The Sound of Music* does not need to have Austrian church bells ringing across a graveyard. Authenticity is fun, but the production needs a soundscape to suit the needs of the text first. The sound designer will draw from the bank of sounds that have been acquired over the course of a career to select one that most fits the emotion of the scene or what will best evoke the appropriate response from the audience.

Audiences have grown to expect a certain range of quality of sound since we are so accustomed to film and music recordings, and to achieve it sound designers have to increase the level of sound in the sound system to cover up the ambient noise of the lights or of the street outside. Microphones are expected now. While some long nostalgically for days before amplification, claiming performers were so much stronger, however audiences could not adequately hear voices over brass and drums. Acoustics help audiences hear better in a given space, but theatres are adapted over time and their acoustics get distorted. Each genre and each medium needs different amplification. Opera's sound requirements are different from a musical's, and different again from a straight play's. Amplification makes the sound more realistic. Building an appropriate sound system is integral to the successful sound design.

The basic sound system

Sound reinforcement in theater has improved massively in the time I have been involved in the business. This process has led to some very nice sounding designs being devised that are both clear and have good vocal intelligibility. However, their basic design concepts are still the same; you hear the performer coming from the stage and the orchestra coming from the pit. Unfortunately, this is becoming ever more difficult. Indeed, with the recent massive increase in the level of general background noise coming from scenery control motors and noisy lighting equipment, the average level a sound system now has to run at to get above basic background noise is becoming ridiculous. Nevertheless, theater is all about human interaction and storytelling and I still believe people like the notion that the singing and acting is coming from the performer on stage. And while modern shows allow us to step out and stretch the boundaries some of the time, essentially the criteria for normal theater musical sound design stays pretty much the same as it ever has.

Nick Lidster

A sound system operates by converting the physical energy of sound waves into electrical energy, increasing the power of the electrical energy using circuitry, and then converting this energy back into physical energy in the form of sound waves. The simple, practical sound system is made up of **input transducers**, which convert sound waves into a **signal**, **signal processing**, which manages the signal, and **output transducers**, which transmit the sounds. In other words, three microphones

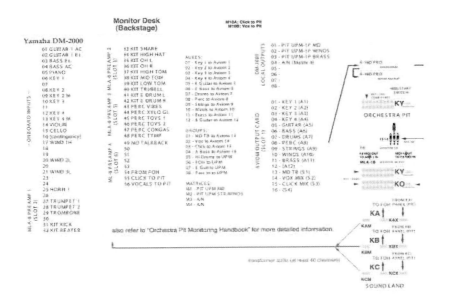

Courtesy of Tony Meola

A sound design is made up of papers and digital media such as system schematics, cue sheets, annotated scripts, musical scores, show disks with pre-recorded music. These demos and cues do not convey what you will get in the spatial acoustics of the theatre, where the voices of the actors, the presence of the audience, and the acoustics of the room will have a transforming effect. Much of what the sound designer does happens live. A soundboard operator monitors the physical sources input and mixes it before it is output to the audience. A clear understanding of which microphones are placed where and what type of experience is being achieved at any moment is integral to a successful performance.

are connected to separate inputs on a **mixing desk**. Each input on the desk provides **pre-amplification**, which amplifies the microphone level signals to **line level**, **equalization**, which provides the means to contour the tonal balance of each microphone, and **level control**, which allows the operator to adjust the relative level of each individual microphone. The mixing desk then combines the inputs to a single line level output. The output of the console is connected to a **power amplifier**, which boosts the console's line level output to a level suitable to drive the loudspeaker. A **loudspeaker** then converts the power amplifier output signal into sound pressure waves. The level of the sound is much higher than that of the original unaided sound. Every sound system is an extension of this basic model.

Transducers are a technology that converts energy from one form into another. Common examples are loudspeakers, microphones, and headphones. **Microphones** convert fluctuating sound waves into an electrical current that is an analog representation of the source sound wave. **Loudspeakers** convert the electrical signal back into physical energy. Devices that actually amplify and change the characteristics of the electrical audio signal are called signal processors. In its simplest form, a signal processor increases the power of the electrical signal coming out of the microphone and going into the loudspeaker. This sort of signal processor is an **amplifier**. Sound systems often include many more types of signal processors, which are used to effect change on any number of different audio signals.

The theatrical environment where the sound system is used can alter the output of the system. For example in a **free-field environment**, such as on an open field, there are very few objects that will reflect the sound – trees, grass, and spectators will tend to absorb sound, rather than reflect it. In these locations the designer has more flexibility than in an enclosed space and can play with the sound system because he or she does not have to worry about reflected sound waves causing acoustic feedback. On the other hand, in a small room with hard walls, the designer has to worry about reflections caused by the amplified sound bouncing off the walls and affecting the overall intelligibility of the system. In a small room with padded walls, the designer will not worry about intelligibility, as the padding will tend to absorb sound rather than reflect it. To work around these constraints designers consider a number of factors including speaker selection and positioning, microphone selection and positioning, and tuning or equalization of a system in a given space.

Whenever you do a show with such a high profile, you have to be prepared to hear from all kinds of people who have all kinds of opinions. My biggest challenge was creating a sound system that fit into the St. James Theatre and would satisfy the desires of my own creative and producing team, Green Day, the general public and lastly, me. I was always confident I would do that, but I also knew it would take the whole preview process. Inexperienced people think that the show will always sound the way it did on the first performance. It's quite a challenge making people relax while that process is unfolding.

Brian Ronan

Brian Ronan put together the sound system for *American Idiot*. In an interview with Ellen Lampert-Gréaux he describes the project as a blend of concert and musical. The sound system was meant to let the audience feel as if they were a part of a huge crowd at a Green Day concert. He also wanted to help the audience connect with the characters by letting the audience listen to the complex lyrics of the piece and understand the storyline. To accomplish this he divided zones onstage and offstage that allowed each area to be adjusted on their own. Performers could hear the music, the singer's words could be heard, or the audience could lose themselves in the rhythm of the music. The setting is a vast cavern with a fire escape and televisions affixed to the walls; its stage is divided into different zones that depict multiple locations. Initially Ronan was concerned with the director Michael Mayer and set designer Christine Jones's positioning of the band around the set, but it was his job to figure out how to make the sounds work for this scenic solution to making the band contribute to the story. Every design choice referred back to the experience that he wanted to create for the audience. For previews he used different microphones and monitored the musicians and singers differently than for the Broadway production. Each space had different acoustical problems and had to be treated differently to achieve the same effects. The sound designer puts together the sound system, and conveys the sound content to the audience, reinforces audibility, and crafts music or effects. By creating a soundscape he or she sculpts an environment of which the audience is not deeply conscious. Its effect should be subtle, drawing attention by taking sound away. A designer can layer background noise – the din of life – by adding and subtracting the racket of birds, bells, and whistles. As well, its contrast, silence, can be used as counterpoint. Continual noise gets filtered out. Thus, the adding and subtracting of sound can craft tension; take it away or bring it back for change or for emphasis. It is a fusion of others' work and ideas in collaboration to help the audience with what is going on in the production. On the stage not only the physics, but the psychological properties of sound become important. It is not simply mechanics – it is a physiological sensation that elicits a psychological response in the audience. The object is to move the audience, to create a world, suggest an environment, or evoke an emotion.

Wicked: A fantasy world with a natural sound

Wicked is a musical adaptation of Gregory Maguire's *Wicked: The Life and Times of the Wicked Witch of the West*, where audiences learn the back-story to Dorothy's adventures in Oz. Maguire's novel uses the world that L. Frank Baum's classic *Wonderful Wizard of Oz* created to show how the perspectives of the witches were formed by their past. His novel is a metaphor for the repressive world of a police state and the position in it of its political elite. Stephen Swartz wrote the music and lyrics and Winnie Holzman wrote the book. *Wicked* chronicles the story of an unlikely friendship between Glinda and Elphaba – a.k.a the good and wicked witches of Oz. The two young women are

173

thrust together as roommates when they begin as Sorcery Students at Shiz University. They are polar opposites. Glinda is a shallow blonde who leads the glamorous life of a popular student, and Elphaba is a girl with a peculiar green complexion who is misunderstood because she is a loner and keeps to herself. While the two manage to develop a friendship it becomes strained when their mutual ambitions come in conflict. Following an encounter with the Wizard of Oz, they reach a crossroads and each chooses to take a very different path as a result of their understanding of the true politics controlling their world. Glinda's unflinching desire for popularity leads her to be seduced by power while Elphaba's determination to remain true to herself and her ideals, and to those around her, has unexpected and shocking consequences for her future. Their life choices secure their public personas as Glinda The Good and Elphaba the Wicked Witch of the West – regardless of whether good and bad are defined as truly black and white.

Swartz discovered the novel in 1995 and finally persuaded Maguire to give him the rights in 1998. The book, lyrics, and score for the musical were developed through a series of readings that tried to condense the complex plot while retaining its dramatic excitement. They took the hated figure of Elphaba and told the story from her point of view, and to have the two witches be roommates in college, but the way in which their friendship and the whole plot develops is different onstage. Characters survive who were murdered in the novel and relationships were simplified. In 2000, Swartz and Holzman recruited producer David Stone, to begin the transition to a full Broadway production, and Joe Mantello was brought in as director. They hired Eugene Lee for scenic design, Susan Hilferty for costume design, Kenneth Posner for lighting design, Tony Meola, for sound design, and Elaine J. McCarthy for projection design. Posner was nominated for a Tony award and Lee and Hilferty won Tonys for their designs.

Wicked was designed for one of the largest theatres on Broadway, the 1,933-seat Gershwin. The volume of the house was a challenge for the design team. Meola has a lot of volume to fill with sound. David Barbour and David Johnson describe how Meola thought that with such a long orchestra floor it would be difficult to get sound into the side seats without making the rest of the house too loud. Another obstacle was that the theatre's ventilation system was too loud. Meola's team had to rebalance the system to bring down the ambient noise in the room to manageable levels. For the music and the voices to reach the back of the house and be understood clearly he chose to install larger loudspeakers. His system was made up of speakers and an **equalization system**, which he chose to get him what he describes as the most real and natural sound. He believes that live qualities of performance are what make the theatre a vital form, and the more technology designers put between the actor and the audience, the farther away sound designers get from what they do best. To accentuate this live illusion he designs the sound to appear as if it is coming from the performer on stage and not from a speaker on the wall. In most of the productions he designs, microphones and loudspeakers are not parts of the story itself, but rather they help tell the story. For example, the Wizard's voice is mostly pre-recorded and played back on cue from the console, but with live processing in the form of pitch shifting down several octaves.

If Madonna is on tour and a piece of the set conflicts with the placement of the speaker, the speaker wins. In the theatre, the sound is usually the last art to be called in and you have to negotiate your place amongst the other artists: the producers, the director, the musical director, the orchestrator and the stars. There's an order in the theatre that has to be observed. Sound has to be deferential, but not submissive.

Tony Meola

Meola divided the sound system into two independent systems, one for the vocals and another for the orchestra. By dividing each group he is able to use a different type of speaker, which suits each type of sound better. Furthermore, he wanted the grouped sounds to come from different locations in the stage space. The instruments' sounds come from the orchestra pit rather than over the proscenium, and the vocals come from center stage where the actor stands rather than from left and right. This enables him to reinforce the live, unmediated quality of the sound design. He explained to *Live Design* that he tries to place the microphones as close to the center of the head as possible, generally running down through the actor's hairline to be as concealed as possible most of the time. The further off-center he placed the microphone, the more high-end sound he lost and had to manually make up for at the console. Hilferty worked closely with Meola insuring that the material in a hat would not interfere and distort the sound going into a microphone fastened in wigs or sideburns. They tested fabrics until they found one that worked. Wires are run through the lace on costumes as camouflage and transmitters are tucked into them. Unlike instrumentalists who have fixed positions, actors move throughout the whole space. The sound operator has to account for this in a live mix so that the audience hears the sound in a manner consistent with real life, allowing them to focus on the actor on the stage rather than on the speakers transmitting their voices.

The orchestra does not have to be in the auditorium with the actors for it to sound natural. Thanks to new technology if the pit lacks space, as it does at the Gershwin Theatre, the designer can microphone the instruments remotely. In this case, the production team was able to expand the pit to give the orchestra some more room, but space was still limited because there is scenery in it. In the end they decided to micro-phone the percussionist and harpist remotely. Sound designers find that scenic designers often take orchestra pit space as if it were stage space. As a collaborator the designer must weigh what is worth it and what is not. In the case of *Wicked* Meola felt that scenery in the pit helped the story, so he was willing to work around it. Meola prior-itizes helping the story and its plotline and the audience's connection to it. Compromise and collaboration are an integral part of incorporating

Photo © Denise Teoh

the sonic world into the visual world of the design. The sound for *Wicked* was a mix of technical manipulation to give the audience a consistent amplification of the actors' voices and organization of the musical sound production. Its success was due to the seamless integration of all of the design elements.

The loudspeakers are hidden within Lee's Clock of the Time Dragon. Speakers are often masked behind scenery or hung from light batons. In this case, the dragon is as tall as a giraffe and is made of painted leather with scales made of overlapping disks of copper, bronze, and iron. There are plenty of places to hide speakers. When it flexes its wings they make a sound like a bellows. Meola wanted to be sure that the loudspeakers were invisible to the audience. This is what contributes to the audience's perception that the sound is natural. Also, they are unaware that the pit is amplified separately from the performers. The live sound is presented as it is expected to be – like it is in the sounds of the recorded cinema.

What sound design adds to a production

The sounds used in theatre take on many forms and are used for a variety of reasons. In theatre production audible events are organized for the purposes of communication – either as music composition or sound design. The sound designer's task consists of amplifying or otherwise manipulating the actor's voice, recreating sounds as they naturally occur, and influencing the emotional content of the drama. Most sound designers agree that adequate audibility is always their first responsibility. However, a good design can transmit the human voice in speech or song, establish locale with ambient noises such as bird song or traffic noises, or establish atmosphere with sounds such as wind and rain. Sound manipulation creates and sustains mood with combinations of devices used for locale and atmosphere, distortion of speech, or soft music.

The use of sound can establish locale, time of year, day or night, weather conditions. It is used to evoke atmosphere, to link scenes, as an emotional stimulus, to reproduce physical happenings with spot cues likes cars arriving, babies crying, or clocks chiming. Furthermore, sound effects are any sound produced by mechanical or human means to create for the audience a noise or a sound associated with the play being produced. For example, a wooden drum made from slats can produce a wind noise. When the drum is turned by crank it makes a noise like a howling wind. Sound effects create, reinforce, or counterpoint the atmosphere or mood; reveal character; or contribute to the advancement of the plot. Sound effects do not have to be faithful reproductions of the subjects concerned.

Sound can enhance the depth and meaning of the play, its atmosphere and mood. Is it designed for acoustic reinforcement? Or are music and environmental sounds used to enhance dramatic impact? For example, for a production of *Sherlock Holmes* the designer Robert Kaplowitz decided to take a sound that the audience would associate with the title character. Holmes plays the violin, so the violin is used as a starting point – though he did not use violin music, rather he used the sounds of the strings to make an aural texture that conveyed ambience and emotion. One way to construct unreal worlds is to play sounds on a sampler. The idea was to add to the action of the play so that the audience could understand what it is that the director wanted them to know. The sound designer will ask how to make the world of the play interesting on an aural level. Is there a rhythmic or tonal way to connect the audience? How is the sound particular to this world? The designer will listen for what is there, for what is not there, to consider whether there is space to add to or make more meaningful. In a musical the designer sets out to discover what the composers are trying to achieve in their score and then figure out how to bring it to an audience. Whether the composer wants to immerse the audience in sound, or punctuate the dialogue, guides the designer in the choices of technology, in the tactics for choosing microphones, and in the concept for the underscoring. The next chapter describes in more detail how the production team works collaboratively to realize the designs for production.

The collaborative process

8

Key Topics:

- How does a group of designers work together to enhance a director's vision?
- The design meeting
- Collaboration in process
- Behind the scenes with the design teams

Case Studies:

- *The Phantom of the Opera* collaboration
- *The Lion King* collaboration
- Organizing John Guare's *Six Degrees of Separation*

This chapter introduces the basic ways in which ideas transform as a result of collaborative development. How does a group of designers work together to enhance the director's vision? What types of compromises must be made to create an organic design where the separate components complement each other? In the end it is impossible to disentangle the end product from the process of collaboration for good or bad. As we have discussed in past chapters, it is not enough to create a unified design. Each designer's part must work in concert with the design components of collaborators to move harmoniously toward the expression of the director's vision. The lines, hues, proportion, and so on must contribute to the overall concepts put forward through setting, costume, lighting, sound, projections, and actor blocking. Each of these components must be considered as the production moves forward through opening night. When all of the designers are in the same room during technical rehearsals, they must make on-the-spot adjustments to their designs. There are always surprises. One tone of hue may work well under the light of the costume shop, but when placed under the stage lighting the hues and values may change in a way that does not convey the original intent of a particular moment or scene.

The proposed structure and format of the actor's environment, derived from the reading of the script, is a statement of the show's direction. This plotting of the flow of movement is the designer's first chore, though it will be augmented and revised by the director and the rest of the design team. Half of the business of design is learning to play well with others. While the designer is the number one collaborator of the director, a committee does not put traditional configurations of theatre together; someone must make the final decision, whether it is the scenographer, auteur, or director. The production team works together to comb through the script to check for all contingencies and business. The designers work to create concrete physical things that function onstage to express the concept of the play. Rendering, modeling, and research are tools for making the play function in three dimensions in concert with the various elements of production.

How does a group of designers work together to enhance the director's vision?

Collaboration is process and part of its joy, as in a journey with friends, but many younger designers are too insecure to be good collaborators. Their work declares itself gorgeously and arrogantly, but forgets that the whole is greater than the sum of its parts, and that the play is the thing – in the long run, the only thing that matters.

Marjorie Kellogg

Collaboration begins with conversation. What does the director imagine? How does the design team understand the characters, the place, and the world? Listening is integral to figuring out what the style is and how the team understands the play or musical. While designers all have their own way of working and imagining, they are flexible in their thinking because they are in constant conversation with others. They must work to bring alive others' ideas in concert with their creative output. Constant adjustment allows for the play to come together in a holistic manner. The order in which the designers become involved is a result of the practicalities of the theatre. Bids for the scenery must go in early, so the set designer is the first collaborator. Next costumes are added because they must be built. Lighting and sound come in next. By no means are these practicalities a matter of one discipline having the definitive interpretation. Rather discussion leads the design team to tailor the visual world of the play around the human characters who will inhabit it. The text provides the details that allow the production team to imagine what the characters look like, what they wear, and how they feel within that environment, what they feel about each other, and how their journey changes them. Together, in concert with each other, the designers imagine the what, when, where, and how.

The design meeting

> In my own work with directors, I never remember who came up with the best idea. Sometimes it was me; sometimes not. In the future, credit should read "production by," and all involved should be credited.
>
> **John Conklin**

The first thing any designer does is to read the script. Some read as if it is radio play, holding back imagery until the director gets involved. While thinking about a production begins well before the first meeting, many enjoy working off the excitement of the director who gets the ideas flowing. As we described in previous chapters, the first meeting may be as small as the scenic designer and the director, or as large as the whole design team and the director. The concerns of scenic designers are considered first because the environment needs to be defined first. After the director understands the shape of the world, then each other element is added. It is the director's job to bring together the team to formulate a complete environment that will make sense to the interpretation offered. Often before the world of the set is defined the director does not know how the characters live within that environment. Collaboration gives definition to vague concepts and preliminary thoughts. Together the production team determines what the show is going to be like.

A director usually just talks. If not, good designers ask lots of questions. What do you want this show to be like? What do you imagine the show to be like for the audience? Every team has a different way of working together, but conversation is at the heart of all collaboration. By the first meeting a designer will have some images, ideas or references to start a dialogue with. Some will come in with research, images, or movies. For example, the costume designer Catherine Zuber likes the director to tell her how he sees each character. She will interview the director about each character in the play. A designer needs to see how the director understands and sees the character so that he or she can honor what the director sees. She will have her own different views from her reading but they need to work off the same point since the other designers, actors, and production team will be guided from the director's perspective. They begin with a slow dialogue over dinner or in a one-and-a-half-hour meeting. For the second meeting a designer will come back with sketches to work from. It is important to honor how each collaborator sees the characters. First sketches of characters emerge in concert with the director. However, once casting takes place the ideas will transform again. Change happens with each added collaborator. One must understand how the team is visualizing the scenes.

> No two people design the same way and there are no two directors who direct the same way. Some directors are much more visually interested and others are more cerebrally interested. As a designer you have to be somewhat of a chameleon and get under the skin of the director. You sort of have to have a love affair with the director because you're creating this piece as a team – there's a director and a lighting designer and a set designer and a sound designer. All of you are really like a cog in the wheel, so you all have to really be in love with each other for the time that you're all working on that project. Sometimes I take along research for the first meeting with a director. If I don't know a director, I will perhaps just go and hear what they have to say and then go back and have another meeting to say we can go this way or that way.
>
> **Jane Greenwood**

Each collaborative team is different, and how they work depends upon the habits of the director. Designers who have the opportunity work together to learn each other's strengths and work intuitively to incorporate all points of view. The set designer will meet first with the director because often determining what the world looks like needs to be conceived first before colors, textures, and moods are thought about. Overall the setting must be scaled to real people. A set is a performance space that is not complete until actors inhabit that space. How do people look in relation to the world of the setting? The ground plan is essential because a set can get in the way of the actors performing within the space. Sets leave room for the inclusion of the actors, the costumes, and the lighting. Set designers imagine how the palettes of the costumer will fit and how the lighting will tie it all together. One might limit the use of colors to allow other elements to exploit the rest of the palette. Sometimes all the designers will meet at that point if they can get everyone in the same room. The set designer wants to get the director to talk about the views of the characters. Directors leave a lot of leeway for the costume designer. A costumer wants to know the tone, feel, or mood of images – is it warm or cool, rough-hewn or slick shiny? The collaborators exchange material continually. Paint chips, fabric swatches, gel samples can all help the team understand which direction they are going in with color. The team tries to imagine the landscape of the world. All designers would love to be involved from the outset listening to see how the ideas are progressing, though financial practicalities often prevent this from occurring. A kernel in those meetings can mature into images.

Collaboration in process

> I absolutely believe in collaboration. It's the drug, the hook that has made me an addict of theatre. I'm not interested in Fine Art, or in crawling away to a studio and doing a painting. It's too isolated. As frustrating as communication can be at times, it's also ecstatically energizing when ideas that come from outside of you draw you outside of yourself as well.
>
> **Michael Olich**

The following case studies show how collaboration enables the production team to hone their interpretations to enhance the story, and how they adapt ideas to balance and support each other's work as well as adapt to the unexpected dilemmas that arise during technical production. Together the director, set designer, costume designer, light designer, sound designer, and other members of the production team find solutions to the goal of how to best evoke the world of the play on stage. There is no single way to go about it. It is a constant struggle to find the most productive working relationships. Sometimes it is as simple as the way in which an idea is presented, so that it is inclusive and presented as an option that one might try. A designer might suggest that he or she was thinking about the scene and propose that the team try some option. The director, musical director, designers, actors, and musicians all feed off of each other, and some of the most amazing transformations take place with the show when they are all locked in a room for twelve hours a day. Many designers feed off this creative exchange.

The Phantom of the Opera collaboration

Set in multiple spectacular locations, the musical *The Phantom of the Opera,* based on Gaston Leroux's novel, tells the story of a mysterious masked figure who lurks in the catacombs beneath the Paris Opera House. Obsessed with Christine, a naive young soprano, he devotes himself to making her into a star by nurturing her talents and by deviously manipulating the management. However, as he falls for her, she falls in love with the handsome Raoul. Enraged, the Phantom nearly kills Christine, but soon decides to intimidate the theatre management into letting her star in the freakish opera he has composed for her and lures her across the underground lake into his secret lair.

One of the *coups de théâtre* of *The Phantom of the Opera* (1986) is a chandelier that comes crashing down. Its context tells the audience where in time they are, and it creates the atmosphere of the Opera in its glory and in its dereliction. The chandelier is a controlling metaphor used through the musical.

It is first used in the auction during the prologue establishing the first narrative frame in 1905. At the end of the auction, the chandelier rises, transporting the audience back to 1881 when the Opera was at its peak. Its most spectacular use comes at the end of the first act when it comes crashing to the stage. To pull this feat off, it took the coordination of the set designer and light designer as well as the technical crew, running crew, and specialists. Like architects, theatre designers need a team of engineers, builders, painters, and carpenters to figure out how to make their designs come to life. Mike Barnett and Will Bowen had to figure out the engineering of these effects. The effect required the work of six different scenery shops over six months painting, constructing the sets, lighting, and finally devising the automation. It involved safety issues, configuring the traveling and tilting bridge platform, and conceiving how the mass of the staircase could be fit within the confines of the theatre's limited backstage. Collaboration is a complicated process requiring negotiation, teamwork, and trust.

In this case the collaborative process began with the producer, Cameron Mackintosh, when he sent a sampling of five designers' work to Hal Prince so they could choose the design team. This packet included Maria Björnson's speculative drawings. Prince chose Björnson's picture out of the pile because despite the opulence of the script her design was minimalist. She chose to use rectangular, wooden louvers and furniture to create a vast architectural performance space. He felt that this simple environment invited the audience in to watch a story. Björnson believes that settings should not sit on stage as decorative façades, but have a dynamic life even without the actors within it. Once Björnson was hired, Richard Pilbrow was considered, but Andrew Bridge ultimately was hired to do the lighting.

As Andrew Lloyd Weber and Hal Prince began hashing out the style of the piece in 1985, Prince and Björnson began the development process by talking extensively over the course of 1985 and 1986 until what Prince regards as a major breakthrough occurred. One evening, he watched a BBC documentary in which crippled men and women were seen in everyday activities. In an interview he recounted that these people had a healthy and uncomplicated way of gratifying their sexual needs. He showed this program to Björnson and they realized that the emotional pull of the Phantom is his erotic aura. They chose to accentuate the eroticism inherent in the source material and find a way to express it through the scenery.

Though Björnson was not known as a conceptualist, collaborators describe her as a great partner, who once the structure was established was able to find freedom within the structure and create marvels. She began the common practice with a new piece of developing her designs for *Phantom* before the script was completed. With instruction from Prince, who had a simple concept of setting it in a black conjurer's box where all of the action seemingly comes out of nothing, her initial designs were placed in a black box. However, Björnson used color, shape, and movement set against that darkness to carry the audience through the course of the play. She used the fluid quality of the black box as a foundation to evoke location. Critics agree that an important component of the play is its strong sense of place. This evocative sense of location was achieved in part because the team visited the Paris Opera House, exploring its heights and depths, and studying the building. The production team reportedly took hundreds of reference photos to help conceive of the set designs, and then supplemented that material with books and films about opera in the Victorian age. They were looking for a sense of the opera house's scale and style. What they were shocked to find was that its rococo grandeur and its hidden shadows gave it a creepy atmosphere. The contrast between its hidden secrets and its Victorian opulence became important to how they imagined the set. Early in the collaboration there was discussion about filling the Phantom's lair with opera memorabilia, costumes, and props he had collected on his visits upstairs to give him a sense of his passion and how long he had been lurking, stealing from the company. However, they found that this excess became overbearing and encapsulated too much of the story rather than supporting the narrative. Instead they pared down the props, choosing simple elements to suggest his psychological state or to foreshadow the action. Elements such as a cracked mirror, a dummy in a wedding dress, and iron bars enclosing the lair inside the black abyss beyond have the effect of suggesting a cage, leading the audience to see Christine as a caged bird. The setting and props did not try to tell the whole story, but rather contribute to the mood and atmosphere in which the action is carried out.

The team chose elements that might suggest more than literal location. The Phantom's search for sexual fulfillment helped not only to shape the show and the performances, but also this notion was the guiding principle that the team used to choose fabrics, props, and the atmospheric lighting. Statues depicting entangled human figures engaged in carnal acts frame the arch of the stage. Björnson then frames this with sumptuous fabric draping. Bridge uses light to accentuate the shadows, and set the lighting at low levels to give a dull and gloomy look to the setting. These choices evoke the sensuous world of the opera and the frustrated love of the central characters. The team decided to use the setting to organize the action. One setting is the elaborate proscenium. These images were a picture frame that focused the audience's attention on the action of the play. The second setting was for the three "cod" operas. These settings are opulent, filled with drops and elaborate costuming full of color constantly in motion. For the rest of the musical the visual details are sparse and open to allow the audience space to imagine what occurs in the dark. The audience's sense of how things ought to be fills in the details of the colors, patterns, and opulence of the staircase.

Collaboration is a necessity when problem solving the obstacles that the design team faces when working on a new piece. The small scale of Her Majesty's Theatre does not easily replicate the grandeur of the Paris Opera. Her Majesty's stage is too shallow to recreate the Garnier staircase. The production team needed to find a means of suggesting a large-scale architectural space while being limited by the volume of the stage space. Eventually with the help of the technical crew they were able to create the impression that the space was larger than it is by putting numerous manikins on the stairs as if they were crowded with people. The scale was important because Björnson wanted to use the staircase as a means to connect the metaphor of a descent into the subconscious. It had to take focus. Bridge explains in an interview that he loved the circular structure as a way to make concrete the character's subconscious desires that were enveloping them. To contribute to this metaphor he developed the idea of a lantern with striations echoing the structure of the stairs as a way of lighting the whole thing. Lighting took on a particularly important role in this play since the team wanted to conjure images out of darkness. Bridge's lighting choices were shaped to provide a menacing atmosphere shrouded in secrets. Audiences were to become aware of unspoken late-Victorian attitudes toward sexuality in the encroaching shadows. They were meant to feel disoriented and troubled and not quite sure why. Prince wanted the lighting to create a perfumed atmosphere where everything is seductive and mysterious. He wanted the show's rhythm to have a strong pulse that would propel it forward. Above all, the design team was encouraged to be contributors and collaborators, to help each other use their imaginations to fill in the spaces they have left blank.

Andrew Bridge describes how he was working off of the gothic style set up by Prince and Björnson. The characters move around in shadows and darkness as well as light, so high contrast is essential to the concept. In this world darkness is just as important as the light. He had to discover a way to link the minimalism of the set design to the light plot. Bridge describes his collaboration with the production team, noting Björnson's use of texture and attention to detail, and Prince's open experimental attitude where the designers could always try unplanned solutions. Most directors tell you that musicals need highly saturated light to pump up the energy as described in the discussion of *Hairspray*. However, in this case Prince asked explicitly to make things darker. Bridge chose to surround the sets with darkness, thus making the lighting often simpler and more economical than one might expect for musical theatre. He used only about four hundred lighting instruments, compared with the seven or eight hundred instruments normally employed in a West End or Broadway musical. He chose lighting instruments whose output he could control to pick out significant detail while leaving the rest of the stage space dim and spooky. It is reported that he tried to complement the spare style of the setting leaving details masked in shadow to stimulate the audience to imagine the details for themselves. The lighting team worked hard to create the effects. At one point when the Phantom crawls across the floor, there is a technician actually on his stomach in the wings directing a spotlight at the Phantom's face.

Collaboration flourishes when there is an understanding on the part of each member of the team that the others involved are to be respected and their authority fully recognized. The motions of carrying out

© Joan Marcus

Visible above the dry ice fog are tiny candles specially designed for this production. The ramp effect couples with rhythmic placement of candelabras (not visible here) and candles give the impression that the Phantom and Christine are traveling by water in the sewers underneath the city. It took collaboration between the set designer, the light designer, and engineers to pull off this effect. As well, sound levels had to be adjusted to account for all of the noise of the hydraulics and extra lights.

the collaboration the different techniques each group will require because of the personalities involved make collaboration a hope, not always an achievement.

Jean Rosenthal

One of the iconic images of the *Phantom* is when the Phantom and Christine travel by gondola to the Phantom's subterranean lair. Hundreds of candles rise up through tiny trap doors in the floor as they travel the canal. To achieve this effect Björnson and Bridge decided to use the nineteenth-century technology such as the original trapdoor system that Her Majesty's Theatre still had. Their solution to how to evoke a Victorian atmosphere was a balance between the practical constraints of a complicated scenic effect and conjuring an imaginary world to suggest the feeling of the experience. They wanted the journey to the lake to be a secret journey that the audience took part in. To give the impression of a long, labyrinthine journey downward, Björnson had to devise a scenic solution to the illusion of travel. She conceived of a piece of moving scenery called the "travelator," which is a ramp that tilts, moves in various directions, backtracks, and leads the gondola from upstage to downstage. Christine and the Phantom appear to float through the mist, and clusters of candles that rise up through the floor. These candles seemingly are conjured out of nothing. These lighting instruments were designed by Bridge. Since he could not use hundreds of candles burning on stage, he used tiny lamps containing even smaller lamps that twinkle in a silicon gel, giving the impression of flickering flame. Also, motorized wheels of gelled material and rotating disks are turned in front of spotlights to create the feeling of light on water or of flickering variations of gaslight. They conceived of the image using the structure of the staircase. They were inspired by a photo of light reflecting in the water in Venice and Björnson's memories of candles seemingly floating in the air in a Greek Orthodox Church. She felt that this image would highlight a sexual connotation akin to religious ecstasy in Christine and the Phantom's journey. Her design is a distortion of reality. It took collaboration between sets and lighting to reach the subconscious of the audience and get an emotional reaction without them realizing that they are feeling the Phantom's sexual energy. Only through collaboration were effective solutions to the design challenges overcome.

The Lion King collaboration

Though collaboration takes place to serve the ultimate decision making of the director and producers, collaborators serve an important function of moving the overall concept and vision to its optimal expression. Compromise and constant critique between the designers and the director allow for the best possible outcome. It is more important to make small constant adjustments over time rather than large ones later when significant amounts of money are at stake. The collaborative process involved in the creation of Disney's blockbuster illustrates how even the most design-aware director is influenced by the production team.

Ever conscious of the potential to make money, Disney Theatrical Productions decided that an adaption of the popular animated film *The Lion King* (1994) could make a successful Broadway musical. They commissioned writers, musicians, and artists to find a viable form to re-imagine the original. Debuting at the Orpheum Theatre in Minneapolis and opening at the New Amsterdam Theatre on Broadway, the musical turned out to be a blend of Broadway-style songs, African rhythms and voices, dances and theatrical techniques drawn from around the world, with masks, costumes that merge the human figure with animal physicality, and larger-than-life puppets. Among the Tony awards it won are awards for Costumes by Julie Taymor and Michael Curry, Scenery by Richard Hudson, and Lighting by Donald Holder. The story is a simple fairytale of a young prince's emotional struggle to grow up and his subsequent rise to power. Simba, a young lion prince, must learn the difference between reckless, youthful adventure and the responsibilities involved in a righteous battle. He begins his journey like a teenager, headstrong and unaware of the consequences of his actions. While his father King Mufasa, an enlightened ruler of all creatures on the African Savanna, preaches about the Circle of Life where everything is connected and that every action we take affects every other living creature, his enemies conspire against him. Simba's evil uncle Scar, with the aid of an army of hyenas, plots to kill both Simba and King Mufasa, and proclaim himself as king. Though Simba survives the coup, he is convinced that he is responsible for his father's death, and so decides to leave the kingdom. While in exile, a warthog called Pumbaa and a meerkat called Timon befriend Simba, and it is through their companionship and protection that he discovers his inner strength and his responsibility to the world around him. When Simba has fully grown and learns that his evil uncle has almost destroyed his kingdom, he is faced with the decision of whether to return. In the end, Simba learns that the environment must be valued and that we must treat each other with respect.

> Collaboration doesn't mean everybody is having a good time together; it means communicating. Collaborating is hard because you have to give things up. You are constantly negotiating.
>
> **Susan Hilferty**

As is typical, the development of the musical for Broadway was a long process that involved staged readings and trials outside of New York. On the way, the production team experimented with visual themes and styles searching for the form that the show would eventually take. The design process started earlier than in most productions when Julie Taymor was hired to develop the piece, since she is an accomplished scenographer in her own right. Working as a director and designer, she collaborated with her design team to develop the final form; however, it was her vision as the director that shaped their efforts. For example, according to Disney promotional material even before the design team was hired, Taymor began to visualize the dominant theme and image of the production to be a circle that stands in for the "Circle of Life." Her initial sketches show the circular form that she suggested to producers that Pride Rock should take. She used this image to sell the idea to the management team, but refrained from developing it further to await collaboration with the eventual set designer. In this case her first collaborator was Michael Curry who helped with the puppets. The rest of the team was hired, although the writers, composers, and choreographers were hired only when the push to get a workshop on its feet came. Mary Peterson was hired as an associate designer and Tracy Dorman was hired as an assistant costume designer. They were to finish the sketches and build more than two hundred and fifty costumes. Richard Hudson was hired for the sets, Don Holder for the lights, and Tony Meola for sound. At the first workshop the team was meant to present costume sketches, prototypes of masks and puppets, and models of scenic designs. These design elements were shown to investors with a reading of selections from the book.

In the old time Hollywood movie studio designers worked side by side in a production studio, but it is rare in the theatre for designers to work in close proximity. Often their teams are located in different cities and they fax, express mail, and email ideas to each other. For this production the whole design team was able to set up a design studio together in New York City. Each team had a space where they could work and they were able to share their research and test ideas as they arose. This made collaboration incredibly easy and allowed the production to develop in a holistic manner. For example, Hudson, born in Africa, became fascinated with African textile design. He dove into research on African textile design and other common symbolic motifs. He would bring these symbolic motifs to show his collaborators. As a result, the costume and lighting teams incorporated many of these images into their designs. They were able to compare patterns from clothing and incorporate the same patterns into the scene design. For example, figures that were replicated on costumes were reproduced on the floor surface and upon the cyclorama as well.

According to published interviews, there were constant discussions about scale, dimension, and traffic flow within the fluid ground plan. For example, Taymor's initial design concept for Pride Rock was a circular wedding cake configuration. When Holder was hired he convinced her that a jagged configuration was necessary to reflect the danger inherent in the plot. Hudson explained that *The Lion King* is not set in any specific time, but rather in the vacuum of their fictional world. This posed a problem as the set design will typically begin by considering the period first as a springboard to creating an understandable world for the audience. Therefore, Hudson had the freedom to go in any direction to evoke the African Savanna. This opened up endless possibilities for the team to conceive of a believable world that helped the audience understand the context of the story. For example, the design team stated that the first challenge was to create an African panorama to serve as a foundation for the action that seemed vast and infinite under a wide-open sky. They had to work within the constraints of a proscenium stage, which is a closed composition, to create an open composition within the frame. Taymor suggested that if side masking were used it might be able to create an illusion that the legs blended with the cyclorama, thereby opening up the panoramic vista. However, another solution emerged out of exchanges between Hudson and Holder. Holder, as a rule, tries to attend as many design meetings as he can, even if the lighting is not discussed specifically. He feels that the best way to understand how to light a show is to get completely immersed in it. During the lengthy set design process for *The Lion King* at a point when Hudson was finalizing a formal design presentation for the producers, Holder decided to light each of the models that were being used. By lighting the models and hearing the critiques of the set design he was able to gain insights that would have been difficult to discover working only on paper. He describes how he gained a deeper understanding of the play. If you search for images of *The Lion King* using search terms such as Taymor, *Lion King*, and savanna, you will find images showing the setting complete with lights, costume, puppets, and actors. Notice how the framework and skin of the animals echoes the textures of the actors' costumes. The soft background stands in contrast to the reflective surface of the stage. The vista is created by shadow and light to give the sense of the open plains.

The relationship between a director and lighting designer is a sensitive one. It should first and foremost be based on a level of mutual trust and respect, which hopefully is the result of a good collaboration from the earliest phases of the design period. It's crucial to establish a healthy rapport with the director way before technical rehearsals begin. Without a good relationship, I find myself constantly wondering about the director's confidence in what I'm doing. This can have a negative effect on my decision-making process, causing me to be somewhat tentative during tech rehearsals. It's most definitely not a good position for a lighting designer to be in.

Don Holder

Taymor's approach to staging the piece, and the overall style of production that was emerging, was a result of the director and costume designer collaboration. Together Hudson and Holder created light boxes that mimicked the light in the density and hue of the lights they planned to place behind the cyclorama. They were able to show how they planned to create a continuum that mimicked the continuous tones of an enveloping sky. By experimenting together with light boxes they were able to figure out how to create the illusion of the African Sahara where shifting hue gave the illusion of a majestic landscape that suggested the nobility of Mufasa's and Simba's reigns. Hudson was open to this level of collaboration because he knows that good lighting can make something dull look pleasant or even beautiful on stage or make something vibrant look ghastly. The collaborative process acknowledges that the color, atmosphere, the texture, everything about the set and costumes are influenced by the lighting choices. It is up to each designer to respond to the other's choices. The circle of Taymor's original configuration transforms into a staircase whose rectilinear shape is softened by the circular shape. The steps serve to evoke the difficult journey that the Lion King must embark upon to reach the summit of Pride Rock. Multiple perspectives convey the sense of the unsettled kingdom. The shapes and volumes serve both as geographic markers and as subtle reminders of Simba's precarious journey.

Another example of the type of problem solving and re-imagining of concepts brought to the table by members of the design team is the scene associated with the "Circle of Life." When Taymor first conceived of a controlling motif for the piece she had suggested a concentric tiered circular promontory. She thought the pure shape of the circle would give the rock power, as it is such a strong shape. However, once Hudson began his own visual analysis he rejected the idea because it was too symmetrical, infusing the world with a stability and structure that it did not have since the kingdom was teetering at the edge of destruction. The philosophy of the circle of life is that life is fragile and can be disrupted. Instead, Hudson wanted to convey a sense of danger through the shape and form of the scenic elements. Hudson had to find a way to convince Taymor that another possibility would be more effective. He did this by showing her another design he had done for a different production which worked along the lines of the effect he wanted to create, suggesting that Pride Rock could work as a revolving spiral staircase. With this solution she could have her circular symbolism, but he was able to fracture it into an asymmetrical shape that appeared more like a jagged rock and made the shape look more organic, like a landscape. This solution resulted in a more powerful Pride Rock by forming a jagged promontory that juts forward. The promontory moved on a turntable allowing the look of the rock to shift as it moves through space as well as shifting lighting effects which could change the images. The circular structure was a reference, but made imperfect much like the situation Simba faced. Through collaboration they were able to refine an idea and set up a structure that could be embellished using lighting. The circle and the curved staircase are married, and African textile patterns give texture to Pride Rock. The cool colors of the savanna were made visually interesting because of the pattern's accent. As well, Pride Rock sits in juxtaposition to the open vista behind. This solution was possible because of the way the collaborators built on each other's ideas. Here a model gives a sense of the composition of the piece with the sets, costumes, puppets, and lighting. While the colors are different than those used ultimately, we get a sense of mood, scale, pattern, and texture. We are able to see how the textile patterns are echoed in the coats of the animals, the rocks, and the costumes. The mountain range at the back takes away from the open feeling of the plain that is present when the vertical and horizontal meet abruptly in a straight line in the background of the stage setting.

Organizing John Guare's *Six Degrees of Separation*

In contrast to the large musical where a spectacular location was essential in the larger themes of the story, *Six Degrees* is more conversational in tone requiring the setting to serve as a context and a means of organizing and defining the action. *Six Degrees of Separation* (1990) was directed by Jerry Zaks and premiered at Lincoln Centre, later moving to the Vivian Beaumont theatre for its Broadway debut. Tony Walton designed the setting with costumes by William Ivey Long, lighting design by Paul Gallo, and sound design by Aural Fixation. The play moves quickly through multiple locations. While the designers had to accommodate the large number of settings they did not think that building elaborate settings was the solution. There were simply too many locations depicted to build them all as distinct locations and simultaneously retain the tone of the play. The design team joined the production process early and typical of a new play, there was little information to indicate setting, costume, or environment. Especially in contemporary plays, it is often the first production that makes sense of the logic of the world of the play. By the end of the production process it seems apparent how the world's transition from one location to the next is possible, but it takes a lot of work to get to that point. Part of this arises because the order of the scenes may be different at the first rehearsal than in the final script, scenes or locations may be cut, and others added. For *Six Degrees*, when the designers first received the play it was in a first draft form written in the style of a screenplay. The production team described their process in an interview with the American Theatre Wing. There was no indication of time, place, or location. They used the action to create a scene breakdown and determined that there were about thirty-five scenic requirements within the text pointing to different places including living rooms, and movie theatres. They had to work out the movement between these locations within rehearsal and to conceive of how a semi-realistic setting could be built to contain all these locations plausibly.

Told as a witty conspiratorial dinner conversation, *Six Degrees of Separation* revolves around Paul, a young African-American con man. He insinuates himself into the lives of the Flan and Ouisa Kittredge. Paul, claiming acquaintance with the Kittredges' children, arrives unannounced at their Central Park apartment. He claims that he was just mugged in the park below and has been stabbed. In the midst of a dinner party, Flan, an art dealer, who is trying to sell a painting by Paul Cézanne, now has this wounded stranger in his home that he has to deal with. Paul, a smooth talker, intrigues everyone with a story that he is in New York to meet his father Sydney Poitier who is directing a film version of *Cats*. Paul continues to charm them with his story, though in reality he is not a Harvard student but obtained details on the Kittredges from another male student he had seduced. Invited to stay beyond the night, eventually Paul abuses their hospitality when he is caught in bed with a hustler. After the Kittredges kick him out they discover that friends of theirs have had similar encounters. Paul starts up another con against Rick and Elizabeth who naively invite him to live with them until his problems with his supposedly wealthy father Flan Kittredge are sorted out. Paul scams Rick out of the couple's money. Soon afterwards Rick commits suicide, and Paul calls the Kittredges for assistance. Ouisa convinces him to give himself up to the police; however, during the arrest, he and the Kittredges are separated. Despite their efforts his fate is unresolved.

Since the play moves rapidly from location to location, the production team was convinced that they were going to lose the attention of the audience if they did not find a way to transition between locations in a rapid fashion. Otherwise they feared that the audience would be faced with long transistion times between scenes as settings were brought onto stage.

To prevent this Walton wanted to pare down each setting. He asked the director if the production team could start by working to see what was absolutely essential. This began a process where they examined each scene. For example, what is needed in a scene in the living room? The director responded that he needed a place to sit. This led to a sofa, and then eventually two sofas. The next question that they had to grapple with was what to do about entrances and exits.

If they were creating fluid spaces that were meant to transform into multiple spaces, how then is the audience supposed to keep track of which location they were in? Likewise, if a scene was brief, was it even necessary to change location? An off-hand comment about characters speaking up from the audience was a solution for this. To make the setting fluid they adopted a red circus-ring style stage, and then they appropriated seats from the audience to be able to include other characters in other locations. For example, it was suggested that they try to place cast in the first two rows. A detective could be sleeping in the audience, and then when a question is asked he stands up and sits down with reaction.

Walton remarked that at first the director hated the idea and then in the middle of the night he called him and agreed that it was a good solution. Sometimes the solution is a result of a physical nature of the problem and other times it is a result of an off-hand comment. It is all part of the importance of being open to listening to the team. They chose to create a bare setting that allows the settings to change fluidly. As well, by subtracting props the audience is able to focus on the characters and their costuming more.

A further complication was that they began the process without the lighting designer, Paul Gallo. Ivey Long and Walton collaborated together to work out the color palette – all they knew was that the color that they were using was red. Both Ivey Long and Walton had conceived of their designs in red, but now they had to coordinate what red. A big red carpet was brought on. When Gallo came on board they tested fabric under the lights on the carpet. To coordinate the designers they drew colors from the palette of the double-sided Kandinsky that is referred to often and is central to the text. As well, they were able to further define and transition between locations using lighting effects. The challenges of the script allowed the team to come up with theatrical solutions. Though the writing was cinematic, the production team embraced the constraints of the theatrical medium to find exciting ways to support and move the story forward.

Collaboration is a process of working as a team to discover the visual world of the play so that audiences will be able to understand the action of the play. By organizing the action and providing visual cues the design elements can enrich a director's vision. Though each element of design is not a fine art, when taken together the visible elements of design can be understood through a lens of aesthetics. The collaborative nature of live performance is in part what gives theatre its vitality. Mastering its elements and principles are just the first step in making exciting theatre. It is an amazing journey.

Behind the scenes with the design teams

Depending on the budget the production team might be quite large. Each designer may have an assistant or associate designer, and they regularly meet with the staff of the theatre as their designs go from concept drawing to full-scale setting, costume, lighting, sound, or projection. There are an assortment of workers who realize the designs for performance, including technical directors, production supervisors, theatre engineers, textile artists, wig masters, prop masters, special effects supervisors, sound and light board operators, and running crew. Each serves a vital function in making real the visual and aural world of the production for audiences. Good design is as much about coordination, negotiation, and good relationships with co-creators as it is a creative endeavor.

As technology improves and new techniques are developed, designers will continue to play with all the technology available as potential expressive tools. New trends in design include the increased role of projections design, performance design, and the increasing preeminence of the scenographer. These changes are the result of making use of new materials and technologies to create vibrant visual and aural worlds for performance. Different types of media need different technical abilities. Theatre Design practice is a vital part of the production process. As we learn how designers view the world and go about their jobs, we can begin to see how the elements and principles of design work in concert to create performances. As long as theatre is a live, collaboratively made art form, the work of designers will continue to thrive. Remember the next time you are looking at a stage setting, costume, or listening to a sound effect that a whole team of creative individuals have spent countless hours making it look so good that you do not even question that these characters live here or wear these clothes.

Glossary

Absorption: is a result of a material that absorbs sound rather than reflects it. Carpet affects high frequencies, and drapes and padded furniture affect low frequencies. Adding absorption can control reverberation in a room, since the more absorption there is the less reverberation occurs.

Abstract shapes: Also known as stylized shapes. Natural shapes that have been altered or simplified to reflect the essence rather than the representation of an object.

Accent light: (1) Illumination used to make something stand out. It may be done with intensity and/or color. (2) A lantern or lighting instrument that provides such illumination.

Accents: In lighting, accents enliven an object with points of light and highlights, or are used as brighteners. Accents are made up of sharply focused beams of light.

Accessory: Items such as gloves, hat, watches, and canes that are used to add detail and character to costumes.

Acoustics: The properties or qualities of sound within different spatial configuration.

Additive color space: The process of producing color through mixing different colors of light. The commonly used additive primary colors are red, green, and blue, and if you overlap all three in effectively equal mixture, you get white light.

Additive mixture: The combination of the three primary color wavelengths of light to form other colors including white.

Alignment: Arranging elements so that their edges are lined up.

Alternation: An instance of patterning where a sequence of repeating motifs are presented in turn, for example, short/long, fat/thin, red/blue, or dark/light.

Ambient beds: Music or sound effects chosen or composed for the play or played under a scene that evoke moods or environments.

Amplifier: A device used in sound systems in which a small amount of input power controls a larger amount of output power. For example, it is used in converting mic-level signals to line level or line level to loudspeaker levels.

Analogous color scheme: Colors which are adjacent to each other on the color wheel. For example, green, yellow green, and yellow, or red, orange, and yellow.

Angled wings: Scenic flats placed on an angle to help accentuate perspective illusion, which were commonly used on the Italian Renaissance stage.

Angular: Sharp cornered objects or objects with multiples sides.

Arena: A stage in the center of a large open space surrounded by the audience.

Asymmetrical balance: Also called informal balance, involves the arranging of objects of differing size in a composition such that they balance one another with their respective visual weights.

Asymmetry: Where the right and left sides of a composition contain different shapes, colors, textures, or other elements.

Atmospheric perspective: A technique of rendering depth or distance in a composition by modifying the tone or hue and distinctness of objects perceived as receding from the proscenium.

Back lighting: See **Backlight**.

Background: The part of a scene or picture that is furthest from the audience.

Background lighting: See **Backlight**.

Backlight: Also called set light. (1) Light from behind the actor or a piece of scenery. (2) The lantern or lighting instrument that provides such illumination.

Balance: Equalization of weight or opposing forces within a composition is the equal distribution of visual weight in a design.

Beam width: Also known as beam spread it is the area of light covered by a light beam. The longer the throw the larger is the beam spread.

Black box: A bare-bones stage of various seating types.

Bold light: A lighting effect noticeable to the audience used to make a grand dramatic statement about the action. It can come in the form or a contrasting color scheme or a dramatic accent that is immediately noticeable.

Box set: A setting of a room comprising three continuous walls made by flats with usable doors and windows and possibly a ceiling.

Brightening: The process of adding light that ranges from a totally dark black to a luminous white. To change the audience's perception or ability to distinguish difference or changes in luminance.

Carbon arc lamp: An arc source in which the arc is formed in air between a pair of carbon electrodes.

Cavea: The seating area in a Roman theatre, divided by social rank.

Changing placement: An alteration in the location of a form or shape.

Changing size: An alteration in the measurement of a form, shape, or volume.

Character types: Different stereotypical characteristics of people such as the ruffian, the innocent, the lover, or the loser.

Chariot-and-pole system: A scenic machine used to coordinate all of the flat changes at once by connecting all of the scenery using ropes and pulleys to a rolling chariot under the stage that could remove and place a scene simultaneously in a single motion.

Color: The visible perception of the wavelengths of light reflected on an object. In other words, the *color* of the light reflected by the performer and the background.

Color harmonies: Colors that work well together, and produce a color scheme that looks attractive.

Color quality: Also known as color rendering. See **Temperature**.

Color rendering: The way in which an object appears beneath a given light source.

Color scheme: Also known as color space. Logical combinations of colors that work well together. Defined as a range of possible colors arranged in a three-dimensional coordinate system.

Color scroller: Also known as a color changer. A lighting accessory attached to the gel frame holder used to change the color projected by stage lighting instruments from afar by moving the color gel into the beam of the light.

Complementary color scheme: Logical combinations of colors that are opposite each other on the color wheel, such as blue and orange, red and green, or purple and yellow.

Complements: Colors that are opposite each other on the color wheel, for example, red and green.

Composition: The arrangement of visual parts within an image used to create a whole.

Compositional location: Relationship of an object or element to the ground plan and other objects.

Compositional movement: The movement of the audience's eye from element to element through a composition.

Concept: The approach the directors and designers will take to communicate their interpretations of a given play in production.

Concept drawings: Sketches that explore the viability of various approaches for a production used for discussion between the director and designers.

Conceptual sound design: The process of conceiving of an abstract soundscape that will complement the themes or atmosphere of a production dictating what sounds or music will be used or composed to create the mood and setting of the production.

Construction drawings: Technical drawings depicting the manner in which scenery is meant to be built.

Continuation: When something like a line, an edge, a curve, or a direction continues from one element to another.

Contrast: The use of dissimilar forms to create interest. In lighting, it is a difference in color or intensity. In set design, it is a difference in scale or texture.

Corseting: The process of creating the construction beneath the dress using bones or other stiff material to create an artificial silhouette.

Costume bible: A guide to building and maintaining costumes kept by the costume shop. It can contain research and renderings, actors' measurements, catalogs that clothes are ordered from, production calendars, and contact lists for performers and production team.

Costume design: The costume designer creates, through selection or construction, a visual idea for each character and the play as a whole.

Costume plot: A list or chart that shows which characters appear in each scene, what they are wearing, and their overall movement throughout the play that helps track the specific costume needs of every character.

Costume scene breakdown: A brief description of each scene charting details such as location, time of day, any important action that goes on to create a costume plot of necessary costume changes.

Creative light: Edward Gordon Craig's concept of light that composes highlights and shadows on the stage.

Cue number: The number indicating where in the script an effect is meant to occur.

Cue synopsis: A list of lighting cues arranged in numerical order used by the light board operator noting where they happen in the script, what happens, and how long it is supposed to last.

Cueing sessions: When lighting effects are honed and labeled during technical rehearsals.

Curved lines: Continuously bending **lines** without angles.

Designer's plans: Drawings that depict every detail of the set as well as provide exact measurements of its components.

Diagonal lines: A straight line inside a shape that goes from one corner to another but is not an edge.

Diffraction: When a sound wave bends around obstacles in its path that are smaller than its wavelength.

Diffused light: A light ray that is reflected from a surface and broken up and scattered into different directions.

Direct light: Light directed downward. See also **Specific light.**

Direction: (1) The angle of the light determines the length and location of the shadows cast by the performer and the three-dimensional props around him or her. (2) In sound it is the location of the sound in space and how sound travels from one location to another.

Distress: A process where set or costume designers make a material look worn, weathered, or aged.

Distribution: The way in which illumination of any color or quantity is spread over a particular background. The distribution of light determines where the stage will be lit.

Dressing the set: Placing props and other accessories on the set.

Duration: The length of time a sound or lighting effect lasts.

Dynamic movement: The way that the elements of design creates a smooth flow from one part of the composition to another, guided by continuations of line or form, and by gradations of color or form.

Echo: When a reflected sound gets delayed and is heard by the listener as a repetition of the direct sound.

Ekkyklema: In the Ancient Greek theatre, a movable platform that could be used to bring or reveal corpses on stage.

Elevations: A view of an object in which the line of sight of the viewer is perpendicular to the object, often called a projection.

Emphasis: Also referred to as **point of focus**, or **interruption**. It marks the locations in a composition which most strongly catches the eye and makes the viewer pay attention.

Equalization: Selectively boosting or cutting bands of frequencies to improve the performance of a sound reinforcement system by emphasizing the frequency ranges most critical for speech.

Equalization system: An audio signal processing device used to modify the frequency response of an audio signal.

Fixed staging: Also known as stationary staging. Mansion stages were set up in available spaces such as courtyards or town squares arranged around the perimeter of the space in the medieval period.

Flat wing: Theatrical scenery painted and positioned on the periphery of the stage in the wings to give the appearance of buildings or other background. Used in the Renaissance to accentuate the illusion of perspective.

Focal Point: see **Emphasis.**

Focus: (1) The session when all the lanterns in the rig are angled in the correct direction, with the correct beam size. (2) Description of how sharply defined a light beam is ("give that profile a sharp focus") (3) Control on projection equipment used to change the focus.

Footlights: Also known as up-lights, light the space and the object from below.

Foreground: The part of a scene or picture that is nearest to and in front of the audience.

Form: Also known as a mass or volume. An object perceived as a three-dimensional shape that has height, width, and depth.

Found, environmental, or **created spaces:** The use of non-theatre buildings, the adaptation of a space to suit the need of an individual production, the use of nature, geography, and architecture to affect the performance environment.

Four controllable properties of light: The qualities of **intensity, distribution, color,** and **movement** are manipulated by lighting designers to modify how lights look on stage.

Free-field environment: A loudspeaker or other sound source operating in an environment in which there are no reflective surfaces around the source.

Front elevations: Scaled mechanical drawings showing the front views of the scenery, where the setting is flattened out and each surface is drawn on a single plane. A scale drawing that gives a front view of the set.

Front lighting: (1) Illumination from the general direction of the audience. (2) A lantern or lighting instrument that provides such illumination.

Full model: A miniature painted version of the set complete with furniture and props used as a guide in the building of the setting.

Functional model: The three-dimensional equivalent of a thumbnail sketch, which is a quickly constructed working model intended to aid in visualizing the basic composition of the scenic design.

Gas lighting: A lighting technique developed in the early nineteenth century that was more easily controlled and burned gas to illuminate the stage.

General light: Also known as main lighting, or indirect light. A non-specific light source such as from a window that washes the space.

Geometric shapes: Shapes such as circles, squares, triangles, and rectangles which are crisp, precise, and mathematical made up of straight edges or consistent curves.

Gesamtkunstwerk: Richard Wagner's concept of the total work of art where all elements of production from the setting, costume, lighting, and music should be controlled by a director's aesthetic vision.

Gradation: Transitional steps in a series of motifs patterned to relate to one another used to create emphasis and a feeling of movement in a design.

Ground plan: A scale drawing showing a view of a set from above detailing the exact location of all items standing on the stage floor and indicating the position of items suspended above.

Hard distribution: Stark shafts of light.

Harmony: A pleasing or congruent arrangement of scenic forms or costume elements , usually achieved by repetition.

Hell Mouth: One of the mansions used in the medieval theatre to depict the gates of hell complete with fire and devils.

High key lighting: A technique in which the overall lighting in the scene is fairly bright and there are no deep shadows.

High saturation: Colors that are close to the pure hue of a color, for example, bright and vivid colors like pure red or pure yellow.

Highlights: Represent the flashes of reflected light from areas that are directly illuminated by a light source.

Horizontal lines: Lines parallel to the plane of the horizon, level, flat.

Hue: The name of a color.

Implied lines: Points in space which are connected or completed by the viewer through closure of disconnected points.

Incandescent lights: A term used to describe a lamp, or a lantern that utilizes such a lamp, that employs the incandescence of a filament as its light source.

Indirect light: Illumination that falls on an area or subject by reflection.

Input transducers: A device such as a microphone that converts sound waves into a signal.

Intensity: The measure of the amount of light reflected in a particular direction.

Level control: A circuit that keeps the output of a microphone or other input transducer constant, even in the presence of large changes in the input allowing the soundboard operator to adjust the relative level of each microphone individually.

Level-set: The process where the director, stage manager, and designers sit in the theatre and program or determine how loud the sound and how bright the lights will be.

Light levels: The control board setting of lighting brightness and intensity at any given moment of production.

Light plot: A plan view of the stage showing where each lighting instrument is hung.

Light primaries: Also known as **additive color space.** Red, blue, and green, and all other colors derived from them.

Lighting designer: The person who plans lighting compositions, lays out light plots, directs the focusing of lanterns, and determines the various intensities, colors, appearance, and cues for a production.

Lighting scheme: The technique used in choosing types of lighting to create particular effects and evoke mood.

Limelight: The first spot light made of limestone which was heated to create an intense but soft beam of light.

Line: An identifiable path of a point moving in space that can vary in width, direction, and length.

Line level: An input found on electronic devices used to receive sound information and measure the strength of an audio signal between components.

Linear perspective: The mathematical system rediscovered in the Renaissance for creating the illusion of space and distance on a two-dimensional surface.

Linear rhythm: The characteristic flow of an individual line in a painting, a costume, or a setting.

Literal movement: Physical movement such as an actor moving across the stage.

Load-in: The process of putting the set together on stage.

Logeion: A raised stage, in front of the *skene*, or scene building in an Ancient Greek theatre.

Loudspeaker: Also known as a speaker. An electroacoustic transducer that produces sound in response to an electrical audio signal input.

Loudspeaker system: The arrangement of speakers within the theatre environment positioned for effect.

Low key: A lighting scheme that employs very little fill light, creating strong contrasts between the brightest and darkest parts of an image and often creating strong shadows that obscure parts of the composition.

Low saturation: Neutral color that is a result of mixing pure colors with either gray or the color's complement.

Mansions: Fixed stage structures used in medieval theatre to represent specific locations, such as Heaven, Hell, or Noah's ark.

Mechane: A crane-like piece of machinery in ancient Greek theatres used to lower an actor playing a god from the roof of the *skene* onto the stage.

Melodrama: The dramatic genre characterized by exaggerated emotions, stereotypical good and evil characters, and climactic plots.

Microphone: An input transducer used for converting acoustic, sound pressure energy into electrical energy.

Mixed lights: Different light sources with different color temperatures are mixed for effect, for example mixing high (blue) and low (yellow) color temperatures to capture the atmosphere of a place.

Mixing desks: Also called mixing consoles or sound boards. An electronic device for combining, routing, and changing the level, timbre, and dynamics of audio signals that are modified to produce a combined output signal for the loudspeaker.

Modeling: Also known as sculpting. Using light for enhancing the three-dimensional qualities of an object, for example in the ways in which highlights and shadowing create form.

Monochromatic color scheme: A color space consisting of different values (tints and shades) of a single color.

Mood: The reflection of the ever changing emotional content of a play.

Motivational lighting: Practical light sources you can see such as candles, fixed light points used to shape and create light so it becomes a storytelling tool to aid the action.

Movable staging: Also called processional staging. Like a parade, when pageant wagons would travel a set route, and the play would be performed at various locations.

Movement: (1) When objects seem to be moving through space over time in a visual design. It comes from the kinds of shapes, forms, lines, and curves that are used. Diagonal lines tend to create the illusion of movement or motion. (2) Movement is any change in the intensity, color, direction, distribution, or texture of the light.

Moving light: Also known as automated light. A luminaire that is robotic and remotely operated from a control console, performing functions such as panning, tilting, focusing, dimming, beam shaping, and coloring.

Moving panoramas: See **Panorama.**

Natural shapes: Also known as organic shapes. Shapes found in nature in flowers, tree branches, or leaves. They are irregular in outline and cannot accurately be described using Euclidian geometry.

Neutral background: A background having no strongly marked or positive characteristics or features. It could be composed of neutral colors that allow the audience to focus on other colors or elements or serve to tone down colors or elements that might otherwise be overpowering on their own.

New Stagecraft: An early twentieth-century American movement influenced by the European avant-garde that moved away from strict pictorial realism to more abstract settings designed to evoke mood and emphasize the language of a play.

Non-objective shapes: Also known as non-representational shapes. Shapes created with no reference to subject.

Orchestra: The dancing place for the chorus in the ancient Greek theatre consisting of a circular area where they chanted and danced, positioned between the audience and the raised stage used by the principals.

Orthographic drawings: Straight-line projection drawings of objects showing three views, typically the top, front, and side, and depicting the "true proportion" of objects to be accurately represented.

Output transducers: Devices that take sound signals and transmit the sounds, for example loudspeakers.

Overlapping: A technique in which the designer creates the illusion of depth on stage by placing one object in front of another.

Pageant wagons: A staging convention used during the medieval period that consisted of a bare platform backed with a plain curtain mounted on a wagon.

Paint elevations: See **Painter's elevations.**

Painted backdrops: Used on the illusionistic stage to represent background locations painted in perspective in tandem with flats placed on the raked stage.

Painted light: Edward Gordon Craig's conception of the painted highlights and shadows on the two-dimensional scenery in nineteenth-century stage design.

Painter's elevations: Scaled paintings of objects in the set of orthographic drawings showing all scenic pieces and elements with the proportions, colors, highlight, and shadow tones, wall textures, and decoration to guide all scenic painting. Sometimes, a painted model is used as a substitute for painter's elevations. It shows the palette and style of the setting.

Panorama: Also known as a cyclorama, or a diorama, it is a background scene painted on a long piece of canvas that is unrolled from one side of the stage to the other, thus giving the impression of motion by presenting a changing landscape.

Parodoi: (singular is *Parados*) In the Ancient Greek theatre these were the entrances into the theatre used by the audience to get into the seating areas as well as by the chorus to enter the orchestra.

Pattern: The repetition of shape or form. It can also reflect the underlying structure of a design by organizing the surfaces or objects in the composition in a consistent, regular manner.

Perceived line: A line that is not present at all but is imagined.

Perception: Becoming aware of the environment and understanding what it means.

Performance designers: Designers who take control of all of the design aspects of different types of performances from a fashion show to a rock concert.

Periaktoi: Early scenic devices of the Greek and Roman theatre, probably consisting of painted prisms that were rotated to indicate a change of scene. Each of the surfaces bore a traditional image to suggest a location, such as waves, trees, or the column of a building. Vertical three-sided or prism-shaped column which could be rotated to present three different scenic pictures.

Pit, box, and gallery: The standard seating configuration of a theatre from about the 1700s, with the pit on the floor of the house, sunk between the stage and lower boxes, the boxes above this, and the gallery at the highest level.

Pitch: The wavelength or frequency of the sound.

Platea: In medieval theatre, the neutral acting area of the mansion stage.

Playback cues: Pre-recorded material set to be played during particular moments in performance.

Playbacks: Pre-recorded material such as a sound effect or an ambient bed that will be played during performance.

Playing areas: The area within the performance space within which the actor may move in full view of the audience. Also known as the acting area.

GLOSSARY

Position: Where something is located in a composition.

Power amplifier: A machine to boost the console's line level output to a level suitable to drive the loudspeaker.

Power relationships: The relative status in terms of class, rank, wealth, or age of a character in relationship to the other characters in the play.

Pre-amplification: The process of amplifying the microphone level signals to line level.

Presentation model: A preliminary model that works to show the designer's idea and provide the detailed information needed for the full-scale creation of the design.

Primary colors: Also known as **primary hues.** The basic colors of red, blue, and yellow that cannot be mixed from others.

Production model: Provides a complete visualization of the scenic designer's concept. Built to scale, fully painted, and completely decorated with all the furniture, props, and set dressing that will be used during the production.

Proportion: Also known as scale. Proportionate size as seen by comparing two lines, objects, or spaces.

Proscenium: The opening serving as a frame that separates the stage from the audience.

Proximity: Grouping elements within a composition by positioning them close together.

Pulpitum: In the Roman Theatre these were platforms on which actors stood to perform in front of the *Scaenae frons.*

Quality: In sound is how pitch and volume combine to give each sound its own distinctive effect.

Quick changes: A rapid change of costume done in the wings during performance.

Raked stage: The slope of a stage floor from the back down toward the front introduced in the Renaissance period to enhance the illusionistic effect of scenes painted in perspective.

Realistic light: Recreating the look of a real lighting situation, such as light from a window or from a lamp.

Rear elevations: Orthographic scale views of the rear unfinished vertical feature of the set so that construction details are clear.

Rectilinear: Moving in, consisting of, bounded by, or characterized by a straight line or lines.

Reflected light: The light that reflects from surfaces of forms onto other surfaces surrounding the form, and is always located on a form's shadow side.

Reflection: When light hits an opaque surface and it bounces off.

Refraction: (1) Where the bending of a sound wave takes place as it passes through some change in the density of the environment. (2) When a beam passing through a transparent object will change direction slightly.

Renderings: Painted scale models or paintings of the set at strategic moments during the play as it might look under stage light.

Repetition: The use of patterning to achieve timed movement and a visual beat, such as a clear repetition of elements in a composition, or it may be a more subtle kind of repetition that can be observed in the underlying structure of the image.

Reverberation: When there are multiple reflections of a sound that maintain a sound in a reflective space for a time even after the direct sound has ceased.

Rhythm: Timed movement of the eye leads the audience from one part of a design to another part, creating movement through repetition of pattern, color, or a regular arrangement of motifs.

Rig: A complete structural assembly for hanging or supporting lighting instruments, scenery, and/or other production equipment.

Saturation: The relative vividness or dullness of a hue as well as a measure of the pureness of a hue.

Scaena: The roofed scenic building at the back of Roman theatres used for a backstage area.

Scaenae frons: In the Roman theatre it was a grand façade that served as a background setting for all plays.

Scale models: A model that is constructed in exactly the same proportions as the full-size finished piece.

Scenography: The design practice where a single designer controls the combined elements of design to create a unified concept.

Secondary colors: Colors made by mixing equal parts of primary colors. For example, green is a secondary color made by mixing yellow and blue.

Secrets: The name for special effects during the medieval period.

Set design: The form and arrangement of the scenery used in a theatrical production.

Shade: The darker value of a hue, resulting from the addition of black to a pure hue.

Shadows: Represented by either the area of an object that is not lit or the area of darkness or shadow that is cast by a lit object.

Shape: A closed contour, an element defined by its perimeter. The three basic shapes are: circle, rectangle or square, and triangle.

Sidelight, Side lighting: (1) Illumination from the general direction of the wings. (2) A lantern or lighting instrument that provides such illumination. (3) A lighting effect that sculpts a subject, revealing contours and textures.

Signal: An electric signal having the frequency of a mechanical wave that can be detected as a sound by the human.

Signal processing: The process of converting analog transmissions into digital signals.

Silhouette: The space of the actor's body and/or the outline of the garment.

Simultaneous staging: A non-realistic style where different scenes are performed in multiple locations at the same time.

Size: The physical dimensions, proportions, magnitude, or extent of an object.

Skene: The scene building whose façade served as a backdrop for all plays in an Ancient Greek theatre.

Sliding flats: Scenery placed in grooves in the stage floor that could be slid on and off stage to depict changes in location.

Soft diffusion: A lighting effect scattering direct light by making it pass through a non-transparent material or by bouncing it off a semi-reflective surface to create an image without shadow.

Soundboard: See **Mixing desks.**

Sound designer: The person in charge of meeting or creating the auditory (all aspects of sound) during productions, including controlling sound levels, sound reinforcement, sound effects, music, and dialogue.

Sound effects: An imitative sound, produced artificially for theatrical purposes.

Sound engineer: Also known as mixer or soundboard operator. The person responsible for some aspect of the sound at live shows who mixes the sound the audience hears.

Sound reinforcement: A sound reinforcement system is the combination of microphones, signal processors, amplifiers, and loudspeakers that makes live or pre-recorded sounds louder and may also distribute those sounds to a larger or more distant audience.

Sound system: The basic sound system made up of input transducers, which convert sound waves into a signal, signal processing, which manages the signal, and output transducers, which transmit the sounds, delivering sufficient sound levels to the audience.

Space: Three-dimensional realm or expanse in which objects are located and events occur.

Specific cueing: The crafting of particular moments within the action to create an effect that influences the mood or feeling within a scene.

Specific light: Also known as direct light. An identifiable lighting source such as a beam of sunlight.

Spotlight: A light that produces a bright narrow beam that can be focused on a particular actor or area of the stage. It is usually mounted so that the beam can be directed as required.

Standing waves: These are a type of interference with the clear transmission of sound. They occur for certain frequencies when the original sound and the reflected sound reinforce each other.

Static movement: Jumps between isolated parts of a composition, attracted by similarities, and simply shifting to shapes with related shape or color.

Storyboard: Sketched or painted pictures of the setting at various times during the action and under different lighting conditions.

Subtractive color mixing: The process of filtering wavelengths of light to create different colors.

Subtractive color space: Subtractive color space is the traditional color space of pigment-based color. In a subtractive color space, the pigments manipulate the wavelengths that our eyes see thus making the absence of any pigment appear white and all pigments blended together appear black.

Symmetrical balance: The equal distribution of weight so that if you were to bisect a composition on its vertical axis both halves would correspond to one another in size, shape, and placement.

Symmetry: The correspondence in size, form, and arrangement of parts on opposite sides of a plane, line, or point; regularity of form or arrangement in terms of like, reciprocal, or corresponding parts.

Technical drawings: Also known as mechanical drawings. These drawings show every piece of scenery to be built, to scale, in a manner sufficient to guide construction.

Technical rehearsals: The first rehearsal in the performance venue where lighting cues, sound cues, fly cues, set changes, set piece movement, prop placement and movement, and curtain timing all need to be worked out.

Technical sound design: The process of building a sound system to fulfil the needs of the production and make sure that the performance can be heard and understood by everyone in the audience.

Temperature: The psychological property of heat or coolness that a color creates.

Textile artist: An artist who works with the costume designer to create two-dimensional designs that can be produced on fabric for use on the stage.

Texture: (1) The surface quality of a material, such as rough, smooth, soft, hard, glossy, or slippery. (2) Texture is the quality of the light; Does it have a soft edge or is it hard edged? Is the field of the light smooth, diffuse?

Theatron: In the Greek theatre this was where the audience sat. It is known as the seeing place.

Three-quarter round: Also known as theatre in the round. The stage is surrounded by audience on all sides.

Thrust stage: A stage that extends into the auditorium so that the audience is seated around three sides The playing area protrudes out into the house with the audience seating on more than one side.

Tint: The lighter value of a hue.

Tone: See **Value.**

Transducers: Electronic devices that convert an input signal into an output signal of a different energy form, for example microphones and loudspeakers.

Translucent drop: Depending on the lighting angle a different scene can be seen by the audience on a backcloth.

Triadic color scheme: A color scheme in which three colors of equidistant distribution on the color wheel are used, for example, red, blue, and yellow.

True views: A technical drawing that shows an object at its true shape and size. meaning all lines are drawn to scale.

Über-marionette: Edward Gordon Craig's ideal actor. He or she would be an egoless "super-puppet," who performed at the bidding of the play's director.

Underscoring: Background music or sound played to add emotion or mood to scene.

Unity: A similar relationship between the meaning and function of the images.

Up-lights: Also known as footlights. (1) Lighting the space and the object from below. (2) A lantern or lighting instrument that provides such illumination.

Value: Also known as tone. Lightness or darkness of a surface.

Value contrast: The relative lightness or darkness of two elements to each other. The further apart the value the higher the contrast.

Value gradation: The progression of a given hue from its darkest value to its lightest used to create the appearance of depth or mass.

Variety: Slight changes in elements that prevent monotony.

Vertical lines: Lines perpendicular to the horizon.

View drawings: One of the orthographic drawings depicting the top, front, and side, and the "true proportion" of objects.

Viewpoint: A position from which something is observed, also known as point of view.

Visibility: The amount of light needed for the audience *to see* the performer.

Volume: The loudness or quietness of the sound.

Voms: Tunnel-like passageways, originally known as vomitoria, leading out of the house of the theatre.

Wash light: (1) An even, overall illumination over a large area. (2) To create such an illumination.

White card model: A simple, unadorned, three-dimensional sketch model made at an early stage in the design process from plain white cardboard.

Wing and groove system: A system used in the Italian Renaissance where a theatre flat wing was positioned in a groove so that it could slide in and out for a scene change.

Bibliography

Adams, Kevin. "Kevin Adams Design," www.ambermylar.com/

American Theatre Wing and XM Satellite Radio. David Rockwell *Downstage Center* #72 (October, 2005); http://americantheatrewing.org/podcasts/index.php

——. "Catherine Zuber," *Downstage Center* #157 (June, 2007); http://americantheatrewing. org/podcasts/index.php

——. "Tony Walton," *Downstage Center* #183 (January, 2008); http://americantheatrewing. org/podcasts/index.php

——. "Ken Billington," *Downstage Center* #196 (April, 2008); http://americantheatrewing.org/ podcasts/index.php

——. "Michael Yeargan: Set Designer of South Pacific," *Downstage Center* #210 (July 15, 2008); http://americantheatrewing.org/podcasts/index.php

——. "Tony Meola: Sound Designer of *Wicked* and *The Lion King*" *Downstage Center* #214 (August 11, 2008); http://americantheatrewing.org/podcasts/index.php

——. "William Ivey Long," *Downstage Center* #216 (August, 2008) http://americantheatre wing.org/podcasts/index.php

——. "Susan Hilferty: Tony Award winning Costume Designer," *Downstage Center* #233 (September 8, 2009); http://americantheatrewing.org/podcasts/index.php

——. "John Lee Beatty: Scenic Designer of *A View From The Bridge* & *Time Stands Still*," *Downstage Center* #256 (February 17, 2010); http://americantheatrewing.org/podcasts/ index.php

——. "Christine Jones," *Downstage Center* #271 (June, 2010); http://americantheatrewing. org/podcasts/index.php

——. "Martin Pakledinaz: Tony Award-winning Costume Designer," *Downstage Center* #281 (August 18, 2010); http://americantheatrewing.org/podcasts/index.php

——. "Natasha Katz," *Downstage Center* #302 (January, 2011); http://americantheatrewing. org/podcasts/index.php

American Theatre Wing. "Technical Director with Mike Cristaldi," *In The Wings* (March 4, 2011); http://americantheatrewing.org/podcasts/index.php

——. "Theatrical Milliner with Lynne Mackey," *In The Wings* (February 18, 2011); http:// americantheatrewing.org/podcasts/index.php

——. "Prop Manager with Desiree Maurer," *In The Wings* (January 21, 2011); http:// americantheatrewing.org/podcasts/index.php

——. "Lighting Supervisor with Dan Montano," *In The Wings* (January 7, 2011); http://americantheatrewing.org/podcasts/index.php

——. "Sound Engineer with Carin Ford," *In The Wings* (October 29, 2010); http://americantheatrewing.org/podcasts/index.php

——. "Model Builder with Steven Kemp," *In The Wings* (October 15, 2010); http://americantheatrewing.org/podcasts/index.php

——. "Wig Maker with Paul Huntley," *In The Wings* (July 23, 2010); http://americantheatrewing.org/podcasts/index.php

——. "Scenic Designer with Ricardo Hernandez," *In The Wings* (May 14, 2010); http://americantheatrewing.org/podcasts/index.php

——. "Textile Artisan with Gene Mignola," *In The Wings* (January 22, 2010); http://americantheatrewing.org/podcasts/index.php

——. "Costume Designer with Carrie Robbins," *In The Wings* (October 21, 2009); http://americantheatrewing.org/podcasts/index.php

——. "Make Up Designer with Angelina Avallone," *In The Wings* (November 6, 2009); http://americantheatrewing.org/podcasts/index.php

——. "Projection Designer with Jeff Sugg," *In The Wings* (October 21, 2009); http://americantheatrewing.org/podcasts/index.php

American Theatre Wing. "Ming Cho Lee," *SDCF Masters of the Stage* (October 8, 2009); http://americantheatrewing.org/podcasts/index.php

American Theatre Wing and CUNY. "Design with Peggy Eisenhauer, Jess Goldstein, David Korins, Derek McLane, Carrie Robbins," *Working In The Theatre* (May, 2006); http://americantheatrewing.org/podcasts/index.php

——. "Design with David Gallo, Donald Holder, Anna Louizos, G.W. Mercier, Catherine Zuber," *Working In The Theatre* (September, 2003); http://americantheatrewing.org/podcasts/index.php

——. "Design with John Arnone, Jane Greenwood, Martin Pakledinaz, Scott Pask, Richard Pilbrow," *Working In The Theatre* (September, 2002); http://americantheatrewing.org/podcasts/index.php

——. "Design with Ken Billington, Robert Jones, William Ivey Long, Thomas Lynch, Tony Walton, David C. Woolard," *Working In The Theatre* (September, 2001); http://americantheatrewing.org/podcasts/index.php

——. "Design with Julie Archer, Christopher H. Barreca, Ruth Maleczech, Aiko Nakasone, Karen Ten Eyck, Angela Wendt," *Working In The Theatre* (September, 1996); http://americantheatrewing.org/podcasts/index.php

——. "Design with Beverly Emmons, Ann Hould-Ward, David Schulder, Tony Walton," *Working In The Theatre* (September, 1994); http://americantheatrewing.org/podcasts/index.php

——. "Design with John Arnone, Elizabeth Fried, Wendall K. Harrington," (September, 1993); http://americantheatrewing.org/podcasts/index.php

——. "Design with Brenda Braxton, Casey Compton, Jules Fisher, Michael Greif, Toni-Leslie James, Ralph Lee," *Working In The Theatre* (September, 1992); http://americantheatrewing.org/podcasts/index.php

——. "Design with Ann Emonts, Mary Louise Geiger, Anthony Holland, Paul King, James D. Sandefur," *Working In The Theatre* (September, 1987); http://americantheatrewing.org/podcasts/index.php

——. "Design with Blu, Lawrence Eichler, Heidi Landesman-Ettinger, Charles Ludlam, Patricia McGourty, Angus Moss, Everett Quinton, Richard Riddell," *Working In The Theatre* (September, 1985); http://americantheatrewing.org/podcasts/index.php

Anderson, Barbara and Cletus Anderson. (1984) *Costume Design.* Fort Worth, TX: Holt, Rinehart and Winston, Inc.

Aronson, Arnold. (1985) *American Set Design.* New York: Theatre Communications Group.

Bablet, Denis, and Joan Miró. (1977) *The Revolutions of Stage Design in the 20th Century.* Paris: L. Amiel, .

Backemeyer, Sylvia, ed. (2003) *Ralph Koltai: Designer for the Stage.* London: Nick Hern Books,

Barbour, David. "Page Turner: Inside the world of War Horse," in *Lighting & Sound America,* (May 2011): pp. 60–9.

——. "Welcome to the 60s: Ken Posner's Lighting Keeps Hairspray Hopping," in *Live Design,* (November 1, 2002).

Barbour, David, and David Johnson. "Hocus Pocus: Wicked on Broadway," in *Live Design,* (February 1, 2004).

Bicât, Tina. (2006) *The Handbook of Costume.* Wiltshire: The Crowood Press.

Blankenship, Mark. "This Dress Tells a Story" *TDF* http://wp.tdf.org/index.php/2010/02/this-dress-tells-a-story/

——. "In: New York," (July 1, 2008); www.susanhilferty.com

Bracewell, John. (1993) *Sound Design in the Theatre.* Englewood Cliffs, NJ: Prentice-Hall.

Brantley, Ben. " 'Cabaret': Desperate Dance at Oblivion's Brink," *New York Times,* (March 20, 1988).

——. "Primary Colors and Abstract Appetites," *New York Times,* (April 2, 2010).

British Library. "National Life Stories: An Oral History of British Theatre Design"; www.bl.uk/reshelp/findhelprestype/sound/ohist/ohnls/nlstheatre/theatre.html

British Theatre Design, 1983–1987: [catalogue of an Exhibition of a Collection by the Society of British Theatre Designers]. Faringdon: Twynam Publishing, 1987.

Brockett, Oscar G, Margaret Mitchell, and Linda Hardberger. (2010) *Making the Scene: A History of Stage Design and Technology in Europe and the United States.* San Antonio, TX: Tobin Theatre Arts Fund.

Brown, Ross. (2010) *Sound: A Reader in Theatre Practice.* Basingstoke: Palgrave Macmillan.

Burian, Jarka. (1971) *The Scenography of Josef Svoboda.* Middletown, CT: Wesleyan University Press.

Burnett, Kate, and Peter R. Hall. (2002) *2d/3d: Design for Theatre and Performance.* London: Society of British Theatre Designers.

Burns, Bree. "Julie Taymor: Breaking the Mold," *Theatre Crafts* (March 1988): pp. 48–53, 68–9.

Cashill, Robert. "Flying the Freak Flag," *Live Design,* (March 1, 2009).

Chivers, Natasha. Natasha Chivers Lighting Design; www.natashachivers.co.uk/

Constable, Paul. "Paul Constable Lighting Design," http://pauleconstable.com/

Cooper, Dan. (1999) "William Ivey Long's Costumes for the Broadway Musical Guys and Dolls"; www.dancooper.tv/fashionfinds_1999/june/pages/william-ivey-long-1.htm

Cote, David. (2005) *Wicked: The Grimmerie, a Behind-the-Scenes Look at the Hit Broadway Musical.* Hyperion.

Courtney, Cathy. (1993) *Jocelyn Herbert: A Theatre Workbook.* London: Art Books International.

Culture Now: art + media+ design. "Derek McLane: An Interview," (last accessed June 2009); www.culturenow.com/site/item.cfm?item=35833

Daley, Dan. "Mixing Sound for Broadway Musicals: Mixing Techniques," *Performing Musician,* January 2008. www.performing-musician.com

Davis, Tony. (2001) *Stage Design.* Crans-Près-Céligny: RotoVision.

Drain, Richard. (1995) *Twentieth Century Theatre: A Sourcebook.* London: Routledge.

Dondis, Donis A. (1973) *A Primer of Visual Literacy.* Cambridge, MA: MIT Press.

Dunham, Richard. (2011) *Stage Lighting: Fundamentals and Applications.* Boston: Allyn & Bacon.

Ebrahimian, Babak. (2006) *Sculpting Space in the Theater: Conversations with the top set, light and costume designers.* Oxford: Focal Press.

Francis, Penny and the National Theatre. "War Horse: Handspring Puppet Company," (October 25, 2007); www.nationaltheatre.org.uk/rss.php?id=15

Fraser, Neil and Simon Bennison. (2007) *The Handbook of Stage Lighting.* Wiltshire: The Crowood Press.

Fox, Jena Tesse. "William Ivey Long: Creating Character Through Costume," http://broad wayworld.com/article/William_Ivey_Long_Creating_Character_Through_Costume_ 20060424

Gillette, J. Michael. (2008) *Theatrical Design and Production,* 6th ed. Boston: McGraw-Hill.

Goodwin, John, ed. (1989) *British Theatre Design:* The Modern Age. London: Weidenfeld & Nicolson.

Grimes, William. "For A Broadway Set Designer, Home is Where the Stage is," *New York Times,* (June 9, 1992).

Hall, Peter and the National Theatre. "Peter Hall on Bacchai," Audio Podcast (May 22, 2002); www.nationaltheatre.org.uk/rss.php?id=12

Hall, Peter Ruthven, and Kate Burnett, eds. (1999) *Timespace: Design for Performance 1995–1999.* London: The Society of British Theatre Designers.

Harada, Kai. "Sound Design Handbook," www.harada-sound.com/sound/handbook/

Henderson, Mark. "Mark Henderson Lighting Design," www.markhendersonlightingdesign. com/markhendersonlightingdesign.com/Home.html

Hilferty, Susan. "Conversation with Theatre Projects for Theatres 2," (September 10, 2008). www.SusanHilferty.com

Holder, Donald. (2003). "Immersing Oneself in Light," unpublished essay.

Horyn, Cathy. "He Dresses the Goddesses of Broadway," *New York Times* (August 30, 2002).

Huntington, John. "How Did They Do That," *Lighting & Sound America,* (April 25, 2005): pp. 42–9.

Ilson, Carol. (1989) *Harold Prince: From Pajama Game to Phantom of the Opera.* Ann Arbor and London: UMI Research Press.

Ishioka, Eiko, and Francis F. Coppola. (2000) *Eiko on Stage.* New York: Callaway.

Jones, Robert E. (1941) *The Dramatic Imagination: Reflections and Speculations on the Art of the Theatre.* New York: Theatre Arts Books.

Keller, Max. (1999) *Light Fantastic: The Art and Design of Stage Lighting.* New York: Prestel Verlag.

Kellogg, Marjorie. (2003) "Proces, A Meditation," unpublished essay.

Kerr, Walter, "The Theater: 'Cabaret' Opens at the Broadhurst," *New York Times,* (November 21,1966).

Koch, Polly, Don Quaintance, and Deborah Velders, eds. (2007) *Between Taste and Travesty: Costume Designs by William Ivey Long.* Wilmington, North Carolina: Cameron Art Museum.

Lassell, Michael, ed. (2002) *Disney on Broadway.* New York: Disney Editions.

Lampert-Gréaux, Ellen. "Q+A: Neil Austin," *Live Design,* (November 4, 2010).

——. "Rockin' Sound For American Idiot," *Live Design,* (June 2, 2010).

Landis, Deborah Nadoolman. (2003) *Costume Design.* Focal Press.

Lapine, James. "*Sunday in the Park with George:* Production History," www.jameslapine.com/ 1984sunday/index.html

Lester, Heather. "*War Horse* Teacher Resource Guide," www.lct.org/content/show/LCT_ WarHorse.TeacherGuide.pdf

Long, William Ivey. "William Ivey Long Studios," www.williamiveylong.com

Long Warf Theatre. "Interview with Michael Yeargan," (last accessed June 2009); http://longwarf.org/off_glass_yeargan.html

McCandless, Stanley. (1958) *A Method for Lighting The Stage*, 4th ed. New York: Theatre Arts Books.

McKenzie, Janet. "Bauhaus: 1919–1933," *Studio International*; www.studio-international.co.uk/reports/bauhaus.asp

McKinney, Joslin, and Philip Butterworth. (2009) *The Cambridge Introduction to Scenography*. Cambridge, UK: Cambridge University Press.

Mellor, David. "A Sound Person's Guide to Lighting," *Performing Musician*, (November 2008): www.performing-musician.com

Meyer Sound. "Meyer Sound Keeps the Audio Consistently *Wicked* in London," (September 2006). www.meyersound.com/news/2006/wicked

——. "A conversation with Nick Lidster," (March 2004): www.meyersound.com/applications/story.php?type=15&id=999

——. "Meyer System Engulfs Audience in WJD Wetherspoon Installs MM-4 Sicked Wizardry," (August 2003). www.meyersound.com/news/wicked_curran/

——. "Interview with Sound Designer Tony Meola," (August 2002). Meyersound.com

Milburn, Rob. (2003) "Process," unpublished essay.

Moiseiwitsch, Tanya, T J. Edelstein, and Alan Barlow. (1994) *The Stage Is All the World: The Theatrical Designs of Tanya Moiseiwitsch*. Chicago: David and Alfred Smart Museum of Art, the University of Chicago, in association with the University of Washington Press.

Moran, Nick. (2007) *Performance Lighting Design: How to Light for the Stage, Concerts and Live Events*. London: Methuen.

Mumford, Peter. "Lighting Dance," *Dance Research* 3.2 (summer 1985): pp. 46–55.

Mumford, Peter. "Peter Mumford Lighting Design," www.petermumford.info/Welcome.html

Nagler, A. M. (1959) *A Source Book in Theatrical History: Sources of Theatrical History*. New York: Dover Publications.

National Theatre, "*Video in War Horse*"; www.nationaltheatre.org.uk/55589/video/ video-in-war-horse.html

National Theatre/ Seventh Art Productions. *Making War Horse* (2009).

New York Public Library. "Celebrating Spectacle: A Conversation with David Rockwell, Julie Taymor, Simon Doonan, instigated by John Hockenberry," (October 20, 2006); www.nypl.org/audiovideo/celebrating-spectacle-conversation-david-rockwell-julie-taymor-simon-doonan-instigated-jo

New York Public Library and the Lighting Archive. "Theatrical Lighting Database," http://lightingdb.nypl.org/

Nightingale, Benedict. "Conjuring an Eerie World for the Phantom," *New York Times*, (January 24, 1988).

Owen, Bobbi. (2005) *The Designs of Willa Kim*. Syracuse, NY: United States Institute for Theatre Technology.

Parker, W. Oren and R. Craig Wolf. (1990) *Scene Design and Stage Lighting*, 6th ed. Fort Worth, TX: Holt, Rinehart and Winston, Inc.

Patel, Neil. "Neil Patel Design," www.neilpateldesign.com/neilpatel_test.html

Patridge, David. "The Cirque of Life," *Live Design*, (January 1, 2005).

Pecktal, Lynn. (1993) *Costume Design: Techniques of Modern Masters*. New York: Back Stage Books.

Pilbrow, Richard. (1997) *Stage Lighting Design: The Art, the Craft, the Life.* New York: Design Press/Quite Specific Media.

Pol, Mic. "Art & Craft In Theatre Sound Design," (July 1996); www.micpool.com/MANIFESTO. html

——. www.micpool.com/STEP_BY_STEP_GUIDE.html

Pollock, Steve. "Sunday in the Park With George: An Artist's Collaboration Brings Seurat to Broadway," *Theatre Crafts* (August/ September 1984): pp. 24–9, 66.

Platform Papers 4. Designers: Bob Crowley Jocelyn Herbert John Napier. London: Royal National Theatre, 1993.

Production Resource Group. "PRG Virtuoso brings light to Sunday in the Park With George,"(May 8, 2008); www.prg.com/news/the-prg-virtuoso-brings-light-to-sunday-in-the-park-with-george/

Reesman, Bryan. "Amplifying American Idiot," *Stage Directions,* (May 2010).

Rich, Frank. "Guys and Dolls; Damon Runyon's New York Lives Anew," *New York Times,* (April 15, 1992).

Rischbieter, Henning, and Wolfgang Storch. (1968) *Art and the Stage in the 20th Century: Painters and Sculptors Work for the Theater.* Greenwich, CT: New York Graphic Society.

Rogoff, Gordon. "Critic and Designer in Conversation: A Talk With Ming Cho Lee," *Theater.* 23.1 (Winter 1992): pp. 28–34.

Rose, Charlie. "A Conversation with David Rockwell," (December 29, 2000); www.charlierose. com/view/interview/3329

Rosenfeld, Sybil. (1973) *A Short History of Scene Design in Great Britain.* Oxford: Blackwell.

Rosenthal, Todd. "Todd Rosenthal Design,"www.toddar.com/clients/rosenthalt/nav/frameset. shtml

Rosenthal, Jean, and Lael Wertenbaker. (1972) *Magic of Light: The Craft and Career of Jean Rosenthal, Pioneer in Lighting for the Modern Stage.* New York: Little, Brown & Co..

"Scenography: The Theatre Design Website." http://sceno.org/

The Scenographer. "Special Issue: Tribute to Maria Bjornson," (October 2009).

Simonson, Lee. (1932) *The Stage is Set.* New York: Harcourt, Brace and Company.

Smith, Rae. "Rae Smith Design," www.raesmith.co.uk/

Smith, Ronn. (1991) *American Set Design 2.* New York: Theatre Communications Group.

Strand News. "Vari-Lite and Strand Lighting Get a Spring Awakening: Lighting Designer Kevin Adams brings his critically-acclaimed lighting design to Broadway," (January 30, 2007); www.strandlighting.com/index.php?src=news&srctype=detail&category=Main&refno=5

Taymor, Julie, with Alexis Greene. (1997) *The Lion King: Pride Rock on Broadway.* New York: Hyperion.

Theatre Development Fund. "Stages," http://wp.tdf.org/

Thomas, Richard K. (2008) *The Designs of Abe Jacob.* Syracuse, NY: United States Institute for Theatre Technology.

——. "The Function of the Soundscape," *TD&T,* 37.1 (Winter 2001): p. 18.

Tilford, Joe. (2010) *The Designs of Joe Tilford: A Retrospective Exhibit of Set Designs.* Syracuse, NY: United States Institute for Theatre Technology.

Tipton, Jennifer. (2003) "Dreaming in Real Time," unpublished essay.

Tubert, Susana. "Jennifer Tipton: Light as Language," *American Theatre* (October 1993): pp. 37 and 126.

Unruh, Delbert. (2008) *The Designs of Jules Fisher.* Syracuse, NY: United States Institute for Theatre Technology.

——. (2006) *The Designs of Ming Cho Lee.* Syracuse, NY: United States Institute for Theatre Technology.

Unruh, Delbert with Marilyn Rennagel and Jeff Davis. (2007) *The Designs of Tharon Musser.* Syracuse, NY: United States Institute for Theatre Technology.

Vear, Tim. "Primer: Acoustic Characteristics of Live Sound Reinforcement," *Pro Sound Web.* (August 6, 2010); www.prosoundweb.com/article/acoustic_characteristics_for_live_sound_reinforcement/

Walter, John W. dir. (2008) *Theatre of War.* DVD.

Warner, Leo, Mark Grimmer, and Lysander Aston. "War Horse Video Design," 59 Productions; http://59productions.co.uk/project?p=1

Warren, Virginia Lee. "Fashion Comes on Strong," *New York Times.* (November 15, 1966).

Wetzsteon, Ross. "The Great New York Show: *Guys and Dolls* Lights up Broadway All Over Again," *New York Magazine* (May 4, 1992): pp. 28–37.

Winslow, Colin. (2006) *The Handbook of Set Design.* Wiltshire: The Crowood Press.

Witchel, Alex. "William Ivey Long Keeps His Clothes On," *New York Times,* (January 29, 2006).

Wolf, Matt. "Sunday in the Park With George," *Variety* (November 30, 2005); www.variety.com/review/VE1117929004?refCatId=33&ref=related

WNET New York. "David Rockewell," *Sunday Arts* www.thirteen.org/sundayarts/profiles-interviews/david-rockwell/79/

Zinoman, Jason. "Who's That Kid Staging Sondheim?" *New York Times,* (February 17, 2008).

Index